# Eliot's Prismatic Plays

## A Multifaceted Quest

Jolly Das

ATLANTIC
PUBLISHERS & DISTRIBUTORS (P) LTD

Published by

**ATLANTIC**

**PUBLISHERS & DISTRIBUTORS (P) LTD**

B-2, Vishal Enclave, Opp. Rajouri Garden,
New Delhi-110027
Phones : 25413460, 25429987, 25466842

Sales Office
7/22, Ansari Road, Darya Ganj,
New Delhi-110002
Phones : 23273880, 23275880, 23280451
Fax : 91-11-23285873
web : www.atlanticbooks.com
e-mail : info@atlanticbooks.com



ISBN 81-269-0770-3



Printed in India
at Syndicate Binders, NOIDA (U.P.)

And do not think of the fruit of action.
Fare forward.

Eliot: *The Dry Salvages*.

This is what my *Acharya*,
Professor Subhas Sarkar,
has always said to me.

I humbly dedicate this book to him.

# Foreword

Not long ago, when I wrote the book, *T.S. Eliot the Dramatist*, was the great master's entity as a playwright given its due recognition. Though the theme of quest in his poetry was noticed and explicated by some critics, it was not pursued or recognized in his drama. My student, Dr. Jolly Das has made a thorough-going and investigative study of Eliot's dramatic creations as part of his individual quest, which has never been done earlier. She has appropriately established how the Christian monistic philosophy came to provide Eliot with the basic platform for this quest—the quest for revival of the much-needed spiritual culture in the modern world.

In this context, the Oriental concept of detachment in spiritual quest and its attendant notion of sacrifice and suffering as enshrined in the Vedantic and Buddhist philosophy that has been incorporated in Eliot's poetry and plays as part of his own personal quest, has been highlighted by Dr. Das to illustrate Eliot's attempt at universalizing his understanding of Christianity as centred in the archetypal image of the Incarnation (in Christ's Passion and Sacrifice).

The centrality of the doctrine of the Incarnation in Eliot's personal life stimulated his desire to use the legendary quest for the Holy Grail as the underpattern of his own quest in his creative writings. This is a very significant aspect of Dr. Das's findings in her study of Eliot's dramatic writings.

Dr. Das's rigorous and insightful study enables us to discover Eliot's own personal quest in his dramas through his experiments with diverse themes and techniques, even poetic language, which are bound up with his spiritual and literary quest. Her study would significantly contribute to a clearer understanding of the great master's contribution to drama and poetry.

**Subhas Sarkar**
*Former Head and Shakespeare Professor of English Rabindra Bharati University, Kolkata*

# Preface

T.S. Eliot has been acknowledged by authors, scholars and critics as the most important personality in twentieth century English literature. He has been the source of inspiration to many authors writing in other languages. His awareness of the unprecedented problems of modern urban people created by the completely new conditions of life, in which they found themselves, propelled him towards a quest for a way of expressing the thoughts and emotions which grew out of such a milieu. This quest was primarily twofold: for self-realization and, for form and articulation.

In the quest for Self-realization, Eliot strove to find a way out of the acedia and spiritual barrenness experienced by modern urban people. He felt that the way shown by the Incarnation in Christ's Suffering and Salvation through the working of the Divine Will (which is an expression of Divine Love) was the way that could be followed for a release from the claustrophobic urban existence. Eliot's understanding of the Incarnation was complemented by his understanding of the Buddha and Lord Krishna's teachings as enunciated in Buddhist texts and the *Bhagavad-Gita*. His deep knowledge of Hindu and Buddhist philosophy enabled Eliot to recognize the essential similarity between Christianity, Hinduism and Buddhism regarding the search for the Ultimate Reality.

Eliot found that he had to forge an appropriate form and mode of articulation to communicate to the contemporary world his awareness of the necessity of this quest for self-realization. Thus, the thematic quest was intertwined with the quest for expression. In this way, Eliot's idea of the role of the poet in society—the concept of tradition and the individual talent—played a key function in his creative writings.

Eliot's Unitarian family and its orthodox environment had a lifelong impact on the playwright who later converted to Anglo-Catholicism, in appreciation of the Incarnation, the validity of which was rejected by the Unitarians. However, the early experience was so deeply embedded in the playwright's being that inspite of his conversion, he remained an introvert. This shy nature, which was essentially romantic, was intelligently camouflaged by the outer austere image which Eliot painstakingly created for his readers—and which led many critics to the conclusion that he was a classicist. It resulted in his creation of the "formalist-realist synthesis" which he strove to achieve in his work.

There was neither any need for Eliot to write an autobiography, nor the need to authorize someone else to write his biography, because his creative writing, although small in volume, is his autobiography, secluded behind the third voice of the interlocutors of the poems and the characters in the plays. The mask of the persona was the essential device of seclusion chosen by the playwright.

The necessity to trace Eliot's development as a dramatist whose personal quest for self-realization, form and articulation got expressed in each succeeding play he wrote, resulted in the present work. It has been a great pleasure to "re-search" Eliot's own work and his wide reading in order to seek for the man behind the literary creations, particularly the plays. During the last decade, I have tried to come closer to the private romantic individual who was T.S. Eliot, carefully and meticulously veiled behind the magnanimous, formal and austere figure of English poetry and criticism.

The present volume has been divided into an introduction, six chapters and a conclusion. The first chapter deals with the early works up to *The Rock*. The next five deal with each of the plays Eliot wrote. Each of these chapters has been divided into sections that deal separately with Eliot's quest for self-realization, for form and for articulation.

I must take this opportunity to acknowledge my gratitude to my *acharya*, Prof. Subhas Sarkar, my debt to whom cannot be expressed in words. I am exceptionally fortunate in gaining the elixir-touch of this ideal *guru* who has made a complete researcher of me—goading me on with his meticulous supervision and training me as a research-scholar. I am humbly grateful to Sir for the Foreword he has written for this book.

I am also indebted to Dr. K.R. Gupta, Chairman, Atlantic Publishers and Distributors (P) Ltd., New Delhi, for his efforts to enable the present book to see the light of day.

**JOLLY DAS**

# Contents

# Introduction

The conscious and meticulous artist in Thomas Stearns Eliot searched for an appropriate form and mode of articulation which could express the personal quest for meaning of life which he undertook in all his poems and plays. Right from his early childhood Eliot seems to have a growing awareness of the contrary forces of materialism and spiritualism which came to influence modern men: as men drifted towards material comforts, they moved away from spiritual fulfillment until a complete spiritual barrenness overtook the urban civilizations of America and Europe. The two World Wars appear to be vain displays of the destructive power that man has incurred with a growing knowledge of technology. They seemed to be expressions of a corresponding spiritual barrenness of the modern urban societies. Eliot's highly perceptive sensibility enabled him to realize that a way had to be found in order to restore spiritual fertility, so that man's existence is fulfilled. The archetypal figure of the Incarnation illuminated the path of Eliot's quest.

When Eliot was a child he sometimes went to the Roman Catholic Church at the corner of Locust Street and Jefferson Avenue in St. Louis, with his Irish nurse, Annie Dunne. The Sunday Mass which he attended during such visits had a far-reaching impact on his personal life. Eliot belonged to one of the leading Unitarian families in St. Louis. His grandfather, William Greenleaf Eliot, was the founder of the Unitarian Church of the Messiah in St. Louis. The Unitarians deny the divinity of Jesus. So, when Eliot witnessed Mass, which centres on the Doctrine of the Incarnation, he was greatly moved. As he grew older,

Eliot felt that in following the ideal example set by Christ, man may regain spiritual fertility. Initially, in his creative writings he emphasized Christ's Suffering and Sacrifice to atone for the sins of men, in order to bring about Salvation—which implied the endurance of austere penance. Later on, with the development of his realization, Eliot came to uphold the Loving and Compassionate nature of Christ, who represents the human version of Divine Love. Eliot's Christian monistic philosophy provided him the basic platform for his quest for a revival of spiritual culture. In the Introduction to G. Wilson Knight's *The Wheel of Fire*, Eliot wrote:

> Now it is only a personal prejudice of mine that I prefer poetry with a clear philosophical pattern; if it has the other pattern as well, to poetry like Shakespeare's [...]. I like a definite and dogmatic philosophy, preferably a Christian and Catholic one, but alternatively that of Epicurus or of the Forest Philosophers of India; and it does not seem to me to obstruct or diminish either the 'poetry' or the pattern.[1]

The Vedic Rishis considered life as 'a divine outflowering', as a movement from mortality to immortality, from mixed light and darkness to the splendour of the divine truth whose abode is in the infinite but can be "arduously built up in man's soul and life through a journey of spiritual quest and an attendant sacrifice."[2] According to the Upanishads, which are commentaries on the Vedas, the *Paramatma* (Eternal Spirit) comes to meet the *Jivatma* (spirit of man) in love, which leads to a harmony that is expressed in a serenity which comes from selflessness and detachment from earthly shackles. This detachment has been emphasized by the Buddha in His Fire Sermon in which He says that the fires of all desires must be extinguished in order to attain salvation in the form of *Nirvana*. The Buddha's sermon is somewhat similar to Christ's Sermon on the Mount.[3]

The centrality of the Doctrine of the Incarnation in Eliot's personal life stimulated his use of the legendary Quest of the Holy Grail as the under pattern of his creative writing. The esoteric aspect of the cult of the Holy Grail is connected with the secret mysterious powers of the Vessel which is the centre of the cult. According to the Oxford anthropologists like Jessie L.

Weston, the Sacrament of the Eucharist is the Christianized version of the Mystic Feast of the Nature cults. The Life-cult of pre-Christian Vegetation-rituals permeates the Christian romance of the Legend of the Holy Grail which is closely associated with Christology and the Doctrine of the Incarnation. 'Life' or fertility cults of non-Christian societies may be interpreted as 'love'—a human representation of Divine Love—in Christian terms. This idea enabled Eliot to widen the scope of his Christian view of the world by incorporating such anthropological notions in his writings. The ritual of the Grail has various layers, beginning with that of the outer symbolism, and moving towards the inner unobservable layers which assume a different form, until one arrives at the centre which is the fixed significance of the Grail as the source of food, implying nourishment (which is chiefly spiritual). James G. Frazer has shown that all the pre-Christian Nature cults are based on a pattern of death and resurrection which is essential for the salvation of the world. The central figure of Christianity, Jesus Christ, thus, appears to be a descendant of these non-Christian Vegetation deities. It may be safely inferred that Christianity is not separate from (it is rather a possible continuation of or improvement on) these earlier cults. Weston points out that "only in the recognition of this one-time claim of essential kinship between Christianity and the Pagan Mysteries that we shall find the key to the Secret of the Grail."[4] The "exoteric"[5] aspect of this cult deals with folk-lore elements. The Quest of the Holy Grail serves as the objective correlative to Eliot's own search for meaning of life and forms the under pattern of all his works right from 'The Love Song of J. Alfred Prufrock' to *The Elder Statesman*.

The natural phenomenon of the cycle of seasons was construed by ancient societies in terms of the fertility myths. Some anthropologists hold the Crucifixion as symbolic of the spiritual rejuvenation of mankind, and therefore, akin to these myths, because sacrifices (human and animal) were performed as symbolic recurrences of the death-rebirth myths. Christ called Himself the last Paschal Lamb to be sacrificed during the Feast of the Passover; the Last Supper is the Feast in which Jesus offers Himself as the sacrificial Lamb whose Blood and Flesh (symbolized by the wine and bread) will cleanse mankind of its sins. The Crucifixion is a token of the working of the Divine Will, through which the Son of God, born as the Son of Man, dies after suffering intense pain, and finally surrendering Himself completely to God's Will. Christ's Death in April (which is springtime) is, thus, a sort of culmination of these anthropological rites on one hand, bringing an awareness of the possibility of spiritual fertility on the other. So, the Chalice or receptacle which Jesus used during His Last Supper comes to bear the symbolic significance of spiritual fertility. The legendary Quest for this lost Grail is, therefore, a figurative search for spiritual fertility. An awareness of these associations of the Incarnation enables Eliot to begin *The Waste Land* with a clear reference to the Crucifixion:

> April is the cruellest month, breeding
> Lilacs out of the dead land, mixing
> Memory with desire, [...][6]

This is the desire to repay Christ which, for the aspirant who seeks the higher Contemplative Life, would be something close to what Becket says when the Knights arrive at the Cathedral, as emissaries of the King, in order to murder him:

> His blood given to buy my life,
> My blood given to pay for his death,
> My death for His death.[7]

As he progresses in his personal quest, Eliot comes to realize that the Way of the Affirmative is as significant as the Way of the Contemplative. In his final play, *The Elder Statesman*, Eliot emphasizes selfless human love as the temporal representative of Divine Love. God sent His Son to live amongst men as the Son of Man in order to serve as the Messiah, mediating between Him and man, by showing men the way to self-realization, through selfless love and humility.

Eliot universalized his understanding of Christianity by enriching it with those vital tenets of Hinduism and Buddhism which come very close to Christianity. All three religions expound the practice of control over the physical self in order to enrich the spiritual self, through the method of the constant practice of humility, selfless love and compassion. Being born in the flesh, even Christ experienced an awareness of the weakness of the physical existence which He spoke about when the Devil tempted Him to act against the Will of God:

> Get thee hence, Satan: for it is written, THOU SHALT WORSHIP THE LORD THY GOD, AND HIM ONLY SHALT THOU SERVE.[8]

At the same time He showed that the strength of the spiritual self can take man closer to God. This exemplar of the Incarnation is used by Eliot in his work: in the early poems he depicts the horror, acedia and infertility of the modern urban civilization and gradually moves towards the expression of the redeeming quality of selfless love in *The Elder Statesman.*

Eliot had no intention to sermonize his readers and auditors, about which he writes: "What I want is a literature which should be unconsciously, rather than deliberately and defiantly, Christian."[9] So, he searched for an appropriate mode of expression which would possess the capacity to convey the various levels of meaning which he desired to share with the readers and auditors who belong to diverse strata of understanding and spiritual awareness.

In his quest for a form of articulation for the purpose of expressing his personal experiences Eliot chose dramatic poetry which expresses better than prose because "dramatic verse alone has as its function the making an immediate, collective impression upon a large number of people gathered together to look at an imaginary episode acted upon a stage."[10] In a letter (dated 2 December 1920) to his mother, Charlotte Eliot, the poet wrote about what he spoke in a lecture entitled 'Modern Audiences of Dramatic Poetry': "[...] I described the sort of audience I should like to have, and the sort I should not want to have, if I were having a verse play produced, and it appeared to be received very well."[11] Two things are clear from this information: that it was as early as 1920 when Eliot was thinking about verse drama, and that the audience was accepting his arguments in favour of such a dramatic form. Eliot opines, through the voice of one of the speakers in 'A Dialogue on Dramatic Poetry' that "We must find a new form of verse which shall be as satisfactory a vehicle for us as blank verse was for the Elizabethans."[12]

It is clear from the seminal essay "Tradition and the Individual Talent" that Eliot was trying to formulate a theory for the creativity of a poet which took into account the relevance of the past for the present and the role of the poet in interpreting this relevance. He fell back on his reading of Dante, the *Upanishads*, H.C. Warren's translation of Buddhist texts, works on mysticism, classical Greek drama, French symbolist poetry, and of course, "the poets and dramatists of the time of Shakespeare and immediately after,"[13] whose work he prefers to that of any other period in English literature. Much of the symbolisms are derived from these sources. The mode of articulation and rhythm of the poetry draw inspiration from the popular forms of entertainment of the contemporary times, like music-hall comedy and jazz music. This complex mode of expression was necessary because, as T.S. Matthews puts it, Eliot put in not less than everything of himself into his poetry, hiding "behind paraphernalia more elaborate than the contrivances of the Wizard of Oz."[14] This can be supported by the dramatist's own words: "The world of a great poetic dramatist is a world in which the creator is everywhere present, and everywhere hidden."[15] However, Eliot was conscious of the difficulties of writing verse plays for the modern auditors, about which he writes in the Introduction to S.L. Bethell's *Shakespeare and the Popular Dramatic Tradition:*

> It must allow the characters to behave inconsistently, but only with respect to a deeper consistency. [...] it must reveal, underneath the vacillating or infirm character, the indomitable unconscious will; and underneath the resolute purpose of the planning animal, the victim of circumstance and the doomed or sanctified being. So the poet with ambitions of the theatre must discover the laws, both of another kind of verse and of another kind of drama. The difficulty of the author is also the difficulty of the audience. Both have to be trained; both need to be conscious of many things which neither an Elizabethan dramatist, nor an Elizabethan audience, had any need to know [...].[16]

Therefore, Eliot's poems and plays were part of the rigorous training to which he subjected himself while undertaking his personal quest for self-realization on one hand and form and articulation on the other. Right from his earliest poems, in the collection entitled *Prufrock and Other Observations*, the dramatic element in the creation of a situation and use of the voices of the personae, can be discerned.

The creation of layers of meaning in his work enabled Eliot to convey his inmost experiences with the help of his wide knowledge in a comparatively small volume of work which reflects his deep understanding of the heritage of both European and Indian literature; this encompasses Sanskrit and Pali texts associated with early Hinduism and Buddhism, as well as the great literary tradition of Europe which begins with the Greeks. The expression of his knowledge comes by way of epigraphs, symbols, images, quotations and references from his sources—all of which contribute to a new understanding of their relevance in the context of the modern urban man's situation. Eliot had written in his dissertation on the philosophy of F.H. Bradley that "Experience is certainly more real than anything else, but any experience demands reference to something real which lies outside of that experience."[17] When he came to express his own experience Eliot found that the use of the "objective correlative"[18] was one of the most effective methods of communication. Eliot's awareness of a European tradition—of the past having an influence on his work and of his work forming some sort of a continuation of that heritage—was in a conscious building up of his own literary world.

Although Eliot's creative literature cannot be said to be voluminous, it has paved the way for much of modern literature, particularly poetry. He stands distinctly amongst the large body of writers in the English language, simply by virtue of a new way of writing about the emotions and experiences of the contemporary urban world. He seemed to express with an enviable aplomb, the apparently inexpressible pent up feelings and thoughts of modern city-dwellers. Eliot was their spokesperson—so close, and yet so distant, with his use of words which were measured and capable of sustaining layers of meaning. The voice they heard in his poems was that of the interlocutor (the persona, or sometimes, the personae) who spoke with the 'third voice' which Eliot described in 'The Three Voices of Poetry' as that of "one imaginary character addressing another imaginary character."[19] Just as the seventeenth century poets fell back on the contemporary colloquial idiom for their chosen mode of articulation in their poems which were conversational in nature, Eliot resorted to the use of the idiom and rhythm of the day-to-day conversation of the modern urban English speaking world for the mode of articulation of his poems and plays. He was conscious of the social function of the poet and the responsibility of the poet to his society. In order to reach out to his target readers and auditors, Eliot had to use a mode of articulation which could be comprehended by them. The closer the idiom of his poetry was to that of the conversation of the auditors, the easier would it be for him to convey his own understanding of the spiritual aridity and acedia of the contemporary urban Western society because "every vital development in language is a development of feeling as well."[20] For the form of his works, Eliot drew largely upon classical literature but for his chosen mode of articulation he counted upon the idiom of contemporary speech—this "formalist-realist synthesis"[21] seems to be a pointer to the romantic self of the poet who sought to express his inmost experiences through a kind of formalism in which he clothed his works. So, the original artistic creations of the poet-dramatist could also be said to express a finely balanced coexistence of romanticism and classicism—rather, a shy romanticism dressed in the austerity of classicism. The entire gamut of Eliot's literary work (which also includes the critical studies) forms the evidence of the personal quest which he undertook with an earnestness which is comparable with that of Aeneas and Dante.

The roots of his quest lie way back in his American past because the idea of a search was an inherent personal experience to him. His curiosity and eagerness to gain knowledge of the meaning of life, of his very existence, made him move from America to Europe as an expatriate searching for his roots in the European background—the traditions of Europe. Octavio Paz states this explicitly, while discussing Eliot and Ezra Pound:

> They went to Europe not as expatriates, but in search of their origins; their journey was not one of exiles but a return to the source.[22]

Eliot was born an American, obtaining his early education in America. Being a devout student of Irving Babbitt, he was seeped in the idea of 'tradition' which was that of a Christian tradition. Eliot's search for self-realization along the path leading back to the roots of the Christian tradition, which is essentially a European one, emerged from his belief that modern writings in English are rooted in this European tradition. At the same time he had also come to the realization that this tradition was not all Christian and European. The Oriental tradition of both Hindu and Buddhist scriptures came to influence him profoundly, though the influence of the Christian tradition was deeper. Eliot clarifies his understanding of 'tradition' in *After Strange Gods*, where he says, "I have wished to use the word to cover much in our lives that is accounted for by habit, breeding and environment."[23] So, he went to Europe, not merely to complete his studies on F.H. Bradley in Oxford, but in quest for roots which Paz makes out clearly:

> The "modernism" of the Anglo-America poets is an attempt to return to the central tradition of Europe—the exact opposite of German and English Romanticism—while French Surrealism carries German Romanticism to its furthest extreme.[24]

Paz goes on to explain this central tradition, using an image:

> Ruins of the Cathedral: the idea of sin, the awareness of death, the knowledge that man is fallen, and exiled in this world and in the next, the vision of oneself as an accidental being in a world of contingency. Not a system of beliefs but a handful of fragments and obsessions.
>
> The modernist tragic-comedy is composed of a dialogue between the body and death, analogy and irony.[25]

Modern man seems to have lost his power of self-exertion. The psychological impulse in the modern society today is towards a materialistic preoccupation. The two World Wars and the onrush of technology have added fuel to man's loss of faith in religion and inner beliefs. The multifarious problems have disintegrated the centre of adherence. As in Robert Browning's 'The Statue and the Bust,' the failure to act, the lack of manliness, is a part of modern existence. Like Browning's lovers, modern men feel that:

> [...] to press a point while these oppose
> Were a simple policy—best wait
> And lose no friends and gain no foes.[26]

Gordon has claimed that "Eliot wrote his own biography, enlarging in poem after poem on the character of a man who conceives his life as a religious quest despite the anti-religious mood of his age and the distracting claims of women, friends and alternative careers."[27] Apparently, there is a kind of religious quest all throughout Eliot's poetry and plays but it is only one facet of a deeper quest for self-realization, which is supported by that for form and mode of communication.

Eliot's Unitarian upbringing was so deep-rooted that in spite of a formal conversion to Anglo-Catholicism in 1927, he could not overcome the restraints imposed upon the self by the strict codes of Unitarianism. As a result, there was a constant conflict between Eliot's outer social self and inner romantic self. He took to the use of personae in his poems in order to devise an outlet for his personal quest for meaning of life in the chaotic and fragmentary modern existence. The primary device for expressing his thoughts turned out to be the "objective correlative" which he defines in the essay, "Hamlet and His Problems":

> The only way of expressing emotion in the form of art is by finding an "objective correlative"; in other words, a set of objects, a situation, a chain of events which shall be the formula of that *particular* emotion; such that when the external facts, which must terminate in sensory experience, are given the emotion is immediately evoked.[28]

Eliot resorted to the use of this technique in his creative literature because he felt that "the more perfect the artist, the more completely separate in him will be the man who suffers and the mind which creates."[29] However, this was easier said than done, and ultimately Eliot's work turned out to be the testimony of his inner struggles which included a queer emotional incapacity to form a stable intimate relation with women outside his family. Eliot came to comprehend the fact that "in an artist these suggestions made by a work of art, which are purely personal, become fused with a multitude of other suggestions from multitudinous experience, and result in the production of a new object which is no longer purely personal, because it is a work of art itself."[30]

Eliot's poetry and plays, complemented by his critical essays, reveal the progress of the artist in him towards a perfection of expression, in lucid terms, of his personal quest for meaning of life, so that it may be easily comprehended by the readers and auditors who belong to different layers of cognizance. This would enable them to share the experiences of the poet-dramatist.

## NOTES AND REFERENCES

1. Thomas Stearns Eliot, "Introduction", *The Wheel of Fire* by G. Wilson Knight (London: Methuen, 1930): xv – xvi.
2. Subhas Sarkar, "The Vedas, Oriental Culture and T.S. Eliot," *Bulletin of the Ramakrishna Mission Institute of Culture* 51.7 (July, 2000): 316.
3. Bible, King James Version, Matthew 5:3 - 7:27; Luke 6:20 - 49.
4. Jessie L. Weston, *From Ritual to Romance* (1920; New York: Doubleday, 1957) 149.
5. Weston, *From Ritual to Romance* 140. Weston clarifies the term "exoteric" as "celebrations openly and publicly performed, in which all adherents of that particular cult could join freely, the object of such public rites being to obtain some external and material benefit, whether for the individual worshipper, or for the community as a whole."
6. Eliot, *The Waste Land, The Complete Poems and Plays** (London: Faber, 1969) 61.
7. Eliot, *Murder in the Cathedral*, CPP 274-75.
8. Bible, Matthew 4:10.
9. Eliot, "Religion and Literature," *Selected Prose*, ed. Frank Kermode (London: Faber, 1975) 100.

* *The Complete Poems and Plays* will be referred to as CPP.

10. Eliot, "The Social Function of Poetry," *On Poetry and Poets* (London: Faber, 1957) 17.
11. Eliot, "Letter to Charlotte Eliot," 2 December 1920, *The Letters of T.S. Eliot*, Vol. 1 (London: Faber, 1988) 424.
12. Eliot, "A Dialogue on Dramatic Poetry," *Selected Essays*, 3rd. ed. (London: Faber, 1951) 57.
13. Eliot, "Letter to Charlotte Eliot, 2 June 1918, *The Letters of T.S. Eliot*, Vol. 1: 233.
14. T.S. Matthews, *Great Tom* (New York: Harper and Row, 1973) 191.
15. Eliot, "The Three Voices of Poetry," *On Poetry and Poets* 102.
16. Eliot, "Introduction," *Shakespeare and the Popular Dramatic Tradition*, by S.L. Bethell (Westminster: P.S. King and Staples, 1944) 9.
17. Eliot, *Knowledge and Experience in the Philosophy of F.H. Bradley* (London: Faber, 1964) 21.
18. Eliot, "Hamlet and His Problems," *The Sacred Wood* (London: Methuen, 1920) 100.
19. Eliot, "The Three Voices of Poetry," *On Poetry and Poets* 89.
20. Eliot, "Philip Massinger," *Selected Essays* 210.
21. Sarkar, *T.S. Eliot the Dramatist* (Calcutta: Minerva, 1972) 3.
22. Octavio Paz, *Children of the Mire*, trans. Rachel Phillips (Cambridge; Massachusetts: Harvard UP, 1974) 123.
23. Eliot, *After Strange Gods* (London: Faber, 1934) 31.
24. Paz vii.
25. Paz 95-96.
26. Robert Browning, *'Men and Women' and Other Writings*, ed. J.W. Harper (London: J.M. Dent, 1975) 64.
27. Gordon, *Eliot's Early Years* 1.
28. Eliot, "Hamlet and His Problems," *The Sacred Wood* 100.
29. Eliot, "Tradition and the Individual Talent," *The Sacred Wood* 54.
30. Eliot, "The Perfect Critic," *The Sacred Wood* 7.

# 1 The Shaping of a Dramatist—The Initial Quest for Form and Meaning

T.S. Eliot's early poems are experiments in dramatic-situation-kind-of-poetry. They are very different from the personal and descriptive poetry of his immediate predecessors. Eliot's poems stand apart from theirs in the technique of presentation where, instead of the poet directly addressing his reader, we find one imaginary persona addressing another imaginary persona, who may even be the other self of the speaker. In doing so Eliot brings back to English poetry the dramatic element found in the poetry of the seventeenth century Metaphysical poets, who exhibited integrity of expression, moving away from the public mode of the traditional expression of romantic feelings to the private mode of articulation. Eliot subscribed largely to this Metaphysical mode which posits three aesthetic points before the poet. The first expects the poet to look at life logically, thereby establishing a relationship between him and the reader through the exercise of the intellect, logically and queryingly. Earlier Romantic poetry took the reader's point of view for granted, but the Metaphysical poets looked upon the reader as a target which means that the poet must have a critical and rational detachment while approaching the reader's world. Secondly, the poet comes to look upon his own self both as an individual and as one of the interlocutors in the poem, using the voice of the persona for the first time in English poetry. Lastly, the world of the poem becomes a world in which the speaker and the listener form a separate entity—this is the world of drama. So, the language of the dramatic mode obviously becomes a colloquial one. John Donne is generally accepted as the forebear of Metaphysical poetry. Discussing him in *The Varieties of Metaphysical Poetry* Eliot states that:

> With Donne the emotion, the feeling, does not simply stop at one point, and verbiage begin; rather, it is never verbiage because there is always *some* emotion or feeling present. We watch a strange kaleidoscope of feeling; with suggested images, suggested conceits, the feeling is always melting, changing into another feeling; we get a kind of unity in flux, which is Donne. There is no *structure* of thought, but every thought is felt, every image has a peculiar feel to it. [...] a very important trick [...] of Donne's shorter poems which [...] leave so much deeper impression, than the longer [...] of first starting a simple and startling idea of direct and easily apprehensible emotional value, and then proceeding to all the variations and changes.[1]

The Metaphysical poets were compelled to forge their own idiom in order to express the variety, complexity and diversity in the worldview which resulted from the impact of rationality, the rapid development of science and the discovery of new lands outside the European world. In Eliot's case the contemporary urban society was sodden with squalor, a sense of vacuity and horror which emerged from an over-enthusiastic pursuit of materialism, and he found the dramatic mode of expression used by the Metaphysical poets congenial for his own purpose of expressing this picture of the malaise of modern man.

Eliot wanted to reach out to as large a readership as was possible, for which the personal tone in poetry was unsuitable. An element of detachment or impersonality was the prerequisite for the type of expression he was aspiring after. The business of art is to embody "impersonal emotion,"[2] for poetry, according to Eliot, "is not a turning loose of emotion, but an escape from emotion."[3] He explains that the poet can reach this state of impersonality by a complete surrender to the work to be done. Since drama is the most objective of all the forms of literature, demanding from the author a sense of detachment by which he is able to be loyal to his work, Eliot chose this form right from his very early poetic ventures, modifying it to portray fragments of pictorial representations, with the help of images, of the condition of the modern city dweller, which was also the state of the target readers of his poetry, who would realize and might even identify themselves with the personae in the poems. These poems solve Eliot's problem of expressing the feelings of horror, squalor and boredom which were the common experience of a decayed society, by avoiding any direct involvement of their creator.

*Prufrock and Other Observations*, the early poems of Eliot, show a distinct concern for the inherent weakness of modern man, nourished and circumscribed by urban society. They deal with the complex problem of man's self-evasion which has arisen from the mechanical and easy-going habits of modern society. An inadequate sense of good and evil has misguided their steps in life since their morals are adhered to simply by way of habit and not on the basis of religious sanction. Most modern men are the victims of an overwhelming sense of incapacity, which springs from mental indecision. Eliot thinks that there are two possible ways out of this state of chaos: one leading through discipline towards salvation, the other through a complete surrender to the elemental passions towards damnation, making one aware of the other self within oneself (the real self of evil) which in turn will lead towards salvation. A reading of Charles Baudelaire's *Fleurs du Mal* initiated Eliot into this concept of a new metaphysic of evil. Sarkar says that this was an idea that had something to do with the concept of Satanism:

> Baudelaire's poetry is quite often the allegory of modern man's sin, suffering and deprivation that represents a new sense of beauty that suffers from a sense of corruption which is closely associated with Satanism.[4]

So, in the world of evil and inherent Original Sin, anticipated by Baudelaire and presented by Eliot, man is exiled from the state of innocence and divine beauty. However, Eliot did not stop with the portrayal of a fragmented world in *Prufrock and Other Observations*, for his quest was for a universal harmony.

Thus, we find that Eliot's concept of poetry is inseparable from his social consciousness which has bred in him a zest for a ruthless analysis of the social ills that have resulted from the lack of faith in the objective and absolute values. In the early poems, starting with 'The Love Song of J. Alfred Prufrock,' the anarchy, boredom and squalor of contemporary life, with occasional flashes of horror, stir the readers out of their complacency. These poems cannot stand on their own as poems of faith. However, this overwhelming sense of emptiness and frustration urges the mind to be conscious of the spiritual realities which are a religious awareness in a nascent stage. It marks the beginning of Eliot's search for something stable on which modern men could take their stand and realize their relative merits. Religion is neither a fanaticism nor a craze; it is in the blood of man. Eliot's sense of religion is closely allied to his sense of history (a sense of the timeless as well as the temporal) which has imparted universality and comprehensiveness to his vision. The fragmentariness, sordidness, materialism and lack of spiritual awareness which Eliot found in St. Louis, his birthplace, turned out to be the characteristic of the entire Western civilization which he came to encounter when he travelled to Europe in the early years of the twentieth century.

The St. Louis where Eliot spent his early years up to 1905 was a strange combination of disjointed ugliness and amiability on the one hand and a tradition of liberalism and earnest scholarship on the other, which passed into the civic life of the city in spite of an element of vulgarity. Matthews describes the city very accurately:

> [...] it is really more like a two-headed monster. Downtown St. Louis, strung out along the western bank of the Mississippi, is miles away from the residential district [where the Eliots lived among other aristocratic households with their exclusive grandeur], and these two areas are connected, or separated, by half-deserted and decaying slums.[5]

The population of 1,86,000 was, like all other parts of developing America, a heterogeneous mixture of immigrants from Europe. The development of St. Louis had been rapid. When Eliot's grandfather, William Greenleaf Eliot, came to the city from Boston, he described himself as "a silver shilling among copper pennies"[6] to express his distinction amidst an inferior population. His aim in coming was to do good by civilizing St. Louis where he founded the Unitarian Church of the Messiah, several educational institutions including Washington University and hospitals. The first sixteen years of Eliot's life here were spent in absorbing impressions from his family life and getting his bearings in a perplexing world in which his God was Unitarian and authoritarian.

In spite of the strong orthodoxy of his family he did catch a few glimpses of the liturgical order and the richness of the Mass in a small Catholic Church on the corner of Jefferson Avenue and Locust Street to which his Irish nurse, Annie Dunne, occasionally took him. It must be mentioned here that the Unitarians are a Protestant sect who reacted against the Trinitarian view of God and believed in His singleness, Christ being only His Son and the Holy Ghost non-existent.

In spite of the restraints of his family and a close supervision of his mother, Charlotte Eliot, and his sisters, Eliot was a mischievous little boy who reported to his father about his older brother Henry's activities which sometimes went into indulgences strictly forbidden by Henry Ware Eliot, their father. However, Eliot was bright, thoughtful and reserved, living up to the expectations of the family. There were, thus, two facets within the young Thomas Eliot: the rigidly conformist Puritan and the adventurous romantic, the latter suppressed by the former. With his sensitiveness and superior intellect Eliot was aware of his St. Louis upbringing which combined family discipline with a keen observation of the urban life of the city.

The pressure of his Unitarian background stunted the emotional growth of the young poet. Excessive individualism, encouraged by the faith, prevented normal social relations, particularly with women. Hence, Eliot suffered from a sense of rootlessness and an awareness of the isolation and alienation of individuals from each other which resulted in the fragmentariness of modern urban society. He began to seek for an adequate mode of expressing his understanding of this situation, to face the tension between his experience and its expression. For this Eliot struck upon the novel device of the use of the voice (sometimes voices, creating a polyphony) which represents levels of awareness. He arrived at an idea of this device from his acquaintance with the poems of the French Symbolists of the nineteenth century, to which he was introduced by Arthur Symons's book *The Symbolist Movement in Literature*. A first-hand acquaintance with their works enabled him to express, in an ironic and slangy language borrowed from Laforgue and Corbiere, the picture of a cosmopolitan world of squalor, horror and boredom, resulting from a loss of faith and man's failure to arrive at a unified sensibility of experience.

He found that the modern city-dweller was haunted by a multiplicity of experiences which impinged on his mind like multiple voices to wake him up to an awareness of his commitments and failures. This is expressed by Eliot through the device of an "internal monologue"[7] in which man's split personality gets articulated through conflicting thoughts, images and associations which represent the modern city-dweller who is confronted by his timidity to assert himself. So he utters, "Do I dare / Disturb the universe?"[8] The dramatic element is emphasized in the early poems by the subtle use of irony and the deliberate subversion of the conventional poetic idiom in order to convey an experience which helps us to see the world around us afresh. The irony is made forceful and revealing by the background of the city dweller's life that is marginalized by the paraphernalia of modern culture:

> After the sunsets and the dooryards and the sprinkled streets,
> After the novels, after the teacups, after the skirts that trail along the floor.
> And this, and so much more?—
> It is impossible to say just what I mean![9]

There is the absence of a sequential order in the development of the poems. So, in this poem we have references to such diverse ideas as surgery, Michaelangelo's paintings, Prince Hamlet, Lazarus and the occasional romantic vision of mermaids.

In order to express the element of impersonality in his poems, Eliot makes use of voices which are detached and fragmentary in nature, unrolling through neat provocative poetic images the psychological complexity of the urban man's mind. So, one finds in Eliot's early poetry a new world of experience, hitherto unchartered by poetical articulation—a new structure of poetic rhythm which grows out of the fusion of thought and feeling, emotion and intellect. By using the formula of objectification of emotions into the form of art, Eliot has set the ball rolling in his quest for articulation (in poetry) of the most complex and difficult experiences of the modern city-dweller.

Images which are evocative rather than descriptive are used as the chief tool of articulation in Eliot's poetry. These images are also sufficiently symbolic so that they may evoke the requisite emotions in the readers. As Eliot's imagination is essentially dramatic, he believes in the objectification of the emotional contents of the multiplicity of experiences. The poet's artistic success depends largely on how he communicates these emotions 'impersonally' through objective correlatives and in presenting the equivalents for diverse emotions; the poet has to undergo a process of continual self-sacrifice or depersonalization. Therefore, the objective correlative is for Eliot, a dramatic mode of expressing emotions. The imagery in his poetry is an integral part of the total process of appropriate expression. In the nascent experiments that form *Prufrock and Other Observations* Eliot makes use of this process which conveys the fragmentariness of man's existence with the help of broken, apparently unconnected, images. In these poems Eliot offers the most ironical sketches of urban life. Here are men and women craving love and companionship, caught in the dilemma of self-expression and also in the hopeless void created by their own conflicting desires. The images mostly chosen for these poems are drawn from dreary evening scenes, vacant rooms, wayside restaurants, dirty streets and yellow smog. Right through the scheme of these images, applied variously in these poems, is an ever-present underlying note of irony which is near-Laforguian in nature. In internalizing his poems and in his use of the colloquial idiom, Eliot was following the French Symbolist poets who, according to Symons, were in "revolt against exteriority, against rhetoric, against a materialistic tradition."[10] The slangy, neologistic, colloquial idiom of these poets, particularly Jules Laforgue, came to have a deep impact on the early poetry of Eliot. It was Laforgue who saw the "pathetically ludicrous"[11] in the automatic life of his time, expressing it through an ironic tone in his poems. Eliot borrowed this tone from him. Thus, the ruling principle of most of Eliot's early poetry is the contrast in the imagery between the present life with its monotony and indecision and the instinctive simplicity of primordial existence. Eliot's idea of tradition which involves not only the pastness of the past but also its presence[12] strikingly asserts itself in the pattern of images that sets the tone of *Prufrock and Other Observations*.

'The Love Song of J. Alfred Prufrock' is the most expressive of these poems. Throwing overboard the conventional form of poetic expression, the poet begins the poem with a clever ironical twist leaving the reader to guess who the 'I' and 'you' might be. The poem takes on the shape of an "internal monologue"[13] in which man's split personality gets articulated through conflicting thoughts, associations and images. The poem begins with a pathological image of "a patient etherised upon a table"[14] as if the whole poem is related to the operation theatre. The poem actually undertakes a clinical operation of the inner being of Prufrock, a modern city-dweller. By juxtaposing the image of the etherised patient with that of the evening "spread out against the sky"[15] Eliot fuses the conventional with the modern. The images of "restless nights in one-night cheap hotels / And sawdust restaurants with oyster shells"[16] intensify the sense of futility and anarchy in the modern existence that lacks a sense of direction. The vacillation and timidity of Prufrock is presented in the description of the street leading to an "overwhelming question."[17] The inevitable tension between the experience and the medium is represented in the novel experiments with poetic articulation through the use of objective description, narration, aside, confession and impersonal commentary through concrete imagery, occasional soliloquy and use of irony. 'The Love Song of J. Alfred Prufrock' is the most effective experiment in modernism in poetry which embodies all these elements.

'Portrait of a Lady' depicts romantic images set against a background of music which is the inharmonious "out-of-tune of a broken violin"[18], "cracked cornets"[19] or "a street-piano, mechanical and tired."[20] The romantic images are incomplete, arising out of the young man's sense of indecision, timidity and inaction. Animal imagery, a recurring symbol in Eliot's poetry for all that is instinctive in man, is quite often the effective instrument of irony that settles the tone of the poem:

> And I must borrow every changing shape
> To find expression [...] dance, dance
> Like a dancing bear,
> Cry like a parrot, chatter like an ape.[21]

The likely discomfiture of the young lover who has failed to develop any relation with the 'Lady' has been successfully hinted at.

In 'Preludes' is exhibited the novel method of stringing together a number of disparate images which unfold like a film and produce upon the reader the impact of a sequence of emotions. The different parts of the poem present in close succession a sense of waste and boredom and a glimpse of horror, corruption and a tragic yearning for adjustment. The striking image that comes almost at the beginning, "the burnt-out ends of smoky days,"[22] quite successfully translates an abstract idea into a decidedly mundane and commonplace experience. In the second part there is the image that is richly suggestive of a sense of horror and disgust:

> One thinks of all the hands
> That are raising dingy shades
> In a thousand furnished rooms.[23]

The third part offers the picture of a society woman who clasps "the yellow soles of feet / In the palms of both soiled hands,"[24] around whom a number of images weave an atmosphere of corruption and dismay. Most significant of all the images in this poem, however, is the one in the last section: "The notion of some infinitely gentle / Infinitely suffering thing,"[25] which is one of the finest symbolic expressions in literature of the personality of Jesus Christ. It is juxtaposed with the sordidness and vacuity of modern man.

The society woman in 'Rhapsody on a Windy Night' is haunted by the tension between the outer and inner worlds as she stands at her doorway which represents the threshold between the two. She seems to represent the grim irony of modern urban existence:

And you see the corner of her eye
    Twists like a crooked pin.[26]

She suffers enormous pain, being unable to escape from the quicksand of the sinful, wicked and perverted world. When she is alone, she recalls the sordid images of the world she is compelled to cater to—a world which will discard her like a "Broken spring"[27] once it has done with her. There is an almost surrealistic design of discontinuous mental impressions in the poem. The Laforguian images seem to enhance its ironic tone:

Midnight shakes the memory
As a madman shakes a dead geranium.[28]

*Prufrock and Other Observations* can be read as one long poem on the condition of urban man, presented with an element of impersonality on the part of the poet who felt that one "cannot create a very large poem without introducing a more impersonal point of view, or splitting it up into various personalities."[29] Eliot's purpose in depicting this sordid and barren world in the quasi-dramatic mode was to portray an intense awareness of the suffering of modern man, for he knew that "the essential advantage for a poet is not to have a beautiful world with which to deal: it is to be able to see beneath both beauty and ugliness; to see the boredom, and the horror, and the glory."[30] Thus, with the help of dramatically presented poetic images Eliot gives the reader glimpses of the harsh reality of modern urban society.

While *Prufrock and Other Observations* presents the fragmentariness, anarchy, sordidness and futility of modern man, *Gerontion, The Waste Land* and *The Hollow Men* portray a spiritual sickness. In *Gerontion*, the poet expresses dissatisfaction with the negative attitude to life. The persona of Gerontion, the old man, finds fault with the vanities and ambitions of city-dwellers who lack moral scruples. He points out how "Unnatural vices/Are fathered by our heroism."[31] The dry intellectual pursuits of these men lead them nowhere:

[...] Think at last
We have not reached conclusion, when I
Stiffen in a rented house. [...][32]

Gerontion almost categorically declares how the dry intellect has been the root of all evils. Modern man has murdered romantic visions in this spiritually arid land. In the midst of utter desolation he sees the terrors of suffering and the troubles of a search for reinstatement in God's trust:

I would meet you upon this honestly.
I that was near your heart was removed therefrom
To lose beauty in terror, terror in inquisition.
I have lost my passion: why should I need to keep it
Since what is kept must be adulterated?[33]

The poet offers a plea for resuscitation of an honest emotional existence through Gerontion:

Tenants of the house,
Thoughts of a dry brain in a dry season.[34]

So, Gerontion waits for the release of the waters of life that will fertilize the barren souls which are like the arid land of the Fisher King. In this barrenness there is no faith, no hope and no relief from suffering. It creates sinful men who are unaware of their growing alienation from God. Having observed the life of the metropolis in America and Europe, Eliot came to believe that modern men belonging to the cities have been rendered emotionally impotent by the imposing complexities of life, lacking self-confidence to face squarely the chaos in the world around them. They are tempted to place a great deal of priority on their material pursuits. Hence, Eliot thinks that only a moral conversion can redeem them. The laziness and tendency for evasiveness that has taken hold of them can be combated with a seriousness of purpose and morally sound living. It was Ezra Pound who dissuaded Eliot from prefixing *Gerontion* to *The Waste Land*. Critics feel that the execution of Eliot's plan would make the close relation of the two poems clearer since both of them are associated very closely with the Grail Legend.

A deeper analysis of this spiritual aridity is undertaken in *The Waste Land*, which after drastic editing by Pound, took a form that resembles the movements of a five-act play—each of its five parts contributing to the development of the theme. The indifference of the city-dweller is reflected in Eliot's description of the city:

> Unreal city,
> Under the brown fog of a winter dawn,
> A crowd flowed over London Bridge, so many,
> I had not thought death had undone so many.
> Sighs, short and infrequent, were exhaled,
> And each man fixed his eyes before his feet.
> Flowed up the hill and down King William Street,
> To where Saint Mary Woolnoth kept the hours
> With a dead sound on the final stroke of nine.[35]

The weight of the mechanical civilization seems to hang heavy on the mind of these modern men. The huge stretch of urban civilization has been characterized by Eliot as the land of the Fisher King as found in the Grail Legend which he came across in Weston's book, *The Quest of the Holy Grail,* in which Weston explains:

> Thus we can now understand how the wasting of the land can be connected with, and directly caused by, the death, or infirmity, of the King, and how the achievement of the Quest, by restoring to health (and [...] to youth) the personage upon whose vitality, the vitality of the land

> depends, can restore these wastes to verdure [...] the achieving of the Quest has restored the rivers to their channels, and caused the dried-up waters to flow. This is precisely the feat which our earliest Aryan forefathers ascribed to their divine hero, Indra; the 'Freeing of the Waters' is the greatest boon that can be bestowed upon man.[36]

The Fisher King of the Grail Legend symbolizes, in Eliot's poem, the sophisticated modern man who has become spiritually barren. He uses the Legend of the Quest of the Holy Grail and the idea of 'Freeing of the Waters' from anthropology as the basic infrastructure of his work and conducts his personal quest for meaning of life in a similar manner, on the spiritual plane.

The symbol of the Quest of the Holy Grail represents man's quest for salvation. His awareness of the responsibility for the inherited sin and committed sin brings him to the realization of the importance of Christ's Sacrifice on the Cross to redeem mankind. But man, in his present state of spiritual barrenness, cannot see His face which is "wrapt in a brown mantle, hooded."[37]

The Cambridge anthropologists, led by Frazer, offered the thesis that man progresses from the magical, through the religious, to the scientific thought. Frazer's *The Golden Bough* and Weston's *From Ritual to Romance* had a deep influence on Eliot, specially when he wrote *The Waste Land*, the layout of which and a great deal of the incidental symbolism, besides the title, were suggested by Weston's book. The poem opens with a complex of anthropological symbols:

> April is the cruellest month, breeding
> Lilacs out of the dead land, mixing
> Memory and desire, stirring
> Dull roots with spring rain.[38]

The Cambridge anthropologists tried to show how Christianity was actually a continuity of primitive rituals and vegetation rites where sacrifices were performed in order to restore the fertility of the land. Carol Smith takes stock of this when she says:

> The primitive analogies between the fertility of the earth and the fertility of man suggests the unity between human and physical nature at the same time that it provided a connection between the sexual and spiritual fulfillment of man.[39]

Christ's crucifixion in April (the season of spring) is an incident which is not separate from the sacrificial rites which were believed to rejuvenate the fertility of the earth. In his conception of the scheme of things Eliot attached great importance to this idea, thereby broadening the corpus of Christianity and universalizing it by linking it up with the myth of the dying God on the one hand and the legend of freeing of the waters on the other. So, he used anthropology in order to suggest and create the necessary setting for his poems since he knew that there was no common ground of belief in the modern urban existence, and he was conscious of his role as poet.

He chose to divide the poem into five parts which would advance towards a denouement (for the poem exposes modern man's spiritual aridity, studies it, and indicates a way towards spiritual regeneration in the final part) in a manner resembling that of the five-act plays of the Elizabethan and Jacobean dramatists, whom Eliot admired. In *The Waste Land* there is the use of several voices of the personae representing the different levels of awareness of modern men. The first part, 'The Burial of the Dead,' has speakers talking of the spiritual barrenness of the city dwellers. One of them says, "And the dry stone no sound of water,"[40] obviously referring to a spiritual aridity. There is the lover who speaks of his incapability of expressing his true feelings:

> —Yet when we came back, late, from the hyacinth garden,
> Your arms full, and your hair wet, I could not
> Speak, and my eyes failed, I was neither
> Living nor dead, and I knew nothing.[41]

The second part, 'A Game of Chess,' involves many interactive voices. There is the narrator's description of Lil and her exotic room, followed by a conversation between them that unveils her disregard for her husband, Albert, who is in the army, away from home. This gives her ample scope for amorous indulgences:

> He's been in the army four years, he wants a good time,
> And if you don't give it him, there's others will, I said.
> Oh is there, she said. Something o' that, I said.
> Then I'll know who to thank, she said, and give me a straight look.[42]

Lil's careful manipulation of her lifestyle resembles the moves of a game of chess. She represents the modern city-dwellers who lead a luxurious and exuberant life that is devoid of spiritual scruples.

The action rises in the third section, 'The Fire Sermon,' where the persona imagines that he is Tiresias, prophesying in the characteristic manner of the legendary foreseer about the fire of physical and material desires that consume men:

> He, the young man carbuncular, arrives,
> [........................................................]
> The meal is ended, she is bored and tired,
> Endeavours to engage her in caresses
> Which still are unreproved, if undesired.[43]

The carbuncular clerk has a close resemblance with the Knave of Hearts[44] in the tarot pack of cards to which there is a reference in 'The Burial of the Dead' where Madame Sosostris has a "wicked pack of cards."[45] This sickening relationship of a repulsive physicality instigates the speaker to escape from this suffocating environment and float on the Thames, "Supine on the floor of a narrow canoe"[46] in order to get the feel of the flowing river which brings to the reader's mind the idea of the life-giving waters in the legend of the Fisher King. Regeneration can be brought about by recourse to spiritual cleansing through rigorous atonement. In order to point out this way to his readers Eliot refers to St. Augustine in 'To Carthage then I Came.'[47] The need for spiritual purification had been hinted at by Buddha (long before the birth of Christ) in his Fire-Sermon. Eliot uses the symbol of the fire as enunciated in the Sermon which he came to know about from a reading of Warren's translation from the *Maha-Vagga,* which is a central text of early Buddhism.[48] This Sermon, Eliot points out in his notes to *The Waste Land,* corresponds to Christ's Sermon on the Mount. Cleo McNelly Kearns comments on the use of the fire-symbol in the poem:

> It takes up a trope used throughout the *Upanishads* and the *Vedas* and in the *Gita,* but one that has a particular importance to the Buddhist tradition—a trope of fire that refers both to the pain of worldly experience—to the process of purification by which that pain can be overcome.[49]

Thus, Eliot uses the fire-symbol as a rhetorical device in order to make his auditors conscious of their attachment to objects of desire—the causes of suffering which can be overcome by a spiritual regeneration.

In the fourth section, 'Death by Water,' the speaker refers to Phlebas, the drowned Phoenician sailor (who is also mentioned in the first section) who is a type of the Fertility God whose image was thrown into the sea annually to symbolize the death of summer. The sea, therefore, is the accepted symbol of regeneration. Eliot uses this symbolic representation of water to hint at the possibility of a spiritual regeneration which brings the reader to the last section of the poem, 'What the Thunder Said.' Here the speaker, seeking for a way towards spiritual fertility, utters:

> The awful daring of a moment's surrender
> [..........................................................]
> Fishing, with the arid plain behind me
> Shall I at least set my lands in order?[50]

The search for a union with God leads to rigorous disciplining of the spiritual self, following not only the way of St. John of the Cross or St. Augustine, but also the path defined by the *Brhadaranyaka Upanishad*[51] regarding selflessness, compassion and control:

Datta. Dayadhvam. Damyata.
Shantih shantih shantih.[52]

This, according to the *Upanishad*, was the advice of the Thunder, rumbling over Himavant, to the three kinds of Brahma's creation. To men he says, "Datta" (give). To the *asuras* or demons he says, "Dayadhvam" (be compassionate). To the gods he says, "Damyata" (control yourselves). These will lead to "shantih" or the peace that passes understanding.[53] Knight sums up the theme of *The Waste Land* beautifully when he says that "Advance is through desert and fire to religious grace, as rain. The only explicit religious commitment is conveyed by a use of Sanskrit quotations to denote a spiritual mastery."[54]

It is through the quasi-dramatic mode of poetic articulation and the use of the voices of personae that Eliot brings to the understanding of the reader the supreme importance of self-control—a moral and emotional discipline which leads towards the apocalyptic vision provided by Virgil that is celebrated in the poem. Virgil portrays Aeneas as a man who fulfils his destiny effectively and this understanding left an indelible mark on the mind of Eliot, the creative artist. So, we find that he brings out the tragic irony implicit in the city-dweller's mechanical life before he proceeds towards pointing out a way of salvation from this predicament. Pound excised from *The Waste Land* "much of the confessional elements [...] which Eliot had introduced into the original manuscript as a part of his autobiographical exercise, [and this] would have given the poem a greater sense of cohesiveness and integrity,"[55] points out a critic.

The next poem, *The Hollow Men*, also follows the five-part pattern to describe the inanity and hollowness of urban life. The speakers in the first part are a group of hollow men who declare:

We are the hollow men
We are the stuffed men
Leaning together
Headpiece filled with straw. Alas![56]

This is a perfect expression of the lack of spiritual understanding in modern men. These hollow men are aware of their inability to look with "direct eyes"[57] at the Ultimate Reality. Their fear is expressed in the second part: "Eyes I dare not meet in dreams."[58] They are aware of their incapacity and spiritual aridity. So, in the third section they describe the modern metropolis: "This is the dead land / This is cactus land."[59] The fourth part depicts the image of the "tumid river"[60] on the one hand and "the perpetual star / Multifoliate rose"[61] on the other—one borrowed from the legend of the Fisher King, the other gleaned from the *Divine Comedy*. These images symbolize man's quest for self-realization. However, the hollow men fail to undertake this quest owing to their state of timidity and acedia. Therefore, in the final section they sing:

*Here we go round the prickly pear*
*Prickly pear prickly pear*
*Here we go round the prickly pear*
*At five o'clock in the morning.*[62]

This song, which may be the parody of a nursery rhyme,[63] expresses man's loss of the state of innocence and his futile pursuit of materialism. The disparity between the reality of his present condition and what he could have been if he had practiced self-control is hammered upon the consciousness of the reader:

Between the desire
And the spasm
Between the potency
And the existence
Between the essence
And the descent
Falls the shadow.[64]

The superimposition of ideas and images creates a picture of sordidness which exists not only on the physical level of existence but on the spiritual plane as well. The use of objective correlatives to express this complex experience shows Eliot's sincere search for an apt mode of poetic expression. The brief lines of *The Hollow Men* convey a sense of breathlessness and exasperation with a noticeable absence of sufficient punctuation marks.

*Ash Wednesday*, published in 1930, is Eliot's confessional poem, written after his inevitable conversion to Anglo-Catholicism in 1927. However, he continues with the use of the third voice of the persona in this poem. It reproduces the same yearning for the love and grace of God which the reader finds in *The Waste Land* and *The Hollow Men*, but with a greater intensity. The final section of *The Hollow Men* emphasized the word 'Between' to express the sense of a hindrance between the aspirant and God. The first part of *Ash Wednesday* emphasizes the word 'Because' pointing out that the obstacle of hesitation and inaction has been overcome. Now there is an ardent plea: "For what is done, not to be done again / May the judgment not be too heavy upon us."[65] There is the Dantesque vision of "The Single Rose"[66] in the second section and an elaborate symbol of the ascent of a spiralling staircase in the third which is also borrowed from Dante. The climbing of the stairs represents an upward movement towards God. The fourth section unfolds the promise of rejuvenation and the fifth refers to God, the Father: "Against the word the unstilled world still whirled / About the centre of the silent word."[67] The final section draws to a close with a line from Dante "Our peace in His will"[68] which leads towards an ardent prayer:

> Suffer me not to be separated
> And let my cry come unto Thee.[69]

The only way towards salvation from the state of spiritual barrenness that modern man finds himself in, is through suffering and salvation which follows the pattern of Christ's Suffering for mankind. Here is a dramatic movement from a sense of hollowness towards union with God. The six-part structure of the poem follows the design of the ascent of the spiralling stairs that Dante uses in *The Divine Comedy*. Unlike *The Waste Land* and *The Hollow Men*, *Ash Wednesday* has six sections, the final one expressing a sincere craving for union with God.

The *Ariel Poems* were written to cater to the Christmas-card trade but they do have something to say to the contemporary reader. The possibility of a wide circulation provoked Eliot to bring to contemporary city-dwellers the awareness of the relevance of Christ's Birth through these poems. In 'Journey of the Magi' (1927), the first of the *Ariel Poems*, the speakers are the three Wise Men of the Orient who have travelled in "The very dead of winter"[70] undertaking a very difficult journey which has become necessary for another Nativity because modern men have come to be like "an alien people clutching their gods."[71] This makes them articulate, "I should be glad of another death"[72] which is another martyrdom for the redemption of sinful men. The speaker in 'A Song for Simeon,' (1928) who is the city-dweller, says, "Not for me the martyrdom, the ecstasy of thought and prayer, / Not for me the ultimate vision."[73] The only way towards salvation and spiritual peace is that which is exemplified by Jesus Christ. This is the way followed by the Christian martyrs, too. It requires humility, a complete submission to God's Will and a detachment from all worldly desires. Eliot's genuine concern for the spiritual awakening in the context of the city-dwellers' irresolute and selfish lifestyle is thrown into relief in 'Animula' (1929):

> The pain of living and the drug of dreams
> Curl up the small soul in the window seat
> Behind the *Encyclopaedia Britannica*.
> Issues from the hand of time the simple soul
> Irresolute and selfish, misshapen, lame,
> Unable to fare forward or retreat,
> Fearing the warm reality, the offered good,
> Denying the importunity of the blood.[74]

The "importunity of the blood" does not lie supremely in His person or ministry or teaching; it lies supremely in His death upon the Cross, according to apostolic teaching and doctrine. Before His arrest and trial, Jesus who knew that His final suffering was close by, gave to His Apostles at the Last Supper the bread and wine as His body and blood, saying, "This do in remembrance of me,"[75] pointing to Himself as the true substitute of the Paschal Lamb. Since then, Christ's blood has been the sign under which God remembers His people in Himself.

The source for 'Marina' (1930), the fourth of the *Ariel Poems*, is Shakespeare's *Pericles,* which is one of his last plays. In these plays of Shakespeare the sea "serves as a reservoir of possibilities."[76] In *Pericles* we find the sea playing a significant role in the reunion of the family of Pericles, King of Tyre, particularly in the discovery of his daughter, Marina, whom he had lost when she was a mere infant. Marina is born at sea, symbolizing rejuvenation. Pericles, the speaker in Eliot's poem, seems to represent modern man with his detachment from the state of bliss: "Those who suffer the ecstasy of the animals, meaning / Death."[77] To him a reunion with Marina symbolizes a return to that state:

> This form, this face, this life
> Living to live in a world of time beyond me; let me
> Resign my life for this life, my speech for that unspoken,
> The awakened, lips parted, the hope, the new ships.[78]

It is through the dramatic device of the third voice which Eliot assigns to the various personae in his poems that he tries to convey the different levels of awareness of the spiritual barrenness of modern urban men. This awareness, injected into the reader's consciousness, will enable the reader to realize the importance of the Crucifixion for which the Nativity was imperative. However, modern men lack the faith to acknowledge a sense of gratitude to Christ, the Son of God born as the Son of Man, for His supreme sacrifice for their sake. In their state of acedia and barrenness they cannot realize the worth of Holy Communion. So, in the pair of fragments entitled *Sweeney Agonistes* Eliot offers us the most significant study of the boredom, squalor and horror of the city life in the late nineteenth and early twentieth centuries, besides an awareness of the spiritual barrenness in modern man that leads to self-understanding which in turn points towards a quest for self-realization and meaning of life.

## II

Eliot presents *Prufrock and Other Observations* in a cinematographic manner with each poem portraying a different, apparently separate feature of the sordid modern world. Eliot's use of the "internal monologue"[79] in his early poems came to reflect a sort of combination of the dramatic monologues of Browning and Laforgue which, according to J. Isaacs, was the result of previous preparation.[80] To this Eliot added an element of detachment while creating the voice of the interlocutor. But, it must be emphasized, that the voices of the different speakers in his poems are Eliot's use of the third voice, which portrays the poet's experimentations in his quest for articulation. Therefore, Elisabeth Schneider's allegation that "Eliot's early verses [...] including the shorter poems of the *Prufrock* volume, are nearly all as impersonal and unromantic"[81] obviously damages a clear understanding of the poet's aim, for impersonality was his stance to veil a romantic nature. However, Schneider records Eliot's own words regarding Davidson's poems when Eliot, discussing Davidson, explained that:

> He got the idea that one could write poetry in an English such as one could speak oneself. A colloquial idiom.[82]

Eliot even wrote a preface[83] to a collected edition of Davidson's poems, the idiom of which (both slangy and colloquial) came to influence Eliot's early poems. Davidson wrote in 'Thirty Bob a Week':

> I couldn't touch a stop and turn a screw,
>     And set the blooming world a-work for me,
>     [.........................................................]
> So p'r'aps we are in Hell for all that I can tell,
>     And lost and damn'd and served up hot to God.[84]

When Eliot's poems, which move from dissociated sensibility towards a unification of sensibility,[85] are read one after another, a complete multidimensional picture evolves. In attempting to experiment with the techniques of appropriate articulation, Eliot found that no adequate form was available to express the multiple levels of understanding he experienced. He felt the urgent need to forge his own poetic idiom, beginning straightaway with 'The Love Song of J. Alfred Prufrock,' using in each successive poem, not the first or second, but the third voice of the interlocutor, which he explains in 'The Three Voices of Poetry' as:

> [...] the voice of the poet when he attempts to create a dramatic character speaking in verse; when he is saying, not what he would say in his own person, but only what he can say within the limits of one imaginary character addressing another imaginary character.[86]

It was through this third voice that Eliot gave vent to his understanding of the contemporary fragmented world. So, we have the voices of Prufrock, the youth in 'Portrait of a Lady,' the old man in *Gerontion*, amongst others. These voices provided the basis of the dramatic-situation-kind-of-poems.

Eliot preferred poetry over prose for expressing himself because he felt that poetry could cover greater ground and a wider variety of implications than prose, conveying something beyond what prose could do.

Having decided upon the voice of the interlocutor as his mode of expression, Eliot embarked upon a quest for form—a form that would suit his purpose of articulating the difficulty of our efforts in throwing into relief the modern spiritual wasteland. He began by following (and not imitating) the form of *verse libre* used by the French Symbolists like Laforgue, Corbiere, Verdenal and Rimbaud in lines like these from 'The Love Song of J. Alfred Prufrock':

> Streets that follow like a tedious argument
>     Of insidious intent.[87]

Conrad Aiken says that "he shows himself to be an exceptionally acute technician"[88] using free rhyme with irregular line lengths. In *Gerontion* he experimented with the possibilities of rhymeless verse:

>     I was neither at the hot gates
> Nor fought in the warm rain
>     Nor knee deep in the salt marsh, heaving a cutlass,
> Bitten by flies, fought.[89]

However, Eliot would not call his verse in the early poems *verse libre* for he clearly states in 'Reflections on *Verse Libre*' that "there is only good verse, bad verse, and chaos,"[90] and in a lecture delivered in 1942, published under the title 'The Music of Poetry,' he clarified this, saying:

> Whether poetry is accentual or syllabic, rhymed or rhymeless, formal or free, it cannot afford to lose its contact with the changing language of common intercourse. [...] When I profess to be talking about the 'music' of poetry, I put such emphasis upon conversation.[91]

Not only melody, but dissonance and cacophony have their significant roles in poetic expression, thereby rendering a rhythm of "fluctuating emotion essential to the musical structure of the whole."[92] While discussing *The Waste Land*, N.L. Rosenthal refers to Eliot's use of this method:

> [...] we have been carried through a process of emotional clarification that is musically ordered, a music of feeling rather than a music of ideas, its dynamics determined by shifts in the intensity and lyric deployment of the successive passages.[93]

Eliot's apathy towards the catch-phrase "free verse" grows from his observation that bad poets try to pass off a great deal of bad prose under this label. For a serious and talented poet there are two tasks—first, to adapt his form to colloquial speech and, second, to elaborate on this. He notes that his work of the years between 1922 and 1942 belongs to a period "of search for a proper colloquial idiom."[94] Perhaps it is for this very reason that he took keen interest in the poems of Davidson.

The words that a poet chooses are the most important part of his quest for articulating the multiplicity of ideas and emotions which are in a constant state of flux within his mind. To Eliot a word is neither ugly nor beautiful. Its beauty lies in its relation with other words "for it is only at certain moments that a word can be made to insinuate the whole history of a language and a civilization."[95] So, the musicality of a poem lies, not solely upon the pattern of the sound, but largely on the secondary meanings of the words that compose it, the melodious effect resulting from a harmony between the two.

He did make ample use of the ironic tone which he came across in the poetry of the French Symbolists. In the early poems up to *The Waste Land* he uses irony as a device of articulating the state of fragmentariness of modern man's spiritual existence in a language which shows obvious signs of being "in the throes of a struggle."[96] Then comes a change in tone as Eliot progresses in his quest for articulation. In *Ash Wednesday* he makes an experiment with a very different mode of expression. Here there is an extensive use of repetitive and incantatory language which gives the poem a lyrical tone, which in many ways is different from that of the *The Waste Land*. There is a repetition of phrases like "Because I do not hope"[97] and other variations.

Unlike in prose, the word in poetry has "absolute value [for it is] incantation, as well as imagery."[98] At the same time "the word is interesting for its own meaning, as well as for what the writer means to mean by it."[99] The significance of articulation lies in the fact that what the poet experiences is not poetry but poetic material for "the writing of the poetry is a fresh 'experience' for him, and the reading of it, by the author or anyone else, is another thing still."[100] These comments, made by Eliot at different phases of his literary career, are a pointer to the fact that he was conscious of the importance of the choice of appropriate expressions to convey to the outer world the complexity of the experiences of his inner being. He explains his task:

> The function of the poet at every moment is to make the inarticulate folk articulate; and as the inarticulate folk is almost always mumbling the speech, become jargon, [...] this purification of language is not so much a progress, as it is a perpetual return to the real.[101]

The quest for articulation made Eliot heavily indebted to the Metaphysical poets who, according to him, were "engaged in the task of trying to find the verbal equivalent for states of mind and feeling."[102] This attempt made them more mature and better poets than their successors. To Eliot's poetry is the expression of immediate and private experience of the poet so that it can be expressed in general conditions in a way which reaches the private experience of the reader, making the three points meet in the understanding of the reader. This is what the Metaphysical poets tried to achieve.

Eliot was a romantic in thought and feeling and a classicist in his poetic technique. So, his is a case of an interesting synthesis of romanticism and classicism—or, a fine combination, a balance of emotion and intellect—may be because of his ingrained affiliation to the Metaphysical poets, on whom he dwelt from time to time.

Andrew Marvell's 'To His Coy Mistress' follows the theme of *carpe diem*, which was used already in an exhaustive manner as a traditional commonplace. The unique quality of the poem lies "where the wit of Marvell renews the theme [...] in the variety and order of the images."[103] That "this wit forms the cresendo and diminuendo of a scale of great imaginative power"[104] is best illustrated by lines like:

> But at my back I alwayes hear
> Times winged Charriot hurrying near,[105]

which remind us of the transitoriness of time and the evanescence of being. Eliot gives these very lines a Laforguian ironical twist when he uses them to describe the sordid materialistic world:

> But at my back from time to time I hear
> The sound of horns and motors.[106]

Modern man treats time in physical terms which is symbolized by the sounds of machines.

The other aspect of Metaphysical poetry that influenced Eliot was the *conceit* which is developed by a quick association of thoughts demanding an equal dexterity in the reader. Discussing the Metaphysical poets, Eliot wrote:

> A thought to Donne was an experience; it modified his sensibility. When a poet's mind is perfectly equipped for its

> work, it is constantly amalgamating disparate experience; the ordinary man's experience is chaotic, irregular, fragmentary.[107]

Donne imbibed the technique of arresting a thought "in order to extract every possible ounce of the emotion suspended in it."[108] He did this in order to highlight those "curious aspects"[109] which would otherwise have remained unobserved. Eliot emphasizes that "It is not so much in the thought, as in the development of the thought, that Donne's metaphysical peculiarity resides."[110] John Donne's method, according to Eliot, follows a movement from "the central to the peripheral, from the passionate to the reflective."[111] The method was so effective that Eliot was drawn towards it, using it, in a modified form in his poetry and drama in order to express himself with the maximum impact upon the reader or the auditor. It was this movement from a "dissociation of sensibility"[112] to "unification of sensibility"[113] that represents the gamut of Eliot's poetic experiences—something he found in the nucleus of the expression of the Metaphysical poets, specially Donne and Marvell. The impact of these poets on Eliot can be traced in lines like "I will show you fear in a handful of dust"[114] and "He knew the anguish of the marrow. The ague of the skeleton"[115] which have "dramatic quality of a high order, not only in dialogue and character creation but in tone of voice,"[116] according to Knight.

Although Eliot used techniques borrowed from the French Symbolists on the one hand and Davidson and the Metaphysical poets on the other, he found no adequate form of poetry or mode of articulation to express the complexity of experiences of the modern urban man. Therefore, he sought for a suitable mode of precise expression. The search began with the early poems which are quasi-dramatic in nature, progressing with each successive creation towards drama proper.

## III

*Sweeney Agonistes*: *Fragments of an Aristophanic Melodrama*, originally published in two volumes of *The Criterion* during 1926-27, was Eliot's first attempt at writing for theatrical performance, although a rudimentary one. He depended largely on Arnold Bennet for its performance in 1934 and Bennet agreed to do the scenario. Eliot's concentration, therefore, rested solely on the dialogue—obviously in verse. In the introduction to his mother's poetic drama, *Savonarola*, published in 1926, Eliot wrote a few significant lines:

> The next form of drama will have to be a verse drama but in new verse forms. Perhaps the conditions of modern life [...] have altered our perception of rhythms. At any rate, the recognized forms of speech-verse are not as efficient as they should be; probably a new form will be devised out of colloquial speech.[117]

Along with his experiments with articulation and verse form, Eliot aimed to reveal several levels of significance through his characters who would reach out in different ways to the several levels of understanding of the contemporary auditors. For the intelligent there was the character of Sweeney who was trying to grapple with the two levels of physical and spiritual existence. Those who were less intelligent among the audience could enjoy the comedy provided by the rest of the characters in a manner which reminded them of the very popular music-hall performances. The experiment with the characters of Wauchope, Horsfall, Klipstein and Krumpacker, whose voices he uses individually and as a Chorus, is the preamble to the series of experiments with the Chorus that Eliot conducts in the plays which follow *Sweeney Agonistes*. Equally significant was his use of the jazz rhythm in the dialogue, spoken to the beats of a drum in order to bring the verse close to the cadence of jazz music, which in turn was close to everyday speech. The effect of this primarily Black-American rhythm on the music of verse, particularly in comedy, was an experiment worth undertaking.

The term "dramatic" had deep implications for Eliot. By it he understood the creation of a harmony in the use of words, "a rhythmic and proportioned totality forming a complete emotional and ideological whole."[118] This is emphasized by the poet himself when he says in 'The Possibility of a Poetic Drama':

> To create a form is not merely to invent a shape, a rhyme or rhythm. It is also the realization of the whole appropriate content of this rhyme or rhythm.[119]

It was the poetry of life which he aimed to uphold in his plays and verse was the best medium for this purpose. It was essential for him to get upon the stage "this precise statement of life [...] a world which the author's mind has subjected to a complete process of simplification."[120] To convey this simplified statement of life, Eliot turned to the rhythms of jazz music because the best of this music had been carried by the Africans to America when they were transported as slaves to the newly discovered land—it was essentially a music of the primitive and simple people.

The beat is the pulse of jazz, effecting a continuity in the rhythm which may be weak, strong, weak, strong, as in "And you wait for a knock and the turning of a lock,"[121] or vice versa, as in "I've been born, and once is enough,"[122] or the resolute one, one, one, one of bop, as in: "Under the bamboo/ Bamboo bamboo."[123] Without this beat music cannot be called jazz. In *Sweeney Agonistes* this drum beat plays on the nerves of the audience, suggesting meanings through the rhythm. To this is added the borrowings from music-hall *turns* which, according to Katharine J. Worth "heighten the sense of isolation: as characters go into their routines, they convey the essential solitariness of the music-hall performer before he makes contact with his audience."[124] So Worth feels that *Sweeney Agonistes* is Eliot's "most radical experiment (of the plays not written for religious occasion)."[125] This is further illustrated in Eliot's own essay on Matthew Arnold where he discusses his concern with rhythm:

> [...] the musical qualities of verse [...] what I call the 'auditory imagination' is the feeling for syllable and rhythm, penetrating far below the conscious levels of thought and feeling, invigorating every word; sinking to the most primitive and forgotten, returning to the origin and bringing

> something back, seeking the beginning and the end. It [...] fuses [...] the most ancient and the most civilized mentality.[126]

In order to penetrate into the level of primitivism in man, Eliot used the jazz rhythm which was primitive, yet close to the cadence of contemporary speech.

*Sweeney Agonistes* may be called a bridge between Eliot's poetry and plays, coming at a time when he was trying to forge a kind of verse suitable for articulation on the stage—poetry that would sound like day-to-day speech. His interest in the theatre and his ardent desire to be a dramatist may be gauged from what he wrote about the poet in the theatre in the Conclusion to *The Use of Poetry and the Use of Criticism*:

> He would like to be something of a popular entertainer, and be able to think his own thoughts behind a tragic or comic mask. He would like to convey the pleasures of poetry, not only to a larger audience, but to larger groups of people collectively; and the theatre is the best place in which to do it. [...] All the better, then, if he could have at least the satisfaction of having a part to play in society as worthy as that of the music-hall comedian.[127]

Music-hall comedy was a very popular entertainment during the early decades of the twentieth century, becoming a serious rival to the theatre with its power to attract audiences. Eliot was intrigued by these musical performances, and he wrote about them in his criticism which included an essay on the great actress of music-hall shows, Marie Lloyd. In 'The Possibility of a Poetic Drama' he writes:

> Our problem should be to take a form of entertainment, and subject it to the process which would leave it a form of art. Perhaps the music-hall comedian is the best material.[128]

The informal interaction between the performers and the audience of music-hall comedies made communication easier. This convenience of articulation and a quick rapport with the audience encouraged Eliot to try his hand at something similar in *Sweeney Agonistes*. The rhythmic speech of the characters follows that of the music-hall performances, besides the beat of jazz music, as in the Chorus:

FULL CHORUS: WAUCHOPE, HORSEFALL, KLIPSTEIN, KRUMPACKER.
When you're alone in the middle of the night and
you wake in a sweat and a hell of a fright
When you're alone in the middle of the bed and
you wake like someone hit you in the head
You've had a cream of a nightmare dream and
you've got the hoo-ha's coming to you.
Hoo hoo hoo.[129]

Eliot's first attempt at writing drama was met with a wide variety of comments from the critics. Grover Smith says that "Eliot's experiment with drama in *Sweeney Agonistes* constituted a false start."[130] It shows that he failed to perceive the effort behind the poem. Sarkar, on the other hand, appreciates the attempt, saying, "[...] *Sweeney Agonistes* occupies a very significant place in the history of Eliot's development as a dramatist."[131]

The subtitle *Fragments of an Aristophanic Melodrama* is pregnant with meanings. Obviously, the work is unfinished and, therefore, fragmentary in nature. The mode is that of melodrama since the dialogue is accompanied by music and song and there is the hint of a happy ending. However, the term *Aristophanic* in the subtitle is the most important part of it because Eliot falls back on Aristophanes' humour which lies largely in exaggeration, parody and satire, which Eliot directs at the materialism and physicality of modern urban existence. The ancient Greek comic-dramatist gave an amusing turn to a serious discussion in much of his work and this trait is borrowed by Eliot for *Sweeney Agonistes*.

The fact that Eliot was undertaking his personal quest while writing *Sweeney Agonistes* is obvious from his use of the epigraphs—one from an ancient Greek tragedy and another from a medieval Christian mystical treatise—apparently unconnected, but having deep spiritual connections. Sweeney's state in the sordid and barren modern world can be best described with the aid of Eliot's own words when he says that "a man may be nearly crushed by the terrible awareness of his isolation from every other human being [... and be ...] alone with himself and his meanness and futility, alone without God."[132]

The first epigraph from Sophocles's *Choephoroi,* expresses Orestes's spiritual unease:

> ORESTES: You don't see them, you don't—but I see them: they are hunting me down, I must move on.[133]

Eliot's use of this line from the non-Christian Greek playwright is described by Morton D. Zabel as "one of the most important declarations in modern poetry."[134] Marvin Halverson notices Eliot's "awareness of the role of myth in illuminating man's situation."[135] The search for a meaning of life is equally significant to Sophocles and Eliot, showing that age, country or religion has little meaning when man quests for the Ultimate Truth that lies at the core of the meaning of life. Eliot makes use of the Orestes-myth in great detail in *The Family Reunion.* Here, man becomes aware of the fact that Paradiso can be reached from Inferno, via Purgatorio, only in and through suffering.

The first epigraph is complemented by the second, taken from the writings of St. John of the Cross:

> Hence the soul cannot be possessed of the divine union, until it has divested itself of the love of created beings.[136]

St. John of the Cross writes in his mystical treatise, *The Ascent of Mount Carmel*:

> In this detachment the spiritual soul finds it's quiet and repose; for, since it covets nothing, nothing wearies it when it is lifted up, and nothing oppresses it when it is cast down, because it is in the centre of its humility; but, when it covets anything, at that very moment it becomes wearied.[137]

Just as "Datta, Dayadhvam, Damyata"[138] are essential for a quester, so also is detachment, as emphasized by St. John of the Cross and the philosophical teachings of Patanjali,[139] propounded in his *Yogasutra*, where he explains:

> [...] purity is the cessation of the experience which is falsely attributed to the Self. In this state [of purity] Isolation follows [...]. Because there are no more hindrances, there is no fruition of *Karma*. In this state the aspects, their task done, do not again submit themselves as objects—for right to the Self. That is the Self's Isolation. Then the Self having its light within itself becomes undefiled and isolated.[140]

Eliot had read J.H. Wood's translation of Patanjali when he was a student at Harvard. The epigraphs "appear to suggest the theological pattern of the work—the pattern of sin, penance, purgation and mystical union with God which lies beyond the comic surface of social satire."[141] But Marianne Moore, unable to realize the spiritual context of the epigraphs, asks, "If one can choose God as a friend of the Spirit, does not the coffin become the most appropriate friend for the body?"[142] Eliot spoke in the context of his Christian belief but for people of other folds of belief it may not be necessary to die in order to win spiritual union with God. The renunciation of all sorts of attachment is a slow and painful process. Zabel feels that since Eliot's sincerity in this regard is beyond questioning, "he should doubtless be allowed not only the amusement but the thoroughness by which he will achieve that spiritual triumph."[143]

The apparent layer of amusement provided by the melodramatic ingredients of *Sweeney Agonistes* leads to the deeper level of a spiritual quest. Sweeney appears in the "Fragment of an Agon" which is preceded by the "Fragment of a Prologue" where he is mentioned in passing as one of the many visitors of Dusty and Doris. These girls spend their time by playing with the tarot cards as they wait for their visitors, reminding the reader (or auditor) of Madame Sosostris in *The Waste Land*:

> DORIS: Now I'm going to cut the cards for tonight.[144]

The tarot shows that there is a sense of lasting happiness which everyone can achieve and this is exactly what attracts the two girls, who are anxious to know what lies ahead of them. The way in which Eliot uses the tarot in the "Fragment of a Prologue" shows his knowledge of the game, particularly the mystical implications of the cards; for instance, Death, in the major arcana, is the symbol of rebirth and the two of spades, which is the two of swords in the minor arcana of the tarot, shows us how we can balance both mind and heart. Eliot uses certain symbolic representations of the tarot to portray the relationship between these two girls and their male visitors, which verges on lewdness. The "Fragment of a Prologue" shows Dusty and Doris living in Pereira's flat and entertaining other men while evading him. The crass sensuality and implied obscenity in the interaction that the girls have with the visitors, Wauchope, Horsefall, Klipstein and Krumpacker, pave the way for Sweeney's Agon in the fragment which follows in this Aristophanic melodrama.

The Agon, which is an awareness of and conflict between the physical and spiritual selves, exists within Sweeney. This 'debate' between the two adversaries in the persona of Sweeney on the crucial issue of the play is externalized when he articulates:

> Nothing at all but three things
> [..............................................]
> Birth, and copulation, and death.[145]

He feels that he has had enough of this materialistic, sordid, world and says so:

> I've been born, and once is enough.[146]

Orestes sought liberation from the hereditary curse of blood-guilt—an awareness thrust upon him in the form of a spiritual burden. Sweeney seeks liberation from the sinfulness of the modern world of materialism. However, he does not possess the strength of Thomas Becket. So, his spiritual weakness succumbs, at times, before its adversary, the physical self, which is revealed in words which he addresses to Doris:

> I'll carry you off
> To a cannibal isle.
> [.......................]

> I'll convert you!
> Into a stew.[147]

Modern civilized man has failed to overcome the primordial desires which ruled the primitive cannibals—an urge to assert oneself upon the weak and unwilling—and which is also a symptom of spiritual barrenness. Sweeney, representing this aspect of the urban man, says to Doris:

> Any man might do a girl in
> Any man has to, needs to, wants to
> Once in a lifetime, do a girl in.[148]

This shows that, however much he desires it, he has not been able to achieve a spiritual detachment from the physical existence. Eliot writes about this in *After Strange Gods*:

> Most people, no doubt, need to be aroused to the perception of the simple distinction between the spiritual and the material. [...] But most people are only very little alive; and to awaken them to the spiritual is a very great responsibility: it is only when they are so awakened that they are capable of real Good, but that at the same time they become first capable of Evil.[149]

Sweeney's 'agonistes,' or conflict within his inner self, centres on the concepts of life and death, which he tries to articulate in this way:

> Death or life or life or death
> Death is life and life is death.[150]

This is an Aristophanic element for it combines an outer surface of social satire presented through comedy and an inner ritualistic celebration of death and rebirth which, according to F.M. Cornford, underlies comedy.[151] C.H. Smith notices a deeper significance in Eliot's use of the epigraphs and the subtitle:

> Thus Eliot sees in the death-rebirth process of the God, which is the type of the Passion and Resurrection of Christ, a wider meaning than the final death of the body and eternal life of the soul after death. He sees that pattern

> applied to the mystic's process of killing desire in order to bring to birth the spirit.[152]

The words of *Sweeney Agonistes* follow the manner of articulation of the music-hall performers and are accompanied by the beating of a jazz drum. The colloquial idiom and the rhythm of jazz are Eliot's experimentations with articulation and form. Sweeney experiences an acute difficulty in expressing himself before others so that they may be able to understand his 'agon.' This quest for articulation is clear when he says:

> I gotta use words when I talk to you
> But if you understand or if you don't
> That's nothing to me and nothing to you.[153]

The importance of *Sweeney Agonistes* in the development of Eliot, the dramatist, lies, not merely in his quest for self-realization, but also in a quest for form and articulation for which he turned to the use of the contemporary idiom and mode, in the cadences of actual speech and the rhythms of popular music. "Eliot's interest in vaudeville and music-hall is sometimes regarded as a quaint foible; it should, in fact, be regarded as a deep passion,"[154] points out Gareth Lloyd Evans. His awareness of the impersonal quality in the audio-visual art of the music-hall compelled him to respond to its warmth and catchiness. The dance-movements associated with the music-hall and the primitive rhythms of jazz were combined by Eliot in *Sweeney Agonistes* as an experiment with the form of expression for he knew that:

> The drama was originally ritualistic; and ritual, consisting of a set of repeated movements, is essentially a dance. [...] It is [...] possible to assert that primitive man acted in a certain way and then found a reason for it.[155]

A close study of *Sweeney Agonistes* reveals that Eliot had included every important aspect of his quest for self-realization, form and articulation in this fragmentary drama. Knight is absolutely correct when he remarks that "this playlet is dynamite."[156] The only thing he lacked at this time was first-hand knowledge of theatrical presentation. This is the chief reason behind the fragmentariness of *Sweeney Agonistes* and a hurried treatment of his personal quest in it. However, this drawback was soon done away with on his acquaintance with E. Martin Browne, the first product of their lasting partnership being *The Rock*. "Although *Sweeney Agonistes* looks back in its subject-matter, it looks forward in its style"[157] says Helen Gardner. C.H. Smith calls this pair of fragments "Eliot's first dramatic version of the theme of spiritual pilgrimage"[158] which recurs in various features in the major plays. *Sweeney Agonistes* occupies a significant place in Eliot's development as a poet in the theatre.

## IV

When Rev. Webb-Odell requested Eliot to write the words for a pageant-play which would raise funds for church-building and which was commissioned by the Forty-Five Churches' Fund of the Diocese of London, he eagerly accepted the offer. It would be the first full-fledged play in which he would be involved as a dramatist. He did not wish to miss this opportunity of writing a poetic play, for he believed that:

> The ideal medium for poetry, [...] and the most direct means of social 'usefulness' for poetry, is the theatre. In a play of Shakespeare you get several levels of significance. For the simplest auditors there is the plot, for the more thoughtful the character and conflict of character, for the more literary the words and phrasing, for the more musically sensitive the rhythm, and for auditors of greater sensitiveness and understanding a meaning which reveals itself gradually.[159]

He also believed that "art, specifically poetry, had something to do with religion."[160] Since this was a play for a religious cause, he decided that it should be written in poetry. Drama had always lured Eliot who felt it to be the only form of literature which "is most permanent, is capable of greater variation and of expressing more varied types of society, than any other."[161]

There was a religious urge for writing this play, for the constant building of Churches symbolized the building up of one's faith. In this respect "tradition," particularly the Christian tradition was of primary importance to Eliot. He writes:

> Tradition may be conceived as a by-product of right living, not to be aimed at directly. It is of the blood, so to speak, rather than of the brain: it is the means by which the vitality of the past enriches the life of the present.[162]

Eliot felt that tradition and orthodoxy were inseparable, both being essential for the development of complete human beings:

> [...] a *tradition* is rather a way of feeling and acting which characterizes a group throughout generations; and that it must largely be, or that many of the elements in it must be, unconscious; whereas the maintenance of *orthodoxy* is a matter which calls for the exercise of all our conscious intelligence. The two will therefore considerably complement each other.[163]

On the one hand Eliot was aware of a sense of tradition and on the other he got his first taste of the problems of presenting plays on the stage. He realized that "A struggle, more or less unconscious, between the creator and the interpreter is almost inevitable. The interest of a performer is almost certain to be centred in himself."[164]

Written in 1934, nearly seven years after his formal conversion to Anglo-Catholicism, *The Rock* gave Eliot ample scope to express his passion for Christ whose image had an overwhelming influence on him throughout his life. At the same time he could never shake off the effect of his Unitarian upbringing. Therefore, the poet's life was spent in seeking his liberation from the oppressive and austere codes of the sect (to which he originally belonged) that denied the Trinity, paradoxically calling themselves Christians. Although he became an Anglican, the deep-rooted influence of his family and its faith remained concealed within his being. Eliot was trying to overcome an adherence to Unitarianism, the faith of his forefathers. It was a struggle towards complete absorption into Anglicanism. On the one hand, he could never expel Unitarianism from his inner self, on the other, he clung to the idea of Jesus Christ as the First Martyr—God's Son born in the flesh for saving mankind. This resulted in a sort of conflict, within Eliot, between the faith that denied the divinity of Christ and that which centred on His divinity. The quest, on the personal level, was for a meaning of life which would lead to a sort of payment for Christ's Martyrdom. So, the idea of martyrdom recurs in all his plays, although in different forms. This is fundamental to an understanding of Eliot's personal quest. Worth analyses the effect of the conversion on Eliot, the dramatist, as damaging in some ways for she feels that right from *The Rock* "much of his energy went into an effort to extend his range, so as to accommodate, within the drama of alienation natural to him, the opposite experience of communion."[165] Such decisive comments display a lack of understanding of Eliot's inner self and his quest for a meaning of life. The alienation of some important characters in the plays serves as an exterior to an inner craving for communion with God.

Eliot acknowledges his debt to the Rev. Webb-Odell, the Rev. Vincent Howson, Browne, F.V. Morley and Martin Shaw, amongst others, for their co-operation while he wrote "the book of words"[166] for the pageant. "It was the first time poetic drama had really come to the people",[167] says Isaacs. In a letter dated 1 April 1959, Eliot wrote to Browne (who with the Rev. Webb-Odell had written the scenario for *The Rock*) that "THE ROCK gave me a great push forward when we were working on it, as it was my first opportunity to write for the stage at all."[168]

The play highlights Christ's death on the Cross—His martyrdom to save mankind from its sins. The builders of the Church, in building it, are actually building up their faith in God. When the Church will be completed they will perform the Eucharist during Mass, participating in Christ's Martyrdom through the Holy Communion:

THE BUILDER'S SONG

Our lives have been bought
By our Lord on the Cross;
We are those who pay rent
To the temporal powers;

Of our lives misspent
        Our Lord bears the loss
[.......................................]
        We will build the new towers
And fashion the shrine
        In this London of ours
For the Bread and the Wine.[169]

Having a higher degree of spiritual understanding than the builders, Becket says in *Murder in the Cathedral*:

His blood given to buy my life,
My blood given to pay for His death.[170]

However, what is important is the profession of an unwavering faith in God—the level of awareness is secondary to devotion to God. Eliot's idea is interpreted by Grover Smith who explains that "the saint's absorption in the moment of Incarnation brings him no closer to God than does the worker's absorption in the moment of his toil."[171]

In order to make men atone for their sins, God willed that His Son should die on the Cross after intense suffering in the flesh. Christ's Birth was essential for this exemplary purpose. So, it may be said that His Death and His Birth are two faces of the same divine intention. However, being imbued with sin, men stray away from God's fold again and again, only to return to the way of light which the Chorus explains:

Through the Passion and Sacrifice saved in spite of their negative being;

Bestial as always before, carnal, self-seeking as before, selfish and purblind as ever before;

Yet always struggling, always reaffirming, always resuming their march on the way that was lit by the light;

Often halting, loitering, straying, delaying, returning, yet following no other way.[172]

The fact that Eliot conducted his quest for self-realization through the Chorus is established from his own declaration in 'The Three Voices of Poetry':

> The chorus of *The Rock* was not a dramatic voice, though many lines were distributed, the personages were unindividuated. Its members were speaking *for me,* not uttering words that really represented any supposed character of their own.[173]

At the same time he experimented with form and articulation, each of the ten choruses being a different experiment, which Browne remarks upon, saying:

> [...] these Choruses are the most dramatically vital part of the play. They combine prophetic thunder with colloquial speech; and they use the orchestra of varied voices, male and female, to create continual dramatic contrast. The verse-rhythms are equally varied, from the rolling periods of the Old Testament in the King James Version to the crisp phrases of contemporary satire; and at times, the two are combined.[174]

While appreciating Eliot's skill in the handling of the metrical pattern of the choric utterances Gardner says that the choruses have "the simplicity of syntax, the emphatic repetitions, the rhythmical variety which choric verse must possess."[175] Nevill Coghill finds the choruses from *The Rock* "the finest choric speeches in English drama since those of Milton's *Samson Agonistes*."[176] An unsigned review in *The Times Literary Supplement* expresses that "They combine the sweep of psalmody with the exact employment of colloquial words. They are lightly written, as though whispered to the paper, yet are forcible to enunciate."[177] Eliot's command over musical speech in the verse of his play showed a possibility for wider and deeper expressions in poetic drama. Although the standard measure seems to be iambic pentameter which lies interspersed with anapestic substitutions, there is great metrical diversity in the choruses in *The Rock* which contribute to the passages of excitement and incantation. There is a subtle combination of colloquialism and prayer-book, English in the Choruses which imparts a familiarity of contemporary speech rhythms to them on the one hand and a dignity of the chant of prayer on the other, thereby demonstrating the capability of this verse form of a wide range of communication. They lack in dramatic emotion, yet they display a wide range of shifting moods and various shades of powerful emotions. *The Rock* was a series of loosely connected pageants, aimed to involve a large number of eager amateur actors who were hard to handle. So the play, in which there was nearly no action, turned out to be a dramatic failure. The only merit of *The Rock* is borne by the ten beautiful Choruses (which attempt to give some sort of coherence to the play) each one different from the others and carrying evidences of Eliot's quest for a suitable verse form for articulation on the stage. The final Chorus demonstrates his capability of attaining the lyric grandeur of the Choruses in Greek Tragedy:

> You have seen the house built, you have seen it adorned
> By one who came in the night, it is now dedicated to GOD.[178]

Thus, *The Rock* may be said to represent a transitory phase between his early poetry and the yet unformed plays. The emphasis is on the stress rather than on the syllabic count in each line. All the rhythms that Eliot uses in the choruses are familiar to the audience's ear. This helps them to enjoy the cadences of the poetry.

In the Christian concept God is 'the still centre', the 'Word', around whom the entire universe revolves. Eliot clarifies this in *Ash Wednesday*:

> Against the Word the unstilled world still whirled
> About the centre of the silent Word.[179]

Traces of the omnipotent God of pre-Christian faiths can be found in the God of the Old Testament who alone is the creator, preserver and destroyer (like Brahma, Vishnu and Maheswara of the Hindu Trinity rolled into one). The same God becomes benevolent and loving in the New Testament—He is Jesus's Heavenly Father. It is around this God that the Saints, led by Christ, revolve. They are the stars while God is the Sun, emanating His radiance, showing men the way to divine grace through faith and love. The Saints have become martyrs for the atonement of the sins of mankind, paying with their blood their debt to God's Son, which the Chorus explains:

> [...] of the household of GOD, being built upon the foundation
> Of apostles and prophets, Christ Jesus Himself the chief cornerstone.[180]

The theology of the Incarnation is especially characteristic of the Anglican Communion which regards the doctrine of 'the Son of God made man' for us men and for our salvation, as the central theme of Christian theology. It is in the sense that Jesus Christ, the Word of God, of His boundless love, became what men are so that He might make men what He Himself is.

From the anthropological perspective, the sacrifice of Christ as the Paschal Lamb of the Passover, the Eucharistic feast and Holy Communion, are all continuations of vegetation rites of fertility. Frazer writes in *The Golden Bough* about certain practices in agricultural societies where the spirit of the corn, or of other cultivated plants, is commonly represented in human or animal form. In some places the custom of killing annually either the human or the animal representative of the God was performed. Frazer also states that he has found:

> [...] a widespread custom of eating the god sacramentally, either in the shape of the man or animal who represents the god, or in the shape of bread made in human or animal form. The reasons for thus partaking of the body of the god are, from the primitive standpoint, simple enough. The savage commonly believes that by eating the flesh of an animal or man he acquires not only the physical, but even the moral and intellectual qualities which were characteristic of that animal or man.[181]

In the perpetual cycle, martyrdoms occur at regular intervals to remind men of the ways of God and of their own evil ways of living—a martyrdom being an act of penance. The world is reminded of Christ's sacrifice in the "perpetual recurrence of determined seasons"[182] of spring and autumn, of birth and death. In anthropology, winter symbolizes the death, and spring, the rejuvenation of the earth and agriculture. In

Christology, winter brings the birth of Christ and spring his death. This apparent dialectic is the balancing factor in man's spiritual progress towards God.

Man's basic weakness is a tendency to succumb to sinfulness. Christ, the Saviour, showed men the way towards redemption through suffering and love. Eliot harps on this idea in 'The Hippopotamus':

> Flesh and blood is weak and frail,
> Susceptible to nervous shock;
> While the True Church can never fail
> For it is based upon a rock.[183]

It is for the sake of bringing humanity back to the ways of God that the ritual of Holy Communion is performed during Mass. The words of Administration at the Holy Communion remind us that:

> The Body of our Lord Jesus Christ which was given for thee, preserve thy Body and Soul unto everlasting life. Take and eat this in remembrance that Christ died for thee, and feed on Him in thy heart by faith with thanksgiving.[184]

Mellitus says the same thing in *The Rock*:

> MELLITUS. You shall have the white bread to eat. For it is written: except ye eat of the Flesh of the Son of Man, and drink His Blood, ye have no life in you.[185]

Thus, building the church is symbolic of building up of one's faith. However, a church can be built only when God desires so. In one of the pageants, Rahere appears, to explain that he, too, had built St. Bartholomew's Church and Bart's Hospital in adverse conditions. Just as man's spiritual journey towards God is full of hardships, Church building involves many obstacles. Church building is the first step towards spiritual fertility and self-realization, in the wasteland, not only of the modern civilization, but also that which exists within every man. Humility and surrender to God's Will are the pre-requisites of spiritual fertility, besides a strong intention and unwavering faith. The Rock emphasises:

I say to you: *Make perfect your will.*
I say: take no thought of the harvest,
But only of proper sowing.[186]

Repeating the same words later in the pageant play:

I have said, take no thought of the harvest, but only of proper sowing.[187]

This is the core of the *Nishkamakarmayoga* as explained by Krishna to Arjuna on the field of the Battle of Kurukshetra. Eliot had not only read the *Gita*,[188] he had imbibed the philosophy of this central Hindu text. This is expressed in 'The Dry Salvages':

And do not think of the fruit of action.
Fare forward.
[..................................................]
So Krishna, as when he admonished Arjuna
On the field of battle.
Not fare well,
But fare forward, voyagers.[189]

Michael Sayers opines that in this play in which both form and content are uninspiring, Eliot "does not concern himself very deeply with the mystery of our existence; this, it appears, would be contrary to his orthodoxy."[190] That this was a wrong conclusion may be proved by what the dramatist wrote in *After Strange Gods*, in which he observed that "the modern environment is so unfavourable to faith that it produces fewer and fewer individuals capable of being injured by blasphemy."[191] He also added that "the perception of Good and Evil—whatever choice we may make—is the first requisite of spiritual life."[192] This awareness in Eliot enabled him to appreciate the philosophy of the *Gita* and to make it his own, for it is a universal truth that selflessness and humility are the traits of the faithful. Even the Rock speaks of "The perpetual struggle of Good and Evil."[193] Christ, too, had to fight against the temptations of Satan, in the desert.

Man has the weight of a double sin on his shoulders—the inherited Original Sin and the sin that he commits. This evil may be cleansed through humble repentance, penance and faith, in building the Church which is the symbol of Christ, as the Chorus says:

> Of all that was done in the past, you eat the fruit, either rotten or ripe.
> And the Church must be forever building, and always decaying, and always being restored.
> [......................................................]
> And all that is ill you may repair if you walk together in humble repentance, expiating the sins of your fathers;[194]

Being born with the Original Sin, men tend to disown God, claiming that the world is what they have created for themselves. Ethelbert says that men never change very much from their easy ways. Eliot explains in *After Strange Gods* that:

> With the disappearance of the idea of Original Sin, with the disappearance of the idea of intense moral struggle, the human beings presented to us both in poetry and in prose fiction to-day, [...] tend to become less and less real. It is in fact in moments of moral and spiritual struggle depending upon spiritual sanctions, rather than in those 'bewildering minutes' in which we are all very much alike, that men and women come nearest to being real.[195]

If people do away with this struggle then human beings become "vaporous".[196] Eliot knows that what he says here has a bearing on only those who believe in the doctrine of Original Sin. One of the reasons for the spiritual barrenness in modern man is his lack of faith in this doctrine, as a result of which he has moved further away from God and closer to the dust. The Chorus asks:

> Where is the Life we have lost in living?
> Where is the wisdom we have lost in knowledge?
> Where is the knowledge we have lost in information?[197]

After they fell from God's grace, He said to Adam and Eve, "for dust thou art, and unto dust shalt thou return."[198]

Christian faith stresses the idea that man must wait upon God in all commitment and humility. They also serve who only serve and wait—this idea has been developed in great detail in the creation of the Chorus of the Canterbury Women in *Murder in the Cathedral*. Here, Mellitus refers to the idea when he speaks to the Saxons and their king, Sabert, for his ideal is Jesus Christ Himself:

> [...] wishing only to live more lowly and suffer more durely still, remembering the humility and the sufferings of our Lord upon earth, and knowing myself the least of his servants [...]. You must not think, whether God be for you, but whether you be for God.[199]

Sarkar aptly observes that this scene anticipates Becket's Christmas sermon which "interprets the sanctity and importance of martyrdom."[200]

The process of building up of one's faith is neither passive nor pacifist. A positive spiritual commitment, to build up from a strength that comes from within, is essential. Ethelbert wards off the Agitator saying, "I'm proud and 'appy to be buildin' a wall as *you'll* never see the inside of."[201] The Chorus confirms:

> So they built as men must build
>     With the sword in one hand and the trowel in the other.[202]

Even Sanballat, the Horonite, had failed to prevent Nehemiah and his followers from rebuilding Jerusalem. They had succeeded in spite of "enemies without [... and ...] spies and self-seekers within."[203] So, history teaches men to build up their faith in spite of adversities. Eliot presents this idea in the choric utterances, highlighting its significance for the modern world at the same time:

> Remember the faith that took men from home
>     At the call of a wandering preacher.
> Our age is an age of moderate virtue
>     And of moderate vice
> When men will not lay down the Cross
>     Because they will never assume it.
> Yet nothing is impossible, nothing,
>     To men of faith and conviction.

Let us therefore make perfect our will.
O GOD, help us.[204]

Eliot knew that writing religious poetry was not an easy task, particularly when he was doing this for a readership (or an audience) which was mixed. He confesses this in *After Strange Gods*, when he says, "The capacity for writing poetry is rare; the capacity for religious emotion of the first intensity is rare; [...] the existence of both capacities in the same individual should be rarer still."[205] Religious emotion can be best expressed in the building up of the Christian faith which is "forever building"[206] because it is not static. It calls for constant replenishment through one's sincere efforts to restore and redeem faith by constantly applying oneself. Man's search for faith is endless; the quest is continuous. Constant rejuvenation indicates going back to the Quest of the Holy Grail, for salvation. Building of the Temple symbolizes the building up of the Christian faith that has come to be lost in the waste and barrenness of modern material living. Faith will lead to redemption, as *The Rock* explains:

And the Gates of Hell shall not prevail.
Darkness now, then
Light.
Light.[207]

The darkness symbolizes Evil. The basic concepts of Christianity are the Devil and the Almighty God—which implies that one can never realize the greatness and benevolence of God without an awareness of Satan. God redeems mankind back to Himself through Christ because the Original Sin came upon man through the design of Satan. The Fall of Man was, in a way, Satan's machination. Darkness reminds us of Evil which was the aftermath of Satan's evil design to undo the Heavenly creation of the Garden of Eden by seducing Eve to partake of the Fruit of the Tree of Knowledge. This was the root cause of man's suffering because man became a tool in the hands of Satan which led to the Fall from Grace and the suffering on Earth, bringing upon man the experience of physical sufferings (toil and moil). Then, for the Evil committed by mankind it is incumbent upon them to atone for their sins which call for suffering. In the process Christ came to save and help mankind in the way back to God, through His Flesh and Blood. So the Chorus says:

> And we thank Thee that darkness reminds us of light.
>
> O Light Invisible, we give Thee thanks for Thy great glory![208]

Being the best of God's creation, man has the ability to choose between Good and Evil. Since the latter is the easier means to temporal luxury, man falls a prey like Doctor Faustus to the booby-traps of Satan. The Chorus mimes God's displeasure:

> I have given you power of choice, and you only alternate
>
> Between futile speculation and unconsidered action.[209]

It warns man, "Life you may evade, but Death you shall not."[210] The advice to man is to follow the way of light without being too curious of Good and Evil. "If humility and purity be not in the heart, they are not in the home: and if they are not in the home, they are not in the city."[211] But above all is God's Grace, without which man is like a seed which cannot germinate due to lack of fertile soil. However, the quest for meaning of life does not imply a denial of the physical existence. Body and soul, the sensuous and the spiritual, the physical and rational, must co-exist in man, observes the Chorus:

> For Man is joined spirit and body,
>
> And therefore must serve as spirit and body.
>
> Visible and invisible, two worlds meet in Man;
>
> Visible and invisible must meet in His Temple;
>
> You must not deny the body.[212]

But at the same time man must learn to exercise restraint upon the physical self by practising compassion and self-control: "Datta, Dayadhvam, Damyata,"[213] which will lead to "Shantih, shantih, shantih."[214] or the peace that passes understanding, as Eliot explains.

Building up one's faith requires God's aid. The Chorus says, "We build in vain unless the LORD build with us"[215] because the quest for self-realization involves a choice between Good and Evil. Every moment, which is the present also, is a crossing between the past and the future, both of which extend into eternity. The Rock warns man that his preoccupation with the present, particularly the material present, is a pursuit of an illusion and man should remember the reality of the eternal:

> O faint-hearted, and easily unsettled, and easily lost
> In the blinding movement of time, sinking and borne away;
> Remember, all you who are numbered for GOD,
> In every moment of time you live where two worlds cross,
> In every moment you live at a point of intersection,
> Remember, living in time, you must live also now in Eternity.[216]

One has to be brave and selfless. If Christ, the Son of God, could give up His life to save mankind, man can, like Nehemiah and Thomas Becket, pay for His blood with his blood. Nehemiah's words anticipate Becket's in *Murder in the Cathedral*, when he says, "Should such a man as I flee? And who is there, that being such as I, would go into the temple to save his life? I will not go in."[217] The Chorus supports him. Sarkar observes that:

> This urgent call to martyrdom given by the Chorus may serve as the befitting prologue to Eliot's plays which dramatize the theme of martyrdom in their ritual underpattern.[218]

However, Eliot's apprehension about the use of the Chorus is expressed in a letter dated 12 April 1939 to Bonamy Dobree:

> I am by no means sure about the chorus: I mean whether I shall look on it as a permanent element for the future, or whether it is a vestige, something the employment of which has been a help to *me* in finding the way from non-dramatic to dramatic verse.[219]

although he had written in a letter to *The Spectator* (Vol. 152, No. 887) dated 8 June 1934 that "My only serious dramatic aim was to show that there is a possible *role* for the Chorus."[220] The significance of *The Rock* in the career of Eliot, the dramatist, lies in the fact that his involvement in the writing of the book of words for this pageant inspired him to write a play for the Canterbury Festival of 1935, of which he speaks in an interview with John Lehmann, almost twenty years after the performance of *The Rock* at Sadler's Wells Theatre:

> [...] and working on it began to make me interested in writing drama, and led directly to 'Murder in the Cathedral.'[221]

## NOTES AND REFERENCES

1. Eliot, *The Varieties of Metaphysical Poetry*, ed. Ronald Schuchard (London: Faber, 1993) 148.
2. Sarkar, *T.S. Eliot the Dramatist* 27.
3. Eliot, "Tradition and the Individual Talent," *The Sacred Wood* 58.
4. Sarkar, "T.S. Eliot: A Poet in Quest of His Roots," *Manual of First UGC-Sponsored Refresher Course* 1.1 (Benaras: Benaras Hindu University, 1999) n. pag.
5. Matthews 3.
6. Matthews 3.
7. Sarkar, "'The Love Song of J. Alfred Prufrock' as a Modernist Poem," *The Journal of English Studies Association* 1.1 (Burdwan: University of Burdwan, 1998) 1.
8. Eliot, "The Love Song of J. Alfred Prufrock," *Prufrock and Other Observations*, CPP 14.
9. Eliot, "The Love Song of J. Alfred Prufrock," CPP 16.
10. Arthur Symons, *The Symbolist Movement in Literature* (New York: Dutton, 1919) 9.
11. Symons, 306.
12. Eliot, "Tradition and the Individual Talent," *The Sacred Wood* 49.
13. Sarkar, "'The Love Song of J. Alfred Prufrock' as a Modernist Poem," *The Journal of English Studies Association* 1.1.
14. Eliot, "The Love Song of J. Alfred Prufrock," CPP 13.
15. Eliot, CPP 13.

16. Eliot, CPP 13.
17. Eliot, CPP 13.
18. Eliot, "Portrait of a Lady," *Prufrock and Other Observations*, CPP 19.
19. Eliot, CPP 19.
20. Eliot, CPP 20.
21. Eliot, CPP 21.
22. Eliot, "Preludes," *Prufrock and Other Observations*, CPP 22.
23. Eliot, CPP 22.
24. Eliot, CPP 23.
25. Eliot, CPP 23.
26. Eliot, "Rhapsody on a Windy Night," *Prufrock and Other Observations*, CPP 24.
27. Eliot, CPP 24.
28. Eliot, CPP 24.
29. Eliot, "William Blake," *Selected Essays* 321.
30. Eliot, "Matthew Arnold," *The Use of Poetry and the Use of Criticism* (London Faber and Faber, 1964) 106.
31. Eliot, "Gerontion," *Poems 1920*, CPP 38.
32. Eliot, CPP 38.
33. Eliot, CPP 38
34. Eliot, CPP 39.
35. Eliot, *The Waste Land*, CPP 62.
36. Weston, *The Quest of the Holy Grail* (1913; London: Frank Cass, 1964) 80-81.
37. Eliot, *The Waste Land*, CPP 73.
38. Eliot, CPP 61.
39. Carol H. Smith, *T. S. Eliot's Dramatic Theory and Practice* (Princeton: Princeton UP, 1963) 41.
40. Eliot, *The Waste Land*, CPP 61.
41. Eliot, CPP 62.
42. Eliot, CPP 66.
43. Eliot, CPP 68.
44. He brings out those feelings which involve taking the initiative. When we feel those emotional needs banging on the door of our mind, we should go with them. Who knows where they might lead us? If we ignore them, we will just remain bored and unfulfilled. By letting

them guide us we might well have a lot of fun!—Evelyn and Terry Donaldson, *Principles of Tarot* (1996; New Delhi: Harper Collins, 1999) 94-95.

45. Eliot, *The Waste Land*, CPP 62.

46. Eliot, CPP 70.

47. Eliot, CPP 70.

48. Henry Clarke Warren, *Buddhism in Translations* (1896; Delhi: Motilal Banarsidass, 1986) 351-353.

49. Cleo McNelly Kearns, *T.S. Eliot and Indic Traditions* (Cambridge: Cambridge UP, 1987) 75-76.

50. Eliot, *The Waste Land*, CPP 74.

51. Eliot read selected portions of the *Vedas* and *Upanishads* in Sanskrit in the *Twenty Eight Upanishads* edited by Vasudev Laxman and Shastri Phansikar, a book presented to him by his teacher Charles Lanman who had marked out some passages for Eliot's attention. The section from the *Brhadaranyaka Upanishad* which Eliot used in *The Waste Land* was one of these—in Mohit Kumar Roy, "T.S. Eliot and the Gita," *Journal of the Department of English*, Vol. V-VI, No. 1 (Burdwan: University of Burdwan, 1989-90) n.p.

52. Eliot, *The Waste Land*, CPP 75.

53. Swami Madhavananda, trans., *Brhadaryanaka Upanishad* 4th. Ed. (Calcutta: Advaita Ashrama, 1993) 564-67.

54. G. Wilson Knight, *The Golden Labyrinth* (London: Phoenix House, 1962) 362.

55. Sarkar, "T.S. Eliot and Ezra Pound: An Intercontinental Creative Encounter," *Literature and Criticism* 1.1 (Calcutta: The Literary Society of India, 2001) 21.

56. Eliot, *The Hollow Men*, CPP 83.

57. Eliot, CPP 83.

58. Eliot, CPP 83.

59. Eliot, CPP 84.

60. Eliot, CPP 85.

61. Eliot, CPP 85.

62. Eliot, CPP 85.

63. Nursery rhyme : This is the way we brush our teeth,
We brush our teeth, we brush our teeth.
This is the way we brush our teeth,
Every day in the morning.

64. Eliot, CPP 85.

65. Eliot, *Ash Wednesday*, CPP 90.
66. Eliot, CPP 91.
67. Eliot, CPP 96.
68. Eliot, CPP 98.
69. Eliot, CPP 99.
70. Eliot, "Journey of the Magi," *Ariel Poems*, CPP 103.
71. Eliot, CPP 104.
72. Eliot, CPP 104.
73. Eliot, "A Song for Simeon," *Ariel Poems*, CPP 105.
74. Eliot, "Animula," *Ariel Poems*, CPP 107.
75. The Bible, King James Version, Luke 22:19.
76. Sumita Banerjee, "The Sea in Shakespeare's Last Plays," *Literature and Criticism* 1.1 123-24.
77. Eliot, "Marina," *Ariel Poems*, CPP 109.
78. Eliot, CPP 110.
79. Sarkar, *Journal of English Studies Association* 1.
80. J. Isaacs, *An Assessment of Twentieth Century Literature* (London: Secker and Warburg, 1951) 139.
81. Elisabeth Schneider, *T.S. Eliot: The Pattern in the Carpet* (California: University of California P, 1975) 10.
82. Schneider 11.
83. Eliot expressed his debt to Davidson's use of dingy urban images and colloquial idiom in the preface to a selection of Davidson's poems, ed. by M. Lindsay in 1961, singling out for particular praise his best known ballad, the defiant and satiric "Thirty Bob a Week"—from *The Oxford Companion to English Literature,* ed. Margaret Drabble (Oxford: Oxford UP, 1995) 260.
84. John Davidson, "Thirty Bob a Week," *The Poems of John Davidson* ed. Andrew Turnbull, Vol. 1 (Edinburgh: Scottish Academic Press, 1973) 63.
85. Eliot "The Metaphysical Poets," *Selected Essays* 288.
86. Eliot, "The Three Voices of Poetry," *On Poetry and Poets* 89.
87. Eliot, "The Love Song of J. Alfred Prufrock," CPP 13.
88. Conrad Aiken, "Divers Realists," *T.S. Eliot: Critical Assessments*, ed. Graham Clarke, Vol. 2 (London: Christopher Helm, 1990) 12.
89. Eliot, "Gerontion," CPP 37.
90. Eliot, "Reflections on *Vers Libre*," *To Criticise the Critic and Other Writings* (London: Faber, 1965) 189.

91. Eliot, "The Music of Poetry," *On Poetry and Poets* 29.
92. Eliot, *On Poetry and Poets* 32.
93. N. L. Rosenthal, *Sailing Into the Unknown: Yeats, Pound and Eliot* (New York: Oxford UP, 1978) 172.
94. Eliot, *On Poetry and Poets* 32.
95. Eliot, *On Poetry and Poets* 33.
96. Harry T. Antrim, *T.S. Eliot's Concept of Language* (Gainesville: University of Florida P., 1971) 44.
97. Eliot, *Ash Wednesday*, CPP 89.
98. Eliot, *The Varieties of Metaphysical Poetry* 272.
99. Eliot, *The Varieties of Metaphysical Poetry* 130.
100. Eliot, "The Modern Mind," *The Use of Poetry and the Use of Criticism* 126.
101. Eliot, *The Varieties of Metaphysical Poetry* 289-90.
102. Eliot, "The Metaphysical Poets," *Selected Essays* 289.
103. Eliot, "Andrew Marvell," *Selected Essays* 295.
104. Eliot, *Selected Essays* 296.
105. Andrew Marvell, "To His Coy Mistress," *The Metaphysical Poets*, ed. Helen Gardner (London: Penguin, 1987) 251.
106. Eliot, *The Waste Land*, CPP 67.
107. Eliot, "The Metaphysical Poets," *Selected Essays* 287.
108. Eliot, *The Varieties of Metaphysical Poetry* 85-86.
109. Eliot, *The Varieties of Metaphysical Poetry* 86.
110. Eliot, *The Varieties of Metaphysical Poetry* 87.
111. Eliot, *The Varieties of Metaphysical Poetry* 126.
112. Eliot, "The Metaphysical Poets," *Selected Essays* 288.
113. Eliot, *Selected Essays* 288.
114. Eliot, *The Waste Land*, CPP 61.
115. Eliot, "Whispers of Immortality," *Poems 1920*, CPP 52.
116. Knight, *The Golden Labyrinth* 362.
117. Eliot, Introduction, *Savonarola*, by Charlotte Eliot, qtd. in C.H. Smith 51-52.
118. C.H. Smith 50.
119. Eliot, "The Possibility of a Poetic Drama", *The Sacred Wood* 63.
120. Eliot, *The Sacred Wood* 68.
121. Eliot, *Sweeney Agonistes*, CPP 126.

122. Eliot, CPP 122.
123. Eliot, CPP 122.
124. Katherine J. Worth, "Eliot and the Living Theatre," *Eliot in Perspective: A Symposium,* ed. Graham Martin (London: Macmillan, 1970) 154.
125. Worth, *Revolutions in Modern English Drama* (London: G. Bell and Sons, 1972) 55.
126. Eliot, "Matthew Arnold," *The Use of Poetry and the Use of Criticism* 118-19.
127. Eliot, Conclusion, *The Use of Poetry and the Use of Criticism* 154.
128. Eliot, "The Possibility of a Poetic Drama," *The Sacred Wood* 70.
129. Eliot, *Sweeney Agonistes*, CPP 125-26.
130. Grover Smith 171.
131. Sarkar, *T.S. Eliot the Dramatist* 40.
132. Eliot, "Literature and the Modern World," *America through the Essay* (ed. Theodore Johnson and Allen Tate (New York: 1938) 382 qtd. in Grover Smith 117.
133. Eliot, *Sweeney Agonistes*, CPP 115.
134. Morton D. Zabel, "A Modern Purgatorio," *Commonweal* 19 April 1933: 697.
135. Marvin Halverson, *Religious Drama* (New York: Living Age Books, pub. by Meridian Books, 1957) 7.
136. Eliot, *Sweeney Agonistes*, CPP 115.
137. St. John of the Cross, *The Ascent of Mount Carmel* 1:13, *Mysticism*, F.C. Happold (Middlesex: Penguin, 1963) 331.
138. Eliot, *The Waste Land*, CPP 75.
139. He was engrossed in Patanjali's philosophy during his studies at Harvard, of which he wrote in *After Strange Gods*: "...a year in the mazes of Patanjali's metaphysics under the guidance of James Woods left me in a state of enlightened mystification," (London: Faber, 1934) 40.
140. James H. Woods, trans., *The Yoga System of Patanjali* (1914; Delhi: Motilal Banarsidass, 1966) 295-96.
141. Sarkar, *T.S. Eliot the Dramatist* 36.
142. Marianne Moore, rev. of *Sweeney Agonistes*, by Eliot, *Poetry* May 1933: 108.
143. Zabel, *T.S. Eliot: The Critical Heritage* 291.
144. Eliot, *Sweeney Agonistes*, CPP 116.

145. Eliot, CPP 121-22.
146. Eliot, CPP 122.
147. Eliot, CPP 121.
148. Eliot, CPP 124.
149. Eliot, *After Strange Gods* 59-60.
150. Eliot, CPP 125.
151. Francis M. Cornford, *The Origin of Attic Comedy* (London: Edward Arnold, 1914) 13-15.
152. C.H. Smith 71.
153. Eliot, CPP 125.
154. Gareth Lloyd Evans, *The Language Sweeney Agonistes of Modern Drama* (London: J. M. Dent and Sons, 1977) 146-47.
155. Eliot, "The Beating of a Drum," *The Nation and Athaeneum* Vol. XXXIV, qtd. in C.H. Smith 48-49.
156. Knight, *The Golden Labyrinth* 363.
157. Helen Gardner, *The Art of T.S. Eliot* 132.
158. C.H. Smith 74.
159. Eliot, Conclusion, *The Use of Poetry and the Use of Criticism* 153.
160. Eliot, "The Modern Mind," *The Use of Poetry and the Use of Criticism* 125-26.
161. Eliot, "The Possibility of a Poetic Drama," *The Sacred Wood* 61.
162. Eliot, *After Strange Gods* 30.
163. Eliot, *After Strange Gods* 29.
164. Eliot, "The Possibility of a Poetic Drama," *The Sacred Wood* 69.
165. Worth, *Eliot in Perspective*, ed. Martin 155.
166. Eliot, *The Rock* (London: Faber, 1934) 6.
167. Isaacs 152.
168. Nevill Coghill, ed., *The Family Reunion*, by Eliot, Introduction (Oxford: Oxford U.P., 1963) 59.
169. Eliot, *The Rock* 64.
170. Eliot, *Murder in the Cathedral*, CPP 274-75.
171. Grover Smith 179.
172. Eliot, *The Rock* 50.
173. Eliot, "The Three Voices of Poetry," *On Poetry and Poets* 91.
174. E. Martin Browne, *The Making of T.S. Eliot's Plays* (Cambridge: Cambridge UP, 1969) 20.

175. Gardner 133.
176. Coghill, ed., *The Family Reunion*, Introduction 60.
177. "Mr. Eliot's Pageant Play," rev. of *The Rock*, by Eliot, *Times Literary Supplement* 7 June 1934: 404.
178. Eliot, *The Rock* 83.
179. Eliot, *Ash Wednesday*, CPP 96.
180. Eliot, *The Rock* 19.
181. James G. Frazer, *The Golden Bough* (1936; Hertfordshire: Wordsworth Editions, 1993) 494.
182. Eliot, *The Rock* 7.
183. Eliot, "The Hippopotamus," *Poems 1920,* CPP 49.
184. Einar Molland, *Christendom* (London: A.R. Mowbray, 1961) 156.
185. Eliot, *The Rock* 18.
186. Eliot, *The Rock* 9.
187. Eliot, *The Rock* 52.
188. Eliot calls the *Bhagavad-Gita* "the next greatest philosophical poem to the Divine Comedy," within his experience—"Dante," *Selected Essays* 258.
189. Eliot, *Four Quartets*, CPP 188.
190. Michael Sayers, "Mr. T.S. Eliot's 'The Rock'," rev. of *The Rock*, by Eliot, *New English Weekly* 21 June 1934: 230.
191. Eliot, *After Strange Gods* 52.
192. Eliot, *After Strange Gods* 52.
193. Eliot, *The Rock* 9.
194. Eliot, *The Rock* 20-21.
195. Eliot, *After Strange Gods* 42.
196. Eliot, *After Strange Gods* 42.
197. Eliot, *The Rock* 7.
198. The Bible, Genesis 3:19.
199. Eliot, *The Rock* 17.
200. Sarkar, *T.S. Eliot the Dramatist* 45.
201. Eliot, *The Rock* 34.
202. Eliot, *The Rock* 35.
203. Eliot, *The Rock* 35.
204. Eliot, *The Rock* 56.
205. Eliot, *After Strange Gods* 29.

206. Eliot, *The Rock* 78.
207. Eliot, *The Rock* 48.
208. Eliot, *The Rock* 85.
209. Eliot, *The Rock* 29.
210. Eliot, *The Rock* 31.
211. Eliot, *The Rock* 39.
212. Eliot, *The Rock* 76.
213. Eliot, *The Waste Land*, CPP 75.
214. Eliot, CPP 75.
215. Eliot, *The Rock* 30.
216. Eliot, *The Rock* 52.
217. Eliot, *The Rock* 37-38.
218. Sarkar, *T.S. Eliot the Dramatist* 45.
219. Coghill, ed., *The Family Reunion*, Introduction 59.
220. Gerald Weales, *Religion in Modern English Drama* (Philadelphia: University of Pennsylvania P, 1961) 187.
221. Eliot, interview, "T.S. Eliot Talks about Himself and the Drive to Create", by John Lehmann, *New York Times Book Review*, 29 November 1953: 5, in Weales 189.

# 2 The Early Beginning with Religion—The Quest for Meaning in Martyrdom

Although *Sweeney Agonistes* contained all the basic ingredients of Eliot's plays, he did not complete it. On the other hand, in spite of being complete, *The Rock* was not satisfactory to Eliot because he had to write the words for the pageant play which was designed to involve a large number of amateur actors who were difficult to handle. The first full-fledged display of Eliot, the dramatist, was made through the presentation of *Murder in the Cathedral* in the Chapter House of Canterbury Cathedral in 1935. The unique atmosphere of the first presentation of the play was created by the architecture of the Chapter House itself, whose single door was used by some of the actors for appearances on the stage at the other end. This meant that they had to walk down a passage in the midst of the audience and the very mechanism involved the audience in the action of the drama, something absent in subsequent performances of the play in theatres. The involvement of the audience was vital for a play which presented the story of the spiritual and physical preparations of Thomas Becket, Archbishop of Canterbury, for his martyrdom. Becket's quest for self-realization leads him towards an understanding of Jesus Christ as the central symbol of Christianity which, in a way, holds out the key to Eliot's inward quest which is found throughout his works. Jesus is the image of the Son of Man passing into the image of the Son of God. There is a remarkable similarity between Eliot's Becket and Hemingway's Santiago (in *The Old Man and the Sea*) in their gradual evolution towards the role of a martyr. Both are determined to achieve their preconceived goal. Becket returns to

England from France, knowing that he will die for the sake of establishing the power and the glory of the Church. Santiago's humility, natural piety and compassion accompany his sense of endurance and assert man's ceaseless struggle for survival. However, there is a difference between them, which Sarkar points out:

> He is not a Christian martyr like Becket in Eliot's *Murder in the Cathedral* but a martyr for a human cause—his own survival, no less religious in his commitment to the cause than Becket himself.[1]

The modernist idea of martyrdom is that it is a way out but Eliot possibly thought of the relevance of the Incarnation in the modern context, that is, in terms of the modern society—as a way of reaching a higher spiritual condition through understanding (by exercising the intellect) and elevation (in faith). Eliot comes to approach the theme of martyrdom from the common human plane from where he moves on to the spiritual plane. He brought Becket, Archbishop of Canterbury, down to the lay level in order to show his spiritual elevation towards the end of the play. For this Eliot concentrated on the last phase of Becket's life, giving the drama a sense of urgency.

Eliot missed the Christian experience as long as he was in the blindfolded and delimited world of Unitarianism. That spiritual void was more than compensated by the centrality of the idea of Incarnation in his works. Eliot's quest becomes obvious in sudden flashes of Becket's behaviour in *Murder in the Cathedral*, when he becomes almost Eliot himself in his quest for a way towards God, but not in the manner in which Milton and Samson can be likened. Becket comes to arrive at certain levels of understanding—through self-purification—absent in Samson. Milton shows that Samson's fortune was preordained. Becket's slow evolution in *Murder in the Cathedral* was intended. It is out of his love for God and for human beings that Becket aspires to follow Christ the Saviour's path towards martyrdom. The idea of Incarnation was Eliot's primary preoccupation in his own spiritual quest which came to be formalized in his conversion to Anglo-Catholicism in 1927. After his baptism, he explained to Paul Elmer More that "only Christianity helps to reconcile one to life which is otherwise disgusting."[2]

After the success of *The Rock* in 1934, Browne mediated between Eliot and the Reverend George Bell, Bishop of Chichester and Dean of Canterbury, desiring to involve Eliot in writing a play for the Canterbury Festival of 1935, since Browne felt that Eliot had the mentality and the spiritual equipments to write a fitting play for the Festival. Unlike Tennyson's *Becket* which is a historical drama Eliot's play is an externalization of Thomas Becket's spiritual quest for self-realization.

At the time Bishop Bell invited Eliot to write a play for the Canterbury Festival of 1935, he was undergoing a personal crisis. The hasty immature marriage with Vivienne was on the rocks and Eliot had nothing but bitterness and trouble as remembrances of his wedded life.[3] There was Emily Hale on the other side of the Atlantic, waiting with her selfless love, for him to emerge from his shy secluded self and speak the much awaited words of proposal to her. Here he was tied down to a mentally deranged wife whom his inner self wished to desert and yet he (the magnanimous personality of contemporary English literature) had to remain dutiful towards her, arranging for her treatment in an asylum. He was caught in a spiritual whirlwind created by his inner romantic attachment to Emily and his outer austere sense of duty towards Vivienne.

Eliot worked on the play during the winter of 1934; a time when he suffered from an inner torment as a result of his disastrous marriage with Vivienne which Gordon calls "the eighteen-year nightmare of his private life—like a bad novel by Dostoievsky."[4] Those that were close to him could see the torment he underwent although he never shared his inner self with anyone. One such friend, Wyndham Lewis, writes:

> Appearing at one's front door, or arriving at a dinner-rendezvous [...] his face would be haggard, he would seem at his last gasp [...] the harassed and exhausted refugee, in flight from some scourge of God.[5]

Life with Vivienne became unbearable, so much so that in spite of a responsible nature he came to a firm decision of formal separation from his neurotic wife. On 14 March 1933 he wrote to Lady Ottoline Morrell about a deed of separation from her:

> For my part, I should prefer never to see her again; for hers, I do not believe that it can be good for any woman to live with a man to whom she is morally, in the larger sense, unpleasant, as well as physically indifferent. But I am quite aware of putting my own interest first.[6]

Herbert Read noticed Eliot's inner suffering at this time. He writes, "I always felt that I was in the presence of a remorseful man, of one who had some secret sorrow or guilt."[7] The frightening and irrevocable nature of this choice led to a lifetime of misery for him.

The sense of guilt could be pinned down to Eliot's awareness of the fact that he had let down two women by being unable to live up to their expectations. At the same time, in a wider sense, he was aware of a Christian sense of guilt which made him experiment with the character of Thomas Becket, the martyred Archbishop of Canterbury, for a search for meaning of life. Martyrdom, following the pattern of Christ's Sacrifice, had always occupied the core of Eliot's heart. The special significance of the idea of the Incarnation to Eliot can be gauged from the essay, 'Revelation' in which he writes:

> I take for granted that Christian revelation is the only full revelation; and that the fullness of Christian revelation resides in the essential fact of the Incarnation, in relation to which all Christian revelation is to be understood.[8]

It was purely because of his concern with the idea of the Incarnation from a very young age that he finally decided to become an Anglo-Catholic in 1927. The conversion from Unitarianism was no sudden or impulsive action. It was the consummation of a faith. His personal disturbances enhanced this dependence on the personality of Jesus Christ: "The God he needed, on whom he could lean his whole weight, was God who had become man, an infinitely gentle, infinitely suffering incarnate thing, recognizably human, unknowably divine."[9] The offer to write a full-fledged play obviously gave him the opportunity to express his inner troubles without the fear of their being discovered by an ever-inquisitive society. It will not be wrong to say that *Murder in the Cathedral*, the play that externalizes Becket's quest for self-realization, is nothing but an externalization of the inner drama that was in progress within the playwright himself. In order to escape from the personal tension which arose from his feelings for Emily and Vivienne he undertook the experiment with the character of Archbishop Thomas Becket in *Murder in the Cathedral*.

Eliot's family in St. Louis prided itself on its orthodox Unitarianism. But his response to 'The Education of Henry Adams'[10] in a 1919 review was markedly defined when he described the Unitarian mind in terms of the 'Boston Doubt': "A scepticism which is difficult to explain to those who are not born to it. [...] it is not destructive, but it is dissolvent. [...]"[11] This comment clarifies the reason behind his conversion.

Eliot makes Becket's quest for martyrdom follow the pattern of the Quest of the Holy Grail[12] and the quest for communion with God at the end of the contemplative life as described in *The Cloud of Unknowing*. So, unlike Tennyson's Becket, Eliot's protagonist experiences inner tensions and tribulations which torment him on his way to martyrdom. Mohit Kumar Ray rightly observes that:

> The greatness of martyrdom consists in the greatness of the vision and in realization of its value by the sacrifice of one's life, and by affecting a transvaluation of values.[13]

The initial title of the play, *Fears in the Way*, made way for *Murder in the Cathedral* because the latter has the suggestion of a detective thriller and the taste of Christian martyrdom. It is "about a situation and a quality of life; the situation is perpetual and the quality is rare."[14] The first audience in the Chapter House knew the story of thc play; the playwright's mastery lay in his deft handling of the theme and the manner of its treatment. "*Murder in the Cathedral* explores the possibility of the saint within the man,"[15] says Niloufer Harben. The theme provided Eliot with an opportunity of expressing his faith through and in drama. Eda Lou Walton, expecting Eliot to affirm a modern intellectual and scientific outlook, is surprised, finding it difficult to understand "how so analytical an intellect came to acceptance of unquestioning faith."[16] That she fails to delve into the inner being of the dramatist is clear from this remark. The "analytical intellect" was the obvious facet of Eliot's personality. The imperceptible facet was the sensitive romantic self which sought for a representation of Divine Love on Earth and found it in Christ, the Son of God born as the Son of Man in order to experience Passion and Sacrifice—His Suffering and Endurance showing men the way to redemption. Eliot said that a bit of the author may be the germ of a character and that a certain character may bring out latent potentialities in the author.[17] There definitely was a close link between Eliot and Becket, who enabled Eliot to shift "the balance of his new life from the shared course of love to the lone course of religious trial."[18] This trial was Becket's pursuit of the contemplative life that would probably end in union with God.

Eliot's aim in writing *Murder in the Cathedral* was to make the audience aware of the Christian implications of Becket's martyrdom. The intention becomes clear from the dramatist's statement:

> It is not, after all, a commercial endeavour. I wrote it to be performed in Canterbury Cathedral as a religious celebration, and so I would always prefer that it be performed in a consecrated setting. I do not know why anyone would want to see it as entertainment.[19]

Becket is a Christian protagonist—a man with a purpose in life. He is like Virgil's hero, Aeneas. Eliot had found in Aeneas "a virtue—an essential ingredient in his piety—which is an analogue and foreshadow of Christian humility. [...] he is, humbly, a man with a mission; and the mission is everything."[20] He is the antithesis of Achilles or Odysseus, suffering only for himself and acting in obedience to his destiny. That is why he abandons Dido's love and Carthage in order to follow his mission of setting up a new kingdom in Italy, as ordained by God.

Becket's purpose is to prepare himself for the "simple, sudden, God-given"[21] martyrdom. However, the preparation for it will be difficult and long, for it is the spiritual quest which may be consummated in martyrdom. As long as the quest goes on, it will be a "strife with shadows."[22] Becket becomes Eliot's 'persona' for his own quest for self-realization, as he follows the path of the life-contemplative, of denial and detachment, which is the way of the would-be saint. During 1934-35, Eliot believed that this life of denial was the only way towards his own *shantih* (the peace that passes understanding).

The playwright's acquaintance with the outstanding spiritual treatise of the fourteenth century, *The Cloud of Unknowing*, is evident from the ritualistic pattern of *Murder in the Cathedral* which follows *The Cloud of Unknowing* closely. It is a commentary on Denys the Areopagite's idea that "*the most godly knowing of God is that which is known by unknowing.*"[23]

The title of *The Cloud of Unknowing* has been taken from Denys's *Mystical Theology*. God is to be attained not through knowledge, but by the way of ignorance. The unknown author explains in his highly complex work that there are two ways in which this cloud can be pierced. The lower way involves the contemplative naked impulse which shoots up like "a sharp dart of longing love"[24] to penetrate the cloud so that the soul might experience direct union with God. In the higher experience God Himself is the worker and the contemplative the sufferer who receives in the supreme moment "a beam of ghostly light, piercing this cloud of unknowing"[25] that is between him and God. The author explains the significance of the cloud of unknowing:

> This darkness and this cloud, [...] is betwixt thee and thy God, and hindereth thee, so that thou mayest neither see him clearly by light of understanding in thy reason, nor feel him in sweetness of love in thine affection. And therefore shape thee to bide in this darkness as long as thou mayest, evermore crying after him whom thou lovest.[26]

Only the blind stirring of love can beat the dark cloud of unknowing on the way to union with God. Man has to cleanse himself of the Original Sin. The author explains, "And the whiles that a soul is dwelling in this deadly flesh, it shall evermore see and feel this cumbrous *cloud of unknowing* betwixt him and his God."[27] The medieval theologian unfolds, in seventy-five chapters, the book of contemplative life that teaches meekness and humility in love and unknowing, forgetting the material world and contemplating service to God solely for Himself.

Eliot divides the play into two parts—the first is the temptation episode and the second involves Becket's self-purification in preparation for the contemplative life that extends into eternity, unlike the active life that ends with death. It is in the state of darkness that Becket comes to realize the limitations of human knowledge.

Christ, too, was under the shadow of this dark cloud of unknowing when He awaited Death (meaning release from the flesh) upon the Cross on the Hill of Calvary. Following the Higher Contemplative life, He suffered in the flesh, and cried out, "My God, my God, why hast Thou forsaken me?"[28] until God worked His Grace in the form of a shaft of bright light which pierced the Cloud and fell on Christ's face. It was only at this final moment of surrender that Jesus said, "Father, into Thy hands I commend my spirit."[29] Even Christ had to prove that He was worthy of Death. Eliot shows us in *Murder in the Cathedral* Becket's awareness of Christ's Suffering and Sacrifice.

There have been several martyrdoms since the First one and each is a repetition of Christ's Sacrifice for mankind because "We have to remember that the Kingdom of Christ on earth will never be realized, and also that it is always being realized."[30] Therefore, every martyrdom is a witness to man's inborn ingratitude to God and his tendency to commit sin. Conceited as he is, man imagines that he can turn the Wheel of Destiny on which he is a fixed point in reality, provided by God with the freedom to choose between Good and Evil. God is the Still Centre of this Wheel—the word of Light—without whom there would be no "release from action and suffering, release from the inner / And the outer compulsion, [...]"[31] Becket explains that it is:

> [...]                                        Only
> The fool, fixed in his folly, may think
> He can turn the wheel on which he turns.[32]

Martyrdoms are points on this Wheel which exemplify God's Love for erring mankind. The saints are God's elect, blessed with His Grace, because they follow the example of the First Martyr. As for the common folk like the Charwomen of Canterbury, Christian dogmas play an important role in their lives. What T.E. Hulme writes in *Humanism and the Religious Attitude*[33] becomes apt in their case:

> What is important, is what nobody seems to realize—the dogmas like that of Original Sin, which are the closest expression of the categories of the religious attitude. That man is in no sense perfect, but a wretched creature, who can yet apprehend perfection.[34]

The turmoils in his own life enabled Eliot to contemplate the development of the character of Becket as that of an ascetic moving towards martyrdom. Eliot had read works of Catholic asceticism which included the *Confessions* of St. Augustine, *The Dark Night of the Soul* of St. John of the Cross and *The Cloud of Unknowing*. However, he had no first-hand knowledge of the life of a would-be saint. This gives rise to the disparity between what Becket says and what he does. Whatever he says, particularly to the Charwomen, Priests, Tempters and Knights, is in accordance with the ideal life of a would-be martyr as exemplified in Christian texts beginning with the Bible. Becket's actions, on the other hand, are those of a man who is still striving to rise above the level of worldly existence, or else, his behaviour with the Knights in Part II of *Murder in the Cathedral* would express detachment and peace. He would not wrangle with them in response to their challenges and abuses saying:

> Traitor to me as my temporal vassal,
> Traitor to me as your spiritual lord.[35]

There is a chasm between what Becket says and what he achieves. This is the chief weakness in his character which Robert Speaight speaks about: "I must confess, however, that in spite of playing Becket more than a thousand times, I have never felt near to him as a man."[36] When the martyrdom, or 'murder', does take place, it is so sudden that the witnesses, including the audience, are unprepared for it, being distracted by wordly concerns and impatient with waiting for it. Becket explains this to the Second Priest in his debut speech:

> They know and do not know, what it is to act or suffer.
> They know and do not know, that action is suffering
> And suffering action. Neither does the agent suffer
> Nor the patient act. But both are fixed
> In an eternal action, an eternal patience
> To which all must consent that it may be willed
> And which all must suffer that they may will it,
> That the pattern may subsist, for the pattern is the action
> And the suffering, that the wheel may turn and still
> Be forever still.[37]

However, in the initial stages of the play, Becket is preparing himself for the martyrdom. So, his words to the Priest are relevant for him as well as for Eliot. He is "dramatizing, but in no obvious form, an action or struggle for harmony in the soul of the poet,"[38] says the dramatist. Becket has to overcome temptation in his quest for self-realization. Christ, too, was tempted by Satan in the wilderness—"The word in the desert / Is most attacked by voices of temptation."[39] Becket is disturbed by it:

> The impossible is still temptation.
> The impossible, the undesirable.[40]

He knows that he must undergo spiritual suffering in order to be worthy of martyrdom, paying for Christ's blood with his own blood because His blood is the sign under which God remembers His people in Himself. He is aware of his election when he says:

> I have had a tremor of bliss, a wink of heaven, a whisper,
> And I would no longer be denied, [...][41]

Herein lies the triumph of the Cross. Becket knows that if he succeeds in overcoming temptation he will simply have to detach himself from the material world in order to gain salvation.

The Old Testament sacrifice of the Paschal Lamb during the Feast of Passover is converted by Jesus in the New Testament to His sacrifice for which the Last Supper is the Passover. It is through Christ's Suffering on the Cross that Mankind reaches salvation, only to lose this state in committing fresh sins. God's Son was born in the flesh to pay with His life, in and through Suffering, for the sins of mankind in order to bring them back to the ways of God. Weston defines the special characteristic of the central Christian rite of the Eucharist as being:

> [...] a Sacred meal of Communion in which the worshipper, not merely symbolically, but actually, partakes of, and becomes one with, his God, receiving thereby the assurance of eternal life (*The Body of Our Lord Jesus Christ preserve thy body and soul unto everlasting life*).[42]

Becket emphasizes the significance of Holy Communion in his Christmas sermon:

> For whenever Mass is said, we re-enact the Passion and Death of Our Lord; and on this Christmas Day we do this in celebration of His Birth. So that at the same moment we rejoice in His coming for the salvation of men, and offer again to God His Body and Blood in sacrifice, oblation and satisfaction for the sins of the whole world.[43]

The members of the church are stimulated by the Holy Spirit while participating in the body of Christ which was offered on the Cross, and they are enabled by the same Holy Spirit to offer themselves to the Father in Eucharistic sacrifice, "to serve one another in love within the body, and to fulfill their sacrificial function as the body of Christ in the service of the need of the whole world which God has reconciled to himself in Christ."[44] Eliot has devised this play primarily as ritual. The pattern of Jesus' life is turned into a ritual which, in its broad outlines, is repeated in the lives of Christian martyrs. Man's transgression from God's way creates the necessity for further martyrdoms of persons who are on the highest level of spiritual awareness—the contemplative life. Becket explains that men both rejoice and mourn, (in a smaller measure) the death of martyrs. Men mourn for the sins of the world for which the elect become martyrs and rejoice in having another saint. Becket sermonizes, "A martyrdom is always the design of God, for His love of men, to warn them and to lead them, to bring them back to His ways."[45] Becket is ready to atone for the sins of men for he knows that Christ had saved mankind with His Blood:

This is the sign of the Church always,
The sign of blood. Blood for blood.
His blood given to buy my life,
My blood given to pay for His death,
My death for His death.[46]

The play "traces the story of transformation of an earthly-minded and ambitious Archbishop into a true servant of God, a martyr who understands that he is 'A Christian, saved by the blood of Christ.'"[47]

The lack of spiritual awareness in modern people disturbed Eliot. He believed that the disappearance of the concept of Original Sin implied the disappearance of people who are morally conscious. In the absence of control, or 'Damyata', the animal nature in man gets the better of his spiritual self leading him towards the Seven Deadly Sins of which *The Cloud of Unknowing* warns the aspirant in the tenth chapter. Men tend to forget that "Destiny waits in the hands of God, not in the hands of statesmen."[48] Becket needs to free himself from the vice of pride before he proceeds in his quest. The keen First Priest observes:

His pride always feeding upon his own virtues,
Pride drawing sustenance from impartiality,
Pride drawing sustenance from generosity,
Loathing power given by temporal devolution,
Wishing subjugation to God alone.[49]

The only solution lies in complete surrender to God's Will. He knows that suffering is part of an action which involves the working of the Divine Will. It is the mode of the quest for self-realization. Becket knows that he has to make himself the lowest on earth in order to make himself eligible to reach up to God, for it is in ignorance and love that he can pierce the dark Cloud of Unknowing. To Eliot "humility was a virtue, the most highly prized of all,"[50] comments Matthews and Eliot wrote that it is "only in humility, charity and purity—and most of all perhaps humility—can we be prepared to receive the grace of God without which human operations are vain."[51] First of all, temptation has to be overcome. Eliot is speaking for himself when he makes Becket argue with the Tempters. Pride grows out of an attachment to the physical world. Eliot and Becket think that "the soul cannot be possessed of the divine union, until it has divested itself of the love of created beings."[52] Dobree, being revolted by this quotation, told Eliot that he regarded it with horror and the dramatist wrote to him in 1936 that:

> The doctrine that in order to arrive at the love of God one must divest oneself of the love of created beings was thus expressed by St. John of the Cross, you know: i.e. a man who was writing primarily not for you and me, but for people seriously engaged in pursuing the Way of Contemplation. It is only to be read in relation to that way: i.e. merely to kill one's human affections will get one nowhere, it would be only to become rather more a completely living corpse than most people are. But the doctrine is fundamentally true, I believe. Or to put your belief in your own way, that only through the love of created beings can we approach the love of God, that I believe to be UNTRUE. Whether we mean by that domestic and friendly affections, or a more comprehensive love of the "neighbour", of humanity in general, I don't think that ordinary human affections are capable of leading us to the love of God, but rather that the love of God is capable of informing, intensifying and devoting our human affections, which otherwise have little to distinguish them from the "natural" affections of animals. Try looking at it from that end of the glass![53]

So it can be seen that both the playwright and Becket are striving to achieve what Becket theorises upon but fall miserably short of attaining their goal.

The Fourth Tempter offers Becket eternal spiritual power gained through martyrdom. The world is full of sinful men who are seeking redemption. So, after the cannonization a saint may easily exploit their shortcomings, winning fame through the process of redeeming them. The Tempter lures Becket towards seizing overriding power:

Man oppressed by sin since Adam fell—
You hold the keys of heaven and hell.
Power to bind and loose: bind, Thomas, bind,
King and Bishop under your heel.[54]

He is nearly repeating Becket's own words to the Second Tempter who offers him the Chancellorship he had resigned earlier:

No! shall I, who keep the keys
Of heaven and hell, supreme alone in England,
Who bind and loose, with power from the Pope,
Descend to desire a punier power?[55]

The Fourth Tempter is merely blowing away the ashes to reveal before Becket his own desires for glory which he is yet to overcome. This is why many critics call this Tempter Becket's alter-ego. Becket's struggle against the offers made by this Tempter is clear from the way the Tempter chaffs off his stern reply:

THOMAS. Others offered real goods, worthless
But real. You only offer
Dreams to damnation.
TEMPTER. You have often dreamt them.[56]

Becket realizes that he has to overcome this spiritual temptation because:

The last temptation is the greatest treason:
To do the right deed for the wrong reason.[57]

His is not a quest for glorious martyrdom. "In order to be a real martyr one must rise above the temptation of being a martyr,"[58] comments Ray. It is a quest for self-realization, meaning of life, for salvation and an understanding of the Absolute Reality. The Fourth Tempter throws back at Becket his own words about the Charwomen:

You know and do not know, what it is to act or suffer.
You know and do not know, that action is suffering,
And suffering action. Neither does the agent suffer
Nor the patient act. But both are fixed
In an eternal action, an eternal patience
To which all must consent that it may be willed

> And which all must suffer that they may will it,
> That the pattern may subsist, that the wheel may turn and still
> Be forever still.[59]

When the words boomerang on him, Becket realizes that he has to practise humility which will lead him towards the consummation of his quest. "Without humility, submission, and love nothing is possible,"[60] writes Eliot. The exasperation of the four Tempters on being repelled, one by one, is clear from their frustrated exhortation:

> All things become less real, man passes
> From unreality to unreality.[61]

To them the real world is the physical one, for the spiritual world has no meaning in their limited perspective.

Although Eliot was writing *Murder in the Cathedral* for a purely Christian purpose, the play bears overtones of anthropology and the playwright's deep regard for tradition. In *After Strange Gods* Eliot wrote, "Tradition by itself is not enough; it must be perpetually criticized and brought up to date under the supervision of what I call orthodoxy."[62] He explained that the terms 'tradition' and 'orthodoxy' did not have theological connotations here. 'Tradition' "cannot mean standing still."[63] It covers "much in our lives that is accounted for by habit, breeding and environment."[64] He believed that a right tradition must also be a Christian tradition. What he meant is made clear when he called a pagan society (as opposed to a Christian society) one in which "the wrong spiritual values are recognized."[65]

Eliot believed that Christianity is a continuation of ancient fertility cults—a belief which grew from his acquaintance with the works of the Cambridge anthropologists, chief of which were *The Golden Bough* and *From Ritual to Romance*. He felt that one cannot deny Nature if one is to acknowledge faith in God. In 'The Idea of a Christian Society' Eliot writes:

> [...] religion, as distinguished from modern paganism, implies a life in conformity with nature. It may be observed that the natural life and the supernatural life have a conformity to

> each other which neither has with the mechanistic life: [...] I mean only that a wrong attitude towards nature implies, somewhere, a wrong attitude towards God, and that the consequence is an inevitable doom.[66]

God created Nature, man being only a small part of it. Therefore, man must learn to respect Nature. The Christian faith helps man to hold a respect for the religious life and it is precisely for this that Eliot has been "a Christian in the self-discipline of his private life."[67] So it can be easily understood why Eliot sought legal separation from his wife whose overbearing sensuality and possessiveness was too heavy a burden for him. The offer of writing *Murder in the Cathedral* at this time propelled Eliot to experiment with the character of a priest who quests for self-realization along the way of the Contemplative life.

When the Chorus chants "[...] and the land became brown sharp points of death in a waste of water and mud,"[68] the audience recall the image of the wasteland. The arid land of the cursed Fisher King had to wait for the release of the life-giving waters for the restoration of fertility. The underlying pattern in *Murder in the Cathedral* is the quest of the Holy Grail, in all its significance, including the symbols of the lance and receptacle which represent the Cross and man's spiritual being respectively. The consummation of Becket's quest will bring spiritual fertility to mankind who will then experience 'Shantih' or the peace that passes understanding. Becket's martyrdom establishes his reference to the Gospel according to St. Luke, 2:14, in his sermon: "Glory to God in the highest, and on earth peace to men of good will."[69]

Eliot could not understand how some people failed to recognize the central nothingness at the core of life which necessitated faith in God. He believed in the existence of Hell, a fear of which made him turn his back to Hell, and involve himself with ecclesiastical activities because he believed that the Church "exists for the glory of God and the sanctification of souls."[70]

The Church is the House of God on Earth, strong enough to survive adversities. When the Knights force themselves into the Cathedral, Becket faces them with fortitude knowing that he is the keeper of the House of God. His decision is in accordance with the working of the Divine Will. Becket explains to the congregation (which is actually the audience) in his Christmas sermon that Christ had said to His disciples, "Peace I leave with you, my peace I give unto you."[71] Becket's martyrdom will also bring peace to men of good will.

The simple Charwomen of Canterbury are excited and disturbed as participators in the act of martyrdom. Becket tells them that their role in the unfolding of divine dispensation is that of witnesses:

> This is your share of the eternal burden,
> The perpetual glory. [...]
> [....................................]
> Human kind cannot bear very much reality.[72]

Therefore, their lot is to watch and wait. "If Christ is regarded as the fulfillment of death-and-resurrection myths, it is easy to explain the elements of sorrow and exaltation in tragedy, especially in relation to the Christian ritual,"[73] says Probodh Chandra Ghosh. The celebration of Christian Mysteries as a social act, brings worshippers out of their isolation into fellowship with each other in the Church, which is the mystical body of Christ. The liturgical background, the occasion and the venue of the performance of *Murder in the Cathedral* show how the pagan element in tragedy has been reinforced by Christianity, says Ghosh.[74]

This is what happens between the Priests, the Charwomen and even the audience when they witness Becket's spiritual preparation for his martyrdom. Browne played the role of Becket in an emergency version of *Murder in the Cathedral* during the Second World War. He made "many discoveries, especially of his close ties with the chorus. These women, the ordinary faithful Christians, are his anchor."[75]

The final moment of spiritual surrender has been beautifully communicated by Joseph Conrad, one of Eliot's favourite authors, in *Heart of Darkness*. When Kurtz lay dying in the pilot-house of the steamer, the novelist observes:

> Did he live his life again in every detail of desire, temptation, and surrender during that supreme moment of complete knowledge? He cried in a whisper at some image, at some vision—he cried out twice, a cry that was no more than a breath—
>
> "The horror ! The horror!"[76]

Conrad makes Marlow utter after Kurtz dies, "If such is the form of ultimate wisdom, then life is a greater riddle than some of us think it to be."[77] The inability of ordinary human beings (who exist on the lower strata of spiritual understanding) to bear the absolute reality is referred to in 'Burnt Norton', the poem which grew out of the edited parts of *Murder in the Cathedral*:

> Yet the enchainment of past and future
> woven in the weakness of the changing body,
> Protects mankind from heaven and damnation
> which flesh cannot endure.[78]

Men need illusion for survival because the stark reality is unbearable. Absurd Drama emphasizes this need for illusion, best exemplified by Vladimir and Estragon's wait for Godot who never turns up in Samuel Becket's *Waiting for Godot*. However, in Eliot's play waiting is not an illusion. It is a positive act. Becket awaits his death with great patience, by persevering to make himself worthy of death. Therefore, his waiting involves spiritual education which is also undergone in varying degrees by the Priests, the Chorus and the audience. Where Becket says, "Death will come only when I am worthy,"[79] the Chorus is scared, "Not what we call death, but what beyond death is not death, / We fear, we fear [...]"[80] R.P. Blackmur says,"Martyrdom is as far removed from common experience as the state of beatitude to which it leads."[81] The Chorus is unable to express in precise terms, its fears and apprehensions, since the simple Charwomen are unable to choose the right words. All that they can do is to wait and watch (this is their lesson in patience) the working of the Divine Wheel, being fixed on it just like Becket, the Priests, the Tempters, the Knights and, also the audience. Eliot writes in 'Towards a Christian Britain' that "It is through [Christian prophets] that God works to convert the habits of feeling and thinking, of desiring and willing, to which we are more enslaved than we know."[82]

On the physical level, the Knights play the role of the emissaries of King Henry II, deployed to punish Becket for disobeying him. However, Eliot's play attributes another function to them—they are the instruments of the material world who destroy the order of God, murdering the Archbishop inside the consecrated precincts of the Cathedral. At the same time, this act brings about a martyrdom, but the four Knights are reluctant to accept Becket's quest for self-realization, the consummation of which comes in the form of the martyrdom which is his death for the cause of God because he wished subjugation to God alone. Eliot gives the Knights a chance to justify their action. The First Knight, Reginald Fitz Urse, the leader of the foursome who murder Becket, serves as the anchor, introducing the others before the audience. The first to explain is the Third Knight, Baron William de Traci. He says that Becket has put up a "good show"[83] in the end. Their action was their duty towards the State which they performed "being completely disinterested in this business."[84] Next comes the Second Knight, Sir Hugh de Morville, who upholds the reason behind the wrath of the King who desired that Becket should unite the offices of Chancellor and Archbishop. On being made Archbishop, Becket resigned the Chancellorship, thereby destroying the King's expectations of having the highest religious authority in England as his subordinate. The Knight opines:

> Had Becket concurred with the King's wishes, we should have had an almost ideal State: a union of spiritual and temporal administration, under the central government. [...] The moment that Becket, at the King's instance had been made Archbishop, he resigned the office of Chancellor, he became more priestly than the priests, he ostentatiously and offensively adopted an ascetic manner of life, he affirmed immediately that there was a higher order than that which our King, and he as the King's servant, had for so many

> years striven to establish; and that—God knows why—the two orders were incompatible.[85]

In order to set things right, explains this Knight, they have "arrived at a just subordination of the pretensions of the Church to the welfare of the State,"[86] which they expect the audience to share as witnesses. The Fourth Knight, Richard Brito, addresses the eye-witnesses of the scene, saying that Becket had "used every means of provocation; from his conduct, step by step, there can be no inference except that he had determined upon a death by martydom."[87] So, Becket's death was actually "Suicide while of Unsound Mind."[88] This is how the four assassins try to argue their case before the audience, asking them to judge their actions in terms of their allegiance to the King, whose supreme political authority is undeniable. Thus the external conflict in Part II is between the servants of temporal power (represented by King Henry II) and the servant of God, Thomas Becket.

Patricia M. Adair calls the Knights "active instruments of evil."[89] She takes into account the guilt of the Chorus, representing all humanity, for "Theirs is the sin of indifference, apathy, evasion of the great issues, the longing to be left in their own small world, 'living and partly living'."[90]

Becket's cannonization is suggested as the play draws to a close, though it comes as a hasty conclusion to a play that deals with his spiritual quest. In Eliot's drama of martyrdom "Becket's transformation is hardly dramatically achieved or even appears to be convincing, since Thomas's last words to the Knights in response to their challenge and abuses are scarcely befitting a would-be saint."[91] He attains martyrdom and sainthood only after achieving a detachment from temptations, both material and spiritual. This sense of detachment dawns on him suddenly and the play appears to arrive at a hasty conclusion, thereby becoming weak towards the end. The Christian sense of detachment has its parallel in Oriental philosophy of which Hindu mysticism is the crux. The *Bhagavad Gita* says:

> Having brought all (the senses) under control, he should remain firm in yoga [evenness of mind] intent on Me; for he, whose senses are under control, his intelligence is firmly set.[92]

The speaker, Lord Krishna, explains further:

> He who abandons all desires and acts free from longing, without any sense of mineness or egotism, he attains peace.[93]

Only then will man realize that God alone is the doer and he is merely His instrument. The theological implication of the play indicates that man is to suffer imperatively from being born in the flesh—that flesh which is imbued with taints of the Original Sin. In order to become the instruments of the Divine Will, one has to make perfect one's will by attaining a level of detachment. Becket attains self-realization through detachment which culminates in his martyrdom.

The character of Thomas Becket succeeds in attaining the goal of his religious quest. Becket's quest appears to be Eliot's objective correlative for his own individual quest. The broken relationship with his wife and the discipline of religion made Eliot believe that his quest lay along Becket's path. However, Eliot was unable to detach himself from his immediate surroundings and from the society of which he considered himself an integral part. He soon realized that the austere Contemplative life of the Archbishop of Canterbury was possibly not the immediate answer to his personal quest for self-realization. Harry, the protagonist of his next play, *The Family Reunion*, is a very different man from Thomas Becket.

## II

Eliot was searching for the right form of drama and mode of articulation in order to convey his quest for meaning of life to his auditors. The communication would not be in an obvious and straightforward manner but would have to be clothed in literary art, in poetry and drama. This resulted in his experimenting with the various characters in his plays—characters who searched for self-realization—which was a continuation of his quest using the personae in his poems and the characters in the early dramatic endeavours. Eliot found that the scope of self-expression of the personae in the poems was limited. So, he turned to drama which permitted the expression of a wide range of feelings through the characters, who would camouflage the dramatist from the auditors' direct scrutiny. In 'The Possibility of a Poetic Drama' Eliot wrote that "the drama is perhaps the most permanent, is capable of greater variation and of expressing more varied types of society, than any other."[94] A fine opportunity for writing a play came to him like God's gracious gift, in the form of an invitation to write a play for the Canterbury Festival of 1935. Eliot knew that "the essential is to get upon the stage this precise statement of life which is at the same time a point of view, a world—a world which the author's mind has subjected to a complete process of simplification."[95] At the same time one must not ignore the performer's interpretation of the character he plays for he stands between the creator of that character and the auditor. Keeping this element in mind, Eliot became preoccupied with the social usefulness of poetry, which is in a way the relation between literature and theology. If the entire being of the poet went into the making of a poem, the entire being of the reader is affected by it. Eliot says:

> Though we may read literature merely for pleasure, of "entertainment" or of "aesthetic enjoyment", this reading never affects simply a sort of special sense; it affects us as entire human beings; it affects our moral and religious existence.[96]

The various levels of significance were to be conveyed to the audience, maintaining at the same time the different levels of understanding of the characters in the play. Eliot uses a variety of verse forms for this purpose. As Sarkar writes in *T.S. Eliot the Dramatist*, the quarrel between Becket and the Knights is in doggerel.[97] In a 1919 article on Christopher Marlowe, Eliot comments that the Elizabethan playwright breaks up a line in order to gain in dramatic intensity in the last soliloquy in *Doctor Faustus*. Marlowe also developed a new mode of verbal exchange between Faustus and the Devil which Eliot uses in *Murder in the Cathedral* in the dialogue between Becket and the Tempters. Their conversation is in four-stress rhyming verse. The chorus has been given a series of forms starting from three-stress rhymes to more complex ones.[98] Denis Donough says:

> At this point we would show that *Murder in the Cathedral* to which a crucial influence on the development of modern verse drama has frequently been attributed, is an unsuccessful

> play; that its text evades, rather than solves, the problems of dramatic verse; and that its structural flaws are similar to those of certain late nineteenth century verse plays.[99]

His comment makes obvious a total lack of understanding on his part of both Eliot's purpose and the verse pattern of the play.

Eliot was aware that the Shakespearean blank verse, appropriate for the late sixteenth and early seventeenth centuries, was not what the modern audience would accept. He had to innovate his own verse medium which, like Shakespeare's, would suit the language and tastes of the contemporary auditors. Thus began Eliot's experiment with the verse form in serious mainstream drama—it had already been tried out in *Sweeney Agonistes* and *The Rock*. In 'The Three Voices of Poetry' he compares the Choruses of *The Rock* with those of *Murder in the Cathedral*, saying that the former was speaking on his behalf while the latter makes some progress in dramatic development.[100]

The verse pattern of *Everyman* was more suited to Eliot's purpose than that of the nineteenth century dramatists who put the iambic into much use. Instead, he uses the alliterative style of Anglo-Saxon poetry to a certain extent, with occasional rhymes to bring home to his audience the desired effect of the drama, as in Thomas's words:

> Delegate to deal the doom of damnation.[101]

Eliot hoped that anything unusual in the sound of the versification of *Everyman*, used in his work, would be to its advantage, for the rhythm of regular blank verse had distanced itself from the speech of the twentieth century.[102] It was not only for the verse but also in the technique of handling the theme that the anonymous poet of *Everyman* is appreciated by Eliot who felt that English drama from Kyd to Galsworthy has made the mistake of aiming at unlimited realism and it was only "In one play, *Everyman*, [...] We have a drama within the limits of art."[103]

In 'A Dialogue on Dramatic Poetry' Eliot expressed the view that mere dramatic technique will not give the form of the play.[104] When the play unfolds itself before the audience, they ought to perceive that it follows the pattern of the ritual performances of the Mass, for the Mass contains all the ingredients of drama including the three Unities. Eliot used this pattern deliberately because he believed that "drama springs from religious liturgy, and that it cannot afford to depart far from religious liturgy."[105] Besides, he had in mind the architecture of the Chapter House of Canterbury Cathedral where the first performance of the play was to take place. J.L. Styan observes that:

> The whole church became a ritualistic theatre with the chancel as its chief acting area. By such means the ceremonial of the drama acquired a meaning greater than itself, but this is not an experiment easily repeated.[106]

Ronald Peacock says the same thing, that "In *Murder in the Cathedral* [...] ritual belongs both to the inner structure of the play and to its performance."[107] This pattern was followed by the tropes which saw the beginnings of drama in the ritual of the church. But Francis Fergusson goes even further backward while seeking for the source of Eliot's inspiration in the art of plot-construction and states that *Murder in the Cathedral* combines the pagan Greek ritualistic drama with the early Christian liturgical performances.[108] Raymond Williams says that the great formal design of the play is one which needs no imposing on the audience for "it is a formal movement, a succession of balances, which springs naturally from the fundamental relationships within the ritual."[109]

This return to the early sources of drama was because of Eliot's dissatisfaction with the drama of his immediate predecessors. He was aware that a search for an appropriate form was necessary for the expression of his personal quest for meaning of life. He saw that:

> The nineteenth century had a good many fresh impressions; but it had no form in which to confine them.[110]

Eliot was enthralled by the ability of the Greek dramatists to unite the concrete and the abstract in philosophy, thought and feeling, action and speculation in life. Their plays were treasure-houses for a dramatist to fall back on. He turned to them for the framework and inspiration of his major plays because "the beauty of phrase in Greek tragedy is the shadow of a greater beauty—the beauty of thought and emotion."[111]

He was against the use of prose in verse plays except in cases where it was imperative for the sake of the drama. He used prose twice in *Murder in the Cathedral*—once in Becket's Christmas sermon and again in the Knights' justification of their act of murdering him. The sermon, preached in prose, retained the aura of realism. It also brought a release to the audience from the tension of the temptation episode. The explanation of the Knights, in prose, after they murder Becket in the holy precincts of the Cathedral, is set in contrast to the high poetry of the final chorus—"the triviality of parliamentary reason, set against the sublimity of religious emotion."[112] Justifying himself in 'Poetry and Drama' Eliot wrote that "the use of platform prose is intended of course to have a special effect: to shock the audience out of their complacency."[113] Horace Gregory, differing in his opinion, criticizes the stance of the Knights as they justify themselves, as being in the style of the Shavian propaganda plays. In 'The Unities and Eliot' Gregory writes:

> The dramatic reality of Mr. Eliot's *Murder in the Cathedral* suddenly evaporated when its four Knights stepped to the footlights and spoke their reasons for killing Becket as though they had walked out of a script conceived and written by Mr. Bernard Shaw.[114]

Eliot preferred a certain amount of detachment in his auditors rather than an overt involvement in the action of the drama because they should be on the level of complete understanding so that, like Shakespeare's spectators, they have the "necessary advantage of a new clue to the character, in noting the angle from which he views himself."[115] Had Gregory realized this intention of the dramatist, he could have seen the necessity of the Knights' explanatory speeches after the assassination. Edwin Muir notices that "the intellectual fabric of this play is quite unusually consistent and clearly limited, and also imaginatively impressive. But it is the dramatic force that it conveys to the action that is perhaps most striking of all."[116]

## III

The dramatist was aware of the limitation of words to articulate one's experience, particularly those relating to spirituality. This may be because man himself is limited and imperfect. Hulme writes in 'Romanticism and Classicism' that "The great aim is accurate, precise and definite description."[117] Articulation for the precise expression of thought and feeling is difficult because language is communal by nature. So, there are moments when silence communicates better than words. Words, or even music, reach out to the eternal silence in the universe. Eliot thought that words had to wait in religious experience which meant moments of insight of the strongest and deepest feelings which are very rare. His motive behind the creation of the chorus was more than a return to the formal Greek drama. It was to make the audience aware of a spiritual knowledge—the "need to recover a sense of religious fear, so that it may be overcome by religious hope."[118] Eliot was trying to use words in order to "insinuate the whole history of a language and a civilization."[119] It was a persistent quest for articulation. The play is an externalization of the drama that takes place in the theatre of Becket's soul. His internal struggle against temptation in Part I and the struggle towards Christian humility in Part II, conveyed to the Chorus and Priests in particular and the auditors in general, to show the right reason for his dying, can only be achieved through the use of language, which, according to Sean Lucy, "is the verse, which is the action, which is the theme, which is the atmosphere, which is the meaning."[120] The timeless dimension of being is conveyed through the play in the frequent use of Biblical allusions and language.

Eliot knew that the only way to convey the various levels of awareness of the characters in *Murder in the Cathedral* was through the words they articulated. He had to keep in mind the layout of the Chapter House in the Cathedral in Canterbury where the first performance was to take place because the involvement of the audience in such a place would be greater than in typical theatres.

The protagonist of this play is Thomas Becket, God's elect for martyrdom. It is his preparation for this final act that is the drama of the play. His doubts and inner turmoils are expressed in words like "Sin grows with doing good"[121] because, he says:

> While I ate out of the King's dish
> To become servant of God was never my wish.[122]

Now that he wishes to serve God, he cannot overcome the spiritual hurdles that form obstructions to his attaining the state of higher contemplation, of which he is aware, for he says:

> I have therefore only to make perfect my will.[123]

This is the theme of the play, which makes it "a unified work, and a work of great beauty."[124] In making his will perfect, Becket has to learn humility for which he has to purge the pride that still remains within him in the form of an awareness of being the Archbishop of Canterbury. This is externalized by Eliot through the presentation of the characters of the four Tempters, each of whom uses a different mode of articulation to express the various states of psychological and spiritual dilemma that he wished to throw Becket into.

The First Tempter uses alliteration in his speeches which convey a sense of confident self-satisfaction in lines which he utters twice:

> Hoping that your present gravity
> Will find excuse for my humble levity.[125]

The alliteration of the clipped language of the Second Tempter is different from that of the First Tempter:

> Power obtained grows to glory,
> Life lasting, a permanent possession
> A templed tomb, monument of marble.[126]

There is a brief stychomethic exchange between Becket and the Second Tempter:

> THOMAS. Who shall have it?
> TEMPTER. He who will come.
> THOMAS. What shall be the month?
> TEMPTER. The last from the first.
> THOMAS. What shall we give for it?
> TEMPTER. Pretence of priestly power.

THOMAS. Why should we give it?
TEMPTER. For the power and the glory.
THOMAS. No!
TEMPTER. Yes! [...][127]

Grover Smith traces the source of this hot exchange to Sherlock Holmes's 'The Adventure of the Musgrave Ritual' saying that "Eliot got his measure by simple plagiarism"[128] and adding that Eliot had since acknowledged this source which is probably the strange catechism to which each Musgrave had to submit and which was handed over to Holmes in the form of a written paper:

Whose was it?
His who is gone.
Who shall have it?
He who will come.
Where was the sun?
Over the oak.
Where was the shadow?
Under the elm.[129]

However, it must be acknowledged that Eliot did have the dramatic sense to borrow Conan Doyle's technique in a detective-story and use it in a play with a solely religious purpose.

The Third Tempter, representing the country gentry, is "a rough straightforward Englishman"[130] as he claims to be, using simple words that approach the rhythm of jazz which Eliot used in Sweeney Agonistes:

We are for England. We are in England.
You and I, my Lord, are Normans.[131]

The Fourth Tempter is subtle, stealthy and measured when he lures Becket towards a misunderstanding:

Fare forward to the end.
All other ways are closed to you
Except the way already chosen.[132]

The Tempters lure and challenge Becket, which is reflected in their speeches that are confident and aggressive. On the other hand the Priests are eager to protect Becket and their anxiety is expressed throughout the play. When the Knights come to murder Becket, the Priests say:

> PRIESTS. (Severally) My Lord, you must not stop here. To the minster.
> Through the cloister. No time to waste. They are coming back,
> Armed. To the altar, to the altar.[133]

And after the martyrdom takes place they request Becket to be charitable towards them in acknowledgement of the martyrdom they have had the good fortune to witness:

> SECOND PRIEST. Now in the sight of God.

Conjoined with all the saints and martyrs gone before you, Remember us.[134]

It is the Chorus, of Charwomen, which serves as a commentator upon the action of the play, in keeping with the function of the traditional Greek chorus in Aeschylus's tragedies. Jones observes that "Eliot has not just copied Aeschylus; he has given the chorus a new significance in the light of the Christian dispensation."[135] This is what Sarkar calls the "formalist-realist synthesis."[136] Eliot continues with what he had begun in *The Rock*, namely, the experiment with the verse attributed to the Chorus, as a result of which we have a variety of expressions in *Murder in the Cathedral* beginning with the first choric utterance expressing insecurity and apprehension:

> Seven years since the Archbishop left us,
> He who was always kind to his people.
> But it would not be well if he should return.[137]

But they bear the capacity to express their premonitions and opinions without stint:

> We have not been happy, my Lord, we have not been too happy.
> We are not ignorant women, we know what we must expect and not expect.[138]

Their arrival at some sort of enlightenment is expressed in the last four lines of the play as they pray (while a Te Deum is sung in Latin by a choir in the distance):

> Lord have mercy upon us.
> Christ, have mercy upon us.
> Lord, have mercy upon us.
> Blessed Thomas, pray for us.[139]

Commenting on Eliot's skilful use of the diverse possibilities in the Chorus, Styan says, "It was a language which was at the same time a sensuous poetry wooing his audience towards the feeling the play wanted, carrying a useful range of vocal tones, and providing a full set of signals for group movement."[140]

The Knights who murder Becket, giving the play its title, are boisterous and aggressive. Critics have commented extensively on their addresses in prose directed towards the audience whom they consider to be witnesses, involving them as participants in the event of the martyrdom. Their language is that of the temporal and material world of the twentieth century metropolis. Isaacs finds the Knights' slipping out of the play and up to the audience coming as a shock and having an impact similar to that of the music-hall turn.[141] Peter Davison finds the direct address of the four Knights interesting and says that "Eliot employs this brilliantly to tempt the audience to accept the Knights' action and thus, in effect, to share their guilt."[142]

In continuing with his quest for articulation, Eliot wisely uses a variety of rhyme schemes for different purposes in *Murder in the Cathedral*. There are half-rhymes and echoes as well as "gnomic or epigrammatic one liners"[143] as in "I have therefore only to make perfect my will"[144] and "And I am not in danger: Only near to death."[145] The combination of the colloquial and the poetic, immediate significance and remote history, renders the twelfth century martyrdom with a contemporary relevance, bringing the impact of the spiritual significance of the martyrdom with a greater force upon the modern audience. This is why Edward Shillito says that:

> Mr. T.S. Eliot in his new work has won for religious drama a fresh hearing. Whether we admire it or not, we cannot ignore it. In my judgement it is a noble drama of enduring worth.[146]

The worthiness of the play lies in the central action of the murder of Becket in the Cathedral (which is also the venue of the first performance of this play) which juxtaposes the kingdom of God and that of nature, the law of God and the law of man. The latter is represented by the Knights and the former by Becket whose beautiful Christmas Sermon follows the language of the Bible closely:

> Still less is a Christian martyrdom the effect of a man's will to become a Saint, as a man by willing and contriving may become a ruler of men.[147]

The prose of the sermon reflects the calm serenity that Becket aspires after, and is, therefore, radically different from the prose of the Knights' speeches. So, it is seen that Eliot comes to equip Becket with different kinds of speeches to enable him to communicate successfully with various persons at various levels of understanding.

Eliot sought to develop a verse form that would accommodate the colloquial and rhetorical idiom of speech. This quest continues in all his subsequent plays which are set in the drawing-rooms of affluent urban households in keeping with the popular successes on the commercial stage in the early half of the twentieth century. He was able to convert a formalist pattern of speech into something of the modern colloquial and naturalistic utterance through a conscious and deliberate use of different kinds of articulation which he came to develop and refine in his next play, *The Family Reunion*.

## NOTES AND REFERENCES

1. Sarkar, "A Modernist Quest for Martyrdom: Hemingway's 'The Old Man and the Sea' and T.S. Eliot's 'Murder in the Cathedral'," *West Bengal,* Hemingway Birth Centenary Number 16, December 1999: 70.
2. D.L. Edwards, Introduction, *The Idea of a Christian Society and Other Writings*, by T.S. Eliot (London: Faber, 1939) 29.
3. According to Aldous Huxley, there was almost entirely a sexual nexus between them: "One sees it in the way he looks at her. [...] she's an incarnate provocation."—Huxley to Ottoline Morrell, 21 June 1917, in *Ottoline in Garsington*, qtd. in Peter Ackroyd, *T.S. Eliot* (London: Hamish Hamilton, 1984) 63.

4. Lyndall Gordon, *Eliot's New Life* (Oxford: Oxford UP, 1988) 19-20.
5. Wyndham Lewis, "Early London Environment," *T.S. Eliot: A Symposium: from Conrad Aiken, et al.*, ed. R. March and Tambimuttu (London: Frank Cass, 1948) 29-30.
6. Eliot, Letter to Ottoline Morrell, qtd. in Schuchard, Introduction, *The Varieties of Metaphysical Poetry* 242.
7. Herbert Read, "T.S.E. — A Memoir," *T.S. Eliot: The Man and His Work*, ed. Allen Tate (London: Chatto and Windus, 1967) 31.
8. Eliot, "Revelation," *The Idea of a Christian Society and Other Writings* 168.
9. Matthews 103.
10. Jewel Spears Brookes, "Substitutes for Christianity in the Poetry of T.S. Eliot," *T.S. Eliot: Essays from the 'Southern Review,'* ed. James Olney (Oxford: Clarendon Press, 1988) 43.
11. Brookes, in Olney 43-44.
12. In *From Ritual to Romance* and *The Quest of the Holy Grail*, Weston shows that the legend of the quest of the Holy Grail performs the symbolic function of the quest for spiritual fertility.
13. Roy, "Use of Source Material for the Development of the Theme of Martyrdom: Eliot and Tagore, A Comparative Study," *Studies in Literary Criticism* (New Delhi: Atlantic, 2001) 164.
14. Coghill, Introduction, *Murder in the Cathedral*, by Eliot (Oxford: Oxford UP, 1963) 10.
15. Niloufer Harben, *Twentieth Century English History Plays: From Shaw to Bond* (Basingstoke: Macmillan, 1988) 112.
16. Eda Lou Walton, "T.S. Eliot Turns to Religious Verse," *T.S. Eliot: Critical Assessments*, ed. Clarke, Vol. 3: 8.
17. Eliot, "The Three Voices of Poetry," *On Poetry and Poets* 94.
18. Gordon, *Eliot's New Life* 28.
19. William Turner Levy and Victor Scherle, *Affectionately T.S. Eliot: The Story of a Friendship, 1947-1965* (London: J.M. Dent, 1969) 24.
20. Eliot, "Virgil and the Christian World," *On Poetry and Poets* 127.
21. Eliot, *Murder in the Cathedral*, CPP 246.
22. Eliot, *Murder in the Cathedral,* CPP 246.
23. Abbot Justin McCann, *The Cloud of Unknowing* (London: Burns and Oates, 1924) x.
24. McCann 24.

25. Mc.Cann xii.
26. Mc.Cann 26.
27. Mc.Cann 45.
28. The Bible, King James Version, Mark 15: 34.
29. The Bible, Luke 23: 46.
30. Eliot, "The Idea of a Christian Society," *The Idea of a Christian Society and Other Writings* 79.
31. Eliot, "Burnt Norton," *Four Quartets*, CPP 173.
32. Eliot, *Murder in the Cathedral*, CPP 247.
33. Thomas Ernest Hulme, *Speculations*, ed. Herbert Read (London: Routledge and Kegan Paul, 1924) 71.
34. Hulme 71.
35. Eliot, *Murder in the Cathedral* CPP 275.
36. Robert Speaight, "With Becket in 'Murder in the Cathedral,'" in Tate 187.
37. Eliot, *Murder in the Cathedral*, CPP 245.
38. Eliot, qtd. by Gordon 30.
39. Eliot, "Burnt Norton," *Four Quartets*, CPP 175.
40. Eliot, *Murder in the Cathedral*, CPP 248.
41. Eliot, *Murder in the Cathedral*, CPP 272.
42. Weston, *From Ritual to Romance* 141.
43. Eliot, *Murder in the Cathedral*, CPP 260.
44. Everett F. Harrison, *Baker's Dictionary of Theology* (Michigan: Baker Book House, 1960) 331-32.
45. Eliot, *Murder in the Cathedral*, CPP 261.
46. Eliot, *Murder in the Cathedral*, CPP 274-75.
47. Sarkar, *West Bengal*, Hemingway Birth Centenary Number 69.
48. Eliot, *Murder in the Cathedral*, CPP 240.
49. Eliot, *Murder in the Cathedral*, CPP 242.
50. Matthews 93.
51. Eliot, "The Idea of a Christian Society," *The Idea of a Christian Society and Other Writings* 104.
52. St. John of the Cross, qtd. by Eliot, *Sweeney Agonistes*, CPP 115.
53. Bonamy Dobree, "T.S. Eliot: A Personal Reminiscence," in Tate 80-81.
54. Eliot, *Murder in the Cathedral*, CPP 253.
55. Eliot, *Murder in the Cathedral*, CPP 249-50.

56. Eliot, *Murder in the Cathedral*, CPP 255.
57. Eliot, *Murder in the Cathedral*, CPP 258.
58. Roy, "T.S. Eliot and the *Gita*," *Journal of the Department of English*, University of Burdwan 87.
59. Eliot, *Murder in the Cathedral*, CPP 255-56.
60. Eliot, "Towards a Christian Britain," *The Idea of a Christian Society and Other Writings* 121-22.
61. Eliot, *Murder in the Cathedral*, CPP 256.
62. Eliot, *After Strange Gods* 62.
63. Eliot, *After Strange Gods* 24.
64. Eliot, *After Strange Gods* 31.
65. Eliot, "A Sub-Christian Society," *The Idea of a Christian Society and Other Writings* 112.
66. Eliot, "The Idea of a Christian Society," *The Idea of a Christian Society and Other Writings* 80-81.
67. Edwards, Introduction, *The Idea of a Christian Society and Other Writings*, by Eliot 9.
68. Eliot, *Murder in the Cathedral*, CPP 239.
69. Eliot, *Murder in the Cathedral*, CPP 260.
70. Eliot, Appendix, *The Idea of a Christian Society and Other Writings* 101.
71. Eliot, *Murder in the Cathedral*, CPP 260-61.
72. Eliot, *Murder in the Cathedral*, CPP 271.
73. Probodh Chandra Ghosh, *Poetry and Religion as Drama* (Calcutta: The World Press, 1965) 210.
74. Ghosh 210-11.
75. Browne 154.
76. Joseph Conrad, *Heart of Darkness*, ed. Paul O'Prey (1902; London: Penguin, 1983). 111.
77. Conrad 112.
78. Eliot, "Burnt Norton," *Four Quartets*, CPP 173.
79. Eliot, *Murder in the Cathedral*, CPP 271.
80. Eliot, *Murder in the Cathedral*, CPP 273.
81. R.P. Blackmur, "T.S. Eliot: From 'Ash Wednesday' to 'Murder in the Cathedral'," in Clarke Vol. 3: 445.
82. Eliot, "Towards a Christian Britain," *The Idea of a Christian Society and Other Writings* 122.

83. Eliot, *Murder in the Cathedral*, CPP 277.
84. Eliot, *Murder in the Cathedral*, CPP 277.
85. Eliot, *Murder in the Cathedral*, CPP 278.
86. Eliot, *Murder in the Cathedral*, CPP 278.
87. Eliot, *Murder in the Cathedral*, CPP 279.
88. Eliot, *Murder in the Cathedral*, CPP 279.
89. Patricia M. Adair, "Mr. Eliot's 'Murder in the Cathedral'," Clarke, Vol. 3: 483.
90. Adair, Clarke, Vol. 3: 483.
91. Sarkar, *West Bengal*, Hemingway Birth Centenary Number 69.
92. *Bhagavad-Gita*, trans. Sarvepalli Radhakrishnan (1948; New Delhi: Harper Collins, 1993) 125.
93. *Bhagavad-Gita* 128.
94. Eliot, "The Possibility of a Poetic Drama" *The Sacred Wood* 61.
95. Eliot, "The Possibility of a Poetic Drama," *The Sacred Wood* 68.
96. Eliot, "Religion and Literature," *Selected Essays* 396.
97. Sarkar, *T.S. Eliot the Dramatist* 109.
98. Sarkar, *T.S. Eliot the Dramatist* 109.
99. Denis Donough, *The Third Voice* (Princeton UP, 1959) 76.
100. Eliot, "The Three Voices of Poetry," *On Poetry and Poets* 91.
101. Eliot, *Murder in the Cathedral*, CPP 250.
102. Eliot, "Poetry and Drama," *On Poetry and Poets* 80.
103. Eliot, "Four Elizabethan Dramatists," *Selected Essays* 111.
104. Eliot, "A Dialogue on Dramatic Poetry," *Selected Essays* 46.
105. Eliot, "A Dialogue on Dramatic Poetry," *Selected Essays* 47-48.
106. J.L. Styan, *The Elements of Drama* (1960; New Delhi: Vikas, 1979) 107.
107. Ronald Peacock, *The Poet in the Theatre* (London: Macgibbon and Kee, 1961) 7.
108. Francis Fergusson, "'Murder in the Cathedral': The Theological Scene," *Twentieth Century Interpretations of 'Murder in the Cathedral'*, in Clarke Vol. 3: 29.
109. Raymond Williams, *Drama from Ibsen to Eliot* (1952; London: Perigrine, 1964) 250.
110. Eliot, "The Possibility of a Poetic Drama," *The Sacred Wood* 62.
111. Eliot, "Seneca in Elizabethan Translations," *Selected Essays* 68.

112. Sarkar, *T.S. Eliot the Dramatist* 108.
113. Eliot, "Poetry and Drama," *On Poetry and Poets* 81.
114. Horace Gregory, "The Unities and Eliot," in Clarke, Vol. 3, 353.
115. Eliot, "Rhetoric and Poetic Drama," *Selected Essays* 40.
116. Edwin Muir, rev. of *Murder in the Cathedral*, by Eliot, *T.S. Eliot: The Critical Heritage* 321.
117. Hulme 132.
118. Eliot, "The Idea of a Christian Society," *The Idea of a Christian Society and Other Writings* 81.
119. Eliot, "The Music of Poetry," *On Poetry and Poets* 33.
120. Sean Lucy, *T.S. Eliot and the Idea of Tradition* (London: Cohent West, 1960) 187.
121. Eliot, *Murder in the Cathedral*, CPP 258.
122. Eliot, *Murder in the Cathedral*, CPP 258.
123. Eliot, *Murder in the Cathedral*, CPP 271.
124. Muir, *T.S. Eliot: The Critical Heritage* 322.
125. Eliot, *Murder in the Cathedral*, CPP 246, 248.
126. Eliot, *Murder in the Cathedral*, CPP 248.
127. Eliot, *Murder in the Cathedral*, CPP 249.
128. Grover Smith 194.
129. Arthur Conan Doyle, *Sherlock Holmes: The Complete Facsimile Edition* (Hertfordshire: Wordsworth, 1996) 359. Eliot had reviewed Arthur Conan Doyle's *The Complete Sherlock Holmes Short Stories* for *Criterion*, Vol. viii, No. 32 (April 1929) 552.
130. Eliot, *Murder in the Cathedral*, CPP 250.
131. Eliot, *Murder in the Cathedral*, CPP 251.
132. Eliot, *Murder in the Cathedral*, CPP 253.
133. Eliot, *Murder in the Cathedral*, CPP 271.
134. Eliot, *Murder in the Cathedral*, CPP 281.
135. Jones 53.
136. Sarkar, *T.S. Eliot the Dramatist* 3.
137. Eliot, *Murder in the Cathedral*, CPP 239.
138. Eliot, *Murder in the Cathedral*, CPP 257.
139. Eliot, *Murder in the Cathedral*, CPP 282.
140. Styan 52.
141. Isaacs 50.

142. Peter Davison, *Contemporary Drama and the Popular Dramatic Tradition in England* (London: Macmillan, 1982) 53.
143. Glenda Leeming, *Poetic Drama*, Macmillan Modern Dramatists Series (Hampshire: Macmillan, 1989) 96.
144. Eliot, *Murder in the Cathedral*, CPP 271.
145. Eliot, *Murder in the Cathedral*, CPP 271.
146. Edward Shillito, Review, *Christian Century*, in *T.S. Eliot: The Critical Heritage* 328.
147. Eliot, *Murder in the Cathedral*, CPP 261.

# 3 Into the Fold of Naturalism—A Search for Form and Meaning in Family Life

Eliot wrote *Murder in the Cathedral* according to prescription, for the Canterbury Festival of 1935. *The Family Reunion*, staged four years later, was the first play, which he wrote purely for the commercial theatre. Although he used the popular drawing-room setting in this play, it was different from other contemporary plays which made use of the same sort of elite drawing-room background. This naturalistic setting would serve merely as the scaffold to his quest for meaning of life. The framework of the play was to be provided by the Oresteian myth which formed part of Aeschylus's contribution to classical Greek drama. The result was a "formalist-realist synthesis"[1] in the pattern of modern poetic drama. Orestes quested for liberation like Harry but the Greek hero sought for liberation from the family curse of blood-guilt; Harry seeks spiritual liberation and self-realization, his search being that of a Christian who is aware of Christ's sacrifice for mankind.

The formalist element in this modern play is the framework of ritual. Eliot draws upon both Pagan (Greek) and Christian rituals in *The Family Reunion* and synthesizes the two under the shadow of the myth of Orestes, the Eumenides serving as the objective correlative of a consciousness of the past. Nevill Coghill says that *The Family Reunion* was "designed to be a crypto-Christian play"[2] with Pagan overtones. He also says that if Eliot uses the Eumenides as the objective correlative that determines Harry's part in the Monchensey curse, it is a deliberate device "to correspond to the human situation, as seen in the Christian doctrine of the fall of Man, that *we are sinners in a world of sin, and that this sin calls for expiation.*"[3] Eliot made useful and effective use of the dramatic device of the Eumenides (the appearance of the supernatural in Classical Greek drama was an accepted device), modifying the accepted conventional Classical device in order to make them appear relevant and convincing in the naturalistic theatre. The classical myth intertwines with the Christian ritual of sin (Original and committed) since "the very structure of the play is dependent on the liturgical representation of Harry's sense of guilt and his search for liberation."[4] Harry realizes the meaning of the pursuit by the Eumenides only after his return to Wishwood, when he hears about his mother's relationship with his father from Agatha. He had sensed the Eumenides pursuing him wherever he went but he sees them for the first time only after he comes to the seat of the Monchenseys. Maud Bodkin observes that:

> There is a vision of the real pressing on our spirits that only myth and imagery can convey. [...] surely, the myth of the Eumenides—dread pursuers that avenge not private but communal crime—far from being academic, has dreadful relevance.[5]

So Harry understands that his seeing the Eumenides only after his return to Wishwood has some significance, although at this early stage he cannot figure out what it is. Still groping in the dark about his purpose in life, he ejaculates:

> Can't you see them? *You* don't see them, but I see them,
> And they see me. This is the first time that I have seen them.
> [..........................................................................]
> Why should they wait until I came back to Wishwood?
> There were a thousand places where I might have met them!
> Why here? Why here?[6]

The introduction of the Eumenides into the modern naturalistic play gives it a ritualistic dimension for which Harry, like Orestes, "must think in terms of the ritualistic conception of sin,"[7] without which an understanding of the use of myth in *The Family Reunion* is impossible. Possibly Middleton Murry is not correct when he observes that "the fundamental cause of this persistent perplexity lay in the very nature of the poet's effort to reinterpret a theme of Greek tragedy in terms of a modern consciousness. [...] Does a sin endure to be expiated by the next generation?"[8] How very consciously and deliberately Eliot is making use of the supernatural as a part of his own dramatic device with the intention of making the modern audience accept the Eumenides as the objective correlative of Harry's psychological condition, can be realized from his careful use of the Eumenides at critical junctures of the play. He is making use of myth as did James Joyce in his works, particularly *Ulysses*. While talking of Joyce's use of myth, Eliot explains the purpose of its use in contemporary literature:

> In using the myth, in manipulating a continuous parallel between contemporaneity and antiquity, Mr. Joyce is pursuing a method. [...] It is simply a way of controlling, of ordering, of giving a shape and a significance to the immense panorama of futility and anarchy which is contemporary history."[9]

He found in Joyce a kind of modality of the use of myth. Eliot combined myth and the state of the mind of modern man as part of the ritualistic framework of this play. William V. Spanos, in *The Christian Tradition in Modern British Verse Drama*, supports Eliot's use of the Furies who bridge the gap between Original Sin and the Incarnation, between Evil and Good, playing "a major role in transmuting the ephemeral contemporary human event into a quest for redemption."[10] Eliot considered Joyce's work to be penetrated with Christian feeling,[11] contrasting it with Yeats's method whose "'Supernatural world' [...] was not a world of spiritual significance, not a world of real Good and Evil, of holiness and sin, but a highly sophisticated lower mythology,"[12] of which he disapproved. As opposed to Yeats's concept of the supernatural, to Eliot, the supernatural is the Divine Will that presides over the natural world. Therefore, modern man's apathy towards this supernatural order perturbs Eliot, and he expresses his concern:

> What I do wish to affirm is that the whole of modern literature is corrupted by what I call secularism, that it is

> simply unaware of, simply cannot understand the meaning of the primacy of the supernatural over the natural life, of something which I assume to be our primary concern.[13]

Eliot emphasized the doctrine of the Incarnation of the Son of God in Jesus Christ and the sacramental nature of the Eucharist. In order to seek salvation through suffering like Him, man must first be aware of a sense of guilt and sin. Even the *desire* to kill is sin. Eliot expresses his awareness of this primordial urge in many individuals when he makes Sweeney articulate in his characteristic manner:

> Any man has to, needs to, wants to
> Once in a lifetime, do a girl in.[14]

As if in continuation of Sweeney's words, Harry nurtured the idea that he pushed his wife overboard the liner on which they were travelling, thereby suffering from a sense of guilt. So, each time Sergeant Winchell uses the term "her Ladyship" to mean his mother, Harry mistakes it to mean his dead wife. His unstable psychological state at this stage of the play is revealed in his words to Sergeant Winchell:

> Why do you keep asking
> about her ladyship? Do you know or don't you?
> I'm not afraid of you.[15]

It is obvious that Eliot follows Dante's vision of Purgatory while treating the character of Harry in the early stages of *The Family Reunion* for, as Kristian Smidt says, he sees man as "hovering in a twilight between salvation and damnation."[16] Eliot's awareness of this state of man becomes apparent in his writings. Discussing John Marston's *Sophonisba,* Eliot mentions "a pattern behind the pattern into which the characters deliberately involve themselves; the kind of pattern which we perceive in our own lives only at rare moments of inattention and detachment, drowsing in sunlight."[17] The characters in Eliot's plays involve themselves in a similar pattern—symbolized by the Quest of the Holy Grail. In *The Family Reunion*, Mary's voice seems to echo with the sound of the waterfall in the forest, which the quester must look for. Harry says to her:

You seem
like someone who comes from a very long distance,
Or the distant waterfall in the forest,
Inaccessible, half-heard.[18]

The image is the objective correlative of the symbolic relevance of the life-giving waters in fertility myths, used by Eliot to represent Harry's self-realization which will help him to rejuvenate the spiritually arid Wishwood. So, Harry's quest for his identity is hinted at here. He feels that he is destined to seek and suffer for the salvation of his family and for his own identity because he is conscious of a growing awareness of his own and his family's past. He reminds the auditors of Christ's Suffering and Sacrifice for the sake of mankind when he says:

Spring is an issue of blood
A season of sacrifice.[19]

The obvious echoes of the opening lines of *The Waste Land* in Harry's words prove that Christ's Sacrifice had great significance for Eliot. The Crucifixion, arising out of the ritual of the Eucharist during the Last Supper indicates Christ's love for mankind, which Eliot acknowledges in 'East Coker':

The dripping blood our only drink,
The bloody flesh our only food:
In spite of which we like to think
That we are sound, substantial flesh and blood—
Again, in spite of that, we call this Friday good.[20]

Holy Communion during the ritual of the Mass is a reminder of this Sacrifice for the salvation of men. Christianity, to Eliot, was not something to be practised mechanically; it had to be imbibed and asserted. C.H. Smith aptly notices that "The time of the action is late march, the time of the spring fertility ceremonies and, in corresponding Christian terms, of Easter."[21] Many critics, who fail to recognize the message in the play, have no understanding of the Christian references in it. For instance, Frederick A. Pottle feels that "It is too late to bring in the Christian reference at the very end by ritual,"[22] and C.L. Barber discovers in the play "the astonishingly ruthless and unchristian way that its hero pursues his destiny."[23] Such comments indicate a failure to perceive the Christian element in the play which, instead of being superficial (or even absent) as these critics seem to find, is an intrinsic part of the play itself. Harry, as the elect of his family (by virtue of being on the highest level of spiritual awareness), is searching for a way of expiating a family sin on one level, and the imbued Original Sin on the other. He blends the Pagan and Christian elements of the play into a universal whole. His highly perceptive and susceptible mind enables him to gradually realize the presence of the supernatural over the natural world. He realizes that his inner suffering is but a microcosm of the Original Sin which is universal. It appears that this has been pinpointed by a critic who observes that "Eliot has used the doctrine of original sin in *The Family Reunion* to lend an almost semi-mythical support to the very theme of his 'naturalistic' play."[24] This is obvious in Eliot's handling of Harry's character. The quest that Eliot chooses to make Harry undertake requires humility — similar to Becket's in *Murder in the Cathedral*, and to that of certain characters in subsequent plays, of which he writes in 'East Coker':

> To arrive where you are, to get from where you are not,
> You must go by a way wherein there is no ecstasy.
> In order to arrive at where you do not know
> You must go by a way which is the way of ignorance.[25]

In this poem Eliot associates his close knowledge of the technicalities of the theatre with the Christian concept of the Cloud of Unknowing—the waiting for the right moment for surrendering oneself to God's Will. He writes:

> I said to my soul, be still, and let the dark come upon you
> Which shall be the darkness of God. As, in a theatre,
> The lights are extinguished, for the scene to be changed.[26]

As the play unfolds before the auditors it is seen that Harry is prepared for his quest by his aunt Agatha, who plays the role of the priestess in myth, making it evident that:

> The play is built around Harry's discovery of spiritual election. The significance of the other characters depends

> upon their relationship to this central experience. They arrange themselves almost schematically in degrees of spiritual perception.[27]

Just as in *Murder in the Cathedral*, so also here we find various levels of understanding represented by the different characters in the play. Glenda Leeming feels that Eliot "mistakenly dismisses the natural human reaction"[28] to the death of Harry's wife and that he treats Agatha's report about Harry's father's desire to murder his mother as "comparatively unimportant."[29] This is precisely because Harry exists on a high level of spiritual understanding, which Eliot tries to reveal through his apparently strange behaviour to make it a perceptible device for the naturalistic effect (which may even be said to be a clever technical device). He feels that there is something just beyond the margin which he cannot gauge. There is an urge to seek for it. He knows that the journey of the quest has to be undertaken alone. Mary, whose level of understanding is lower than Harry's or Agatha's, tries to comprehend the situation on her own, thereby undergoing suffering in her small way. Harry says to her:

> There is only one way for you to understand
> And that is by seeing. They are much too clever
> To admit you into *our* world. Yours is no better.
> They have seen to that: it is part of the torment.[30]

Mary's role in this play is a reminder of that of the priests in *Murder in the Cathedral* in which play they tried to retain the safety and physical security of Thomas Becket, unconsciously posing as a hindrance to his self-realization through the process of martyrdom. They belonged to the lower stratum of the church order. Initially they were not interested in Becket's role as God's chosen one. Similarly, Mary wanted to hold on to Harry so that he would not leave Wishwood. But the similarity ends here. Since the characters in the later play were more realistic, Mary, with a better spiritual understanding than the Priests, realized that Harry had a mission to fulfil. So, she learns to express her selfless love for him and decides to help him towards a smooth departure from Wishwood.

Dr. Warburton, a character who is far below Harry on the axis of spiritual understanding, says to Harry, "You don't understand me."[31] Obviously, he is correct because Harry's understanding is far superior to his and the two cannot reach the same level of spiritual understanding. Harry's words to him, "The things that are going to happen / Have already happened"[32] are an echo of Eliot's own words in "Tradition and the Individual Talent" where he says that:

> [...] the poet cannot reach this impersonality without surrendering himself wholly to the work to be done. And he is not likely to know what is to be done unless he lives in what is not merely the present, but the present moment of the past, unless he is conscious, not of what is dead, but of what is already living.[33]

So it can be seen that Harry has several levels of understanding (both spiritual and physical) at the same time, articulating which becomes difficult for him, and he says of his mother, aunts (Ivy and Violet) and uncles that:

> They don't understand what it is to be awake,
> To be living on several planes at once
> Though one cannot speak with several voices at once.[34]

His words appear to be enigmatic because he is seeking for the right form of expression for articulating the suffering he is undergoing. Ever since his arrival at Wishwood a few hours ago, his spiritual insight is becoming deeper and the purpose of his quest clearer. Now he knows that his suffering is part of a bigger design, his misery is part of a universal spiritual wasteland—the suffering of modern man in a world bereft of spirituality and faith. He sees his own life as:

> [...] part of some huge disaster,
> Some monstrous mistake and aberration
> Of all men, of the world, which I cannot put in order.[35]

Agatha's understanding is on the second-highest level. She has had one kind of spiritual experience—a brief moment of an all-consuming nature—"a present moment of pointed light / When you want to burn."[36] The other is harder. It is a spiritual journey symbolized by that across a wilderness of hurtful broken stones causing suffering, meant for those with a higher spiritual understanding. It is a lifetime's journey. Harry will have to undertake this, though at the present moment he knows neither.

The difference in their levels of understanding becomes clear in the dialogue between Amy, Harry's natural mother, and Agatha, his spiritual mother, when Amy says to Harry, "So you will run away,"[37] Agatha's reply is:

> In a world of fugitives
> The person taking the opposite direction
> Will appear to run away.[38]

The two sisters have never seen eye to eye ever since Amy suspected Agatha, her youngest sister, of having an affair with her late husband. As a result their voices appear to be discordant.

Agatha knows that Mary and she have levels of understanding superior to those of the others who exist on various strata of the physical plane, which is one world. But Harry now exists on the spiritual level of higher understanding, which is another world. Since Mary and Agatha can comprehend both worlds, Agatha describes their world as "the neutral territory"[39] between these two worlds. Referring to this speech, Gerald Weales says that there are three levels of understanding in the play:

> Harry is the saint or the man on the way to special spiritual knowledge [...] Agatha and Mary will not meet Harry, however, for he will have gone beyond them. The rest of the aunts and uncles form an uncomprehending Chorus that prefers to focus its attention always on the little incident, the polite comfort, the known situation.[40]

Eliot places these characters on various levels of understanding because he was experimenting with *The Family Reunion*, in which he wished to say many things within the limited scope of dramatic presentation. This was his personal quest for meaning of life as well as for a form of presentation and the articulation of the innermost experiences and thoughts. So, one may say that the role and behaviour of Harry seems to have a sort of resemblance with Eliot's personal life. Harry's relation with the women who figure in his life (particularly Amy, Agatha, Mary and his wife) and his behaviour with them seems to reflect the dramatist's own behaviour (or desired behaviour) with the women who played significant roles in his life about the time he was writing this play.

Right from his infancy Eliot, the youngest in the family of six children, found himself in the company of women. His mother, Charlotte Eliot, took great care of her son. His four elder sisters doted on him as did his nurse. Even in his later life Eliot found himself at ease with women. Matthews observes that "women were the people who counted most in Eliot's life."[41] Gordon says the same thing: "In fact, it seems that only with women was Eliot ever fully at ease."[42]

However, his Unitarian family taught him to be austere where sensuality was concerned. This led to a deep horror of women, according to Matthews, which actually is a fear of falling below the expected standard of his family. As a result, "He was fascinated by women and preoccupied by sex, yet in all his poetry Eliot never once managed to convey what Yeats did a hundred times: a feeling of desire for a woman, the sense that a woman is desirable."[43] Although he wrote the King Bolo verses in his early youth he suppressed them at the earliest opportunity when he realized that they were highly improper according to the expectations of the Unitarian standards.

It was because of an awareness of the Unitarian constraint that Eliot could not publicly assert his true feelings for Emily Hale as she waited patiently for him to do so, leading to a strange life-long relation between them. His sojourn into England led to his hasty, sudden courtship and marriage with Vivienne Haigh-Wood. It is assumed that at this time Eliot was suffering from deep depression (probably from being away from home and with the First World War raging in Europe) and that Pound actively encouraged the marriage with the hope of rejuvenating Eliot's spirits in order to enable him to carry on with a literary career in England. Eliot loved Vivienne and was very attentive to his wife. She was intelligent and lively, suggesting the name for Eliot's journal, *Criterion*, and making contributions of at least eleven pieces of fiction, prose and verse to it. Eliot appreciated her intelligence calling her "a woman who had a mind like a man."[44] But she was possessive and insecure to care about his feelings or temperament. Eliot's disillusionment regarding his married life with her is clear from the *Ode* he wrote on 4 July 1918:

> [...] Tortured
> When the bridegroom smoothed his hair
> There was blood upon the bed.
> Morning was already late.[45]

The unpleasant personal reference in this poem made Eliot drop it from subsequent publications. Matthews finds that his love for his wife which was:

> A deep incurable wound in his life, had begun in anxiety and fear—fear and anxiety over the break with his family, his country, his traditions—and grew into a different profound anxiety about her health, her sanity, and the inevitable lessening of his own love. And there was always the competitive stress, himself against the rest of the writing world.[46]

Soon, the inevitable occurred as the couple drifted away from each other. Eliot became aloof, involving himself in his literary world, although he remained dutiful towards her. Matthews calls her Eliot's 'muse.' If she was so, it was for a brief period, for he soon felt that his identity was at a crisis under the overbearing possessiveness of a highly sensuous kind which verged on neurosis. Referring to Harry's ejaculation, "O that awful privacy / Of the insane mind!"[47] Gordon points out that Eliot used these very words to describe his life with Vivienne years later, to his friend Mary Trevelyan. He said "I used to find that, once I got out of the atmosphere, I recovered normality surprisingly quickly. But at the time it seemed as though it would never end."[48] So, when the director of the play, Browne, told Eliot that he found the character of Harry baffling, Eliot's long reply to him sounded like a private testimony. The letter revealed Eliot's horror of women which is "connected with a predisposition to see women as creatures of sexual sin who dare men to consort with them and so receive their ineradicable taint."[49] In spite of Eliot's attempts to conceal the probable likeness between himself and Harry, sensitive auditors like Virginia Woolf were able to discover after watching the play that "The chief poker is Tom."[50]

Soon, Vivienne became nervous and desperate, losing health. Bertrand Russell wrote to Lady Ottoline Morrell that she was fond of Eliot but was impulsive occasionally, "a person who lives on a knife edge, and will end as a criminal or a saint."[51] She was a peculiar woman—intelligent, yet with a feeling of insecurity. She never understood her husband although she imposed herself on him. On the other hand, Emily understood him but never imposed herself on him. As for Eliot, his Unitarian grooming prevented a free and normal relationship with women on a personal or sensual level. Peter Ackroyd writes about the period during 1937-38:

> But if these were all roles he played, they were necessary ones; they protected a man who could be extremely shy and nervous in the company of other people. He suffered from a kind of hypersensitivity which, unchecked or unguarded, would have incapacitated him. On one occasion in this period he was unusually self–revealing in a conversation with Virginia Woolf; she sensed an agonized and lonely man, filled with 'self–torture, doubt, conceit, desire for warmth and intimacy.' This was a man who needed all the help and support from others he could get."[52]

The help came from Emily Hale who "endured with him his prolonged expiation."[53] He could not get Vivienne's spiritual support, yet he was conscious of a sense of duty towards her. This led to an agonized life of celibacy on his part which ended with his second marriage in 1957. Matthews quotes him tearfully saying to Hayward, "I've not a single second of happiness to look back on, and that makes it worse."[54]

Emily Hale came to his rescue from 1930 to 1935. She belonged to his American past and knew him better than most others. Like Mary, she "had to accept a man damaged by his more recent past, and accept too the penitential 'life time's march' that took him away from her."[55] Harry, whose character is Eliot's experimental persona, seems to be partly the dramatist himself. Harry is "absorbed in his own soul, and through him Eliot explored the nature of a hermit in the making."[56]

So, his superior understanding, incomprehensible to most of his family, whose queer behaviour disgusts Harry, makes him turn to the only person who understands him—Agatha. He says:

> Time and time and time, and change, no change!
> You all of you try to talk as if nothing had happened,
> And yet you are talking of nothing else. Why not get to the point
> Or if you want to pretend that I am another person —
> A person that you have conspired to invent, please do so
> In my absence. I shall be less embarrassing to you. Agatha?[57]

The intense storm that surges within him cannot be perceived by his mother, aunts (Ivy and Violet) and uncles, who resemble those auditors who are on the lowest level of comprehension. Their view is expressed by an anonymous criticism in the *Times Literary Supplement*:

> We had imagined a dynamic and cursive drama, learning from the Greek, but moving away from it too. This is the contrary. Characters are erected like statues [...] here and there about the dessicated stage.[58]

The biased critic clearly fails to understand the inner drama of the play, particularly on the stage of Harry's inner being. It is after he leaves the theatre that another critic Desmond MacCarthy gets Eliot's message clearly. He says:

> It is a drama of the inner life. [...] If I had grasped this while in the theatre instead of only when on my return home, I should not have been so perplexed by the play.[59]

The emphasis lies on the significance of his past on Harry's life. Most people fail to realize that the present is posed like a hyphen between past and future, both of which extend into eternity. They lay greater emphasis on the present which Harry points out to Agatha:

> Of the past you can only see what is past,
> Not what is always present. That is what matters.[60]

On the one hand Eliot brings in the idea of going to the roots of European culture in search of one's past, on the other he refers to the Oresteian myth to emphasize the responsibility of Harry as the consciousness of his family, with his greater spiritual understanding. The past is bound to the present which in turn leads to the future. Harry was restless, his purpose undefined. So, he thought that escape was possible if he returned to Wishwood. His arrival was soon followed by the appearance of the Eumenides for the first time. The realization that escape is not for him begins to dawn on him. He has to search for his self–realization, for his roots which lay in his past, even his parents' past. Harry asks:

> How can we be concerned with the past
> And not with the future? Or with the future
> And not with the past?[61]

The present connects the past with the future and becomes part of the past with each passing moment. Elliot writes in "Tradition and the Individual Talent":

> [...] the past should be altered by the present as much as the present is directed by the past [...] who is aware of this will be aware of great difficulties and responsibilities.[62]

Thus Harry, aware of his past and its impact on his present, realizes that he must know more about his father in order to seek for his identity. That his father is important for his quest, that Amy had tried to push her husband into the darkness of obscurity and the oblivion of her sons, that he must know more about him begins to dawn upon Harry gradually, making him realize both his responsibility and the difficulty of his quest. Intense emotions cannot be expressed in exact terms. There is no escape from experiencing such emotions. Harry is the quester whose awareness is incomplete at this stage. So he thinks that he is in a desolate expanse of desert, jostled by the memories of his past; a lonely man seeking liberation from them:

> [...] I talk in general terms
> Because the particular has no language. One thinks to escape
> By violence, but one is still alone
> In an overcrowded desert, jostled by ghosts.[63]

The reason for being the elect of the family as the quester is still not clear to Harry. But he knows that the answers to his queries lie at the end of his journey, in following the Eumenides (Pagan and Greek) or as Harry calls them, the bright angels (Christian and modern). Harry prepares to search for self-realization alone since he realizes that he will not have company. For a long time he was under the misconception that the Eumenides were his pursuers because he could not understand the reason behind their following him around. He came back to Wishwood intending to collect his broken selves together. Soon he realizes his mistake and he contemplates on the appearance of the Eumenides:

> I still have to find out what their meaning is.
> Here I have been finding
> A misery long forgotten, and a new torture,
> The shadow of something behind our meagre childhood,
> Some origin of wretchedness. Is that what they would show me?[64]

Harry's words seem to bear echoes of the playwright's own childhood in St. Louis. Commenting on Eliot's use of the supernatural beings on the modern stage, Coghill says that "The supreme flaw is the daring introduction of the Eumenides as the objective correlative of Harry's guilt and expiation."[65] Theoretically the introduction of the Eumenides is an excellent innovation. But where presentation on the stage is concerned, they do pose as a problem for the director. Eliot confesses in 'Poetry and Drama' that every manner of presenting them proved a failure which is "merely a symptom of the failure to adjust the ancient with the modern."[66] The director of the first presentation, Browne, finds that the Eumenides "cannot involve the audience in an experience which cannot be seen upon the face of the character who alone can mediate it."[67] He considered *The Family Reunion* "a masterpiece, but not a successful play."[68] Coghill obviously falls short of understanding the fact that Harry's character is *not* "the very portrait of a certain kind of soul in the throes of religious conversion."[69] The reference being Eliot's conversion to Anglo-Catholicism. If there are "throes", they are because of Eliot's first marriage. Matthews is probably right when he calls Harry "Eliot's mouthpiece."[70] Harry's inner being suffers intense torments which he cannot articulate properly. But when his quest begins to define itself before him, his purpose made clear, he feels that it is the end of his anxiety and restlessness. He says:

> I feel quite happy, as if happiness
> Did not consist in getting what one wanted
> Or in getting rid of what can't be got rid of
> But in a different vision. This is like an end.[71]

Agatha points out to him that the actual quest for self-realization will begin now:

> And a beginning. Harry, my dear,
> I feel very tired, as only the old feel.[72]

The burden of the knowledge of a sense of guilt has been shifted to Harry who will carry it in his quest like a Cross, on the higher level of spiritual understanding, in search of the Absolute Truth. Their exchange reminds one of 'East Coker,' where the poet writes:

> In my beginning is my end [...][73]

and,

> [...] In my end is my beginning.[74]

This is the acknowledgement of an awareness of the supernatural presiding over the natural world. The burden being transferred, Agatha is spiritually relieved. She is frightened for Harry because she knows the enormity and gravity of his task—a lone journey into the unknown. Without humility Harry will not be able to aspire towards salvation, as Eliot writes in 'East Coker':

> In the middle, not only in the middle of the way
> But all the way, in a dark wood, in a bramble,
> The only wisdom we can hope to acquire
> Is the wisdom of humility: humility is endless.[75]

This is the core of Christianity as exemplified in works like *The Quest of the Holy Grail, The Cloud of Unknowing* and the *Divine Comedy*.

It becomes possible for Harry to reach out to all the lower levels of spiritual understanding. As he begins to humble himself, he learns to show compassion, even towards his mother who had made every effort to tie him to a mechanical, preconceived material existence scheduled in clock-like precision. Human life, so long as it is not a life of spiritual fulfillment, remains arid and futile, like a desert. Harry says:

In and out, in an endless drift
Of shrieking forms in a circular desert
Weaving with contagion of putrescent embraces
On dissolving bone. In and out, the movement
Until the chain broke, I was left
Under the single eye above the desert.[76]

Since Eliot was a determinist, he believed in the closed circuit of events taking place in a man's life. So the desert is 'circular'—meaning fixed and rigid. There appears to be an echo of what Marvell had written in 'To His Coy Mistress': "And yonder all before us lye / Deserts of vast Eternity."[77] The "putrescent embraces" which Harry speaks about, are barren, having no promise. They are repulsive. This is Eliot's voice. He came to develop not only apathy, but also antagonism towards the sensuous nature in women. Emily Hale, who never asserted herself on him, was the one towards whom he could turn for an emotional haven. The bitter experiences with a neurotic wife compelled him to withdraw inside the hard mask of a severe and uncompromising personality whenever he found people, particularly women, trying to be intimate with him. It was close to prying as far as his personal life was concerned and he detested it. Ackroyd tries to explain this behaviour as "a natural *hauteur* or even of a Puritan dislike for self-revelation."[78]

Robert J. Andreach overlooks Harry's traumatic experience in marriage, accusing him of being "incapable of love."[79] He sees Harry's rejection of Mary in this way:

> If his sacrifice were motivated by love of god and, therefore, love of god's creatures, then it would be more meaningful because recognizing that the way of suffering is more important than the possibility of happiness that human love offers, Harry would be rejecting a very real human attraction.[80]

Harry's quest has carried him beyond the stratum of self-centred interest and the level of "real human attraction." His search is for the divine attraction—the Absolute Truth— which will enable him to divest himself of the love of created beings, and seek for the life-giving waters which will restore spiritual fertility. Harry says to Amy, trying to ease her growing anxiety for him by giving her a bare minimum of essential information:

> My advice has come from quite a different quarter,
> But I cannot explain that to you now. Only be sure
> That I know what I am doing, and what I must do,
> And that it is the best thing for everybody.[81]

He is unable to articulate the complex understanding he has had in suitable terms to Amy. He says, "I do not know the words in which to explain it—/That is what makes it harder."[82] The character of Harry Monchensey becomes intriguing because of this inability to articulate his psychological condition, which is a very complex one. The dramatist himself commented on Harry's character, saying, "my hero now strikes me as an insufferable prig."[83]

There seemed to be too much of Eliot in Harry, which turned against a complete development of his character: the required detachment in the playwright was lacking. His personal quest turned out to be a kind of hindrance to the culmination of Harry's search for liberation because Harry's character was the facade behind which Eliot was undertaking his own quest, and Eliot was not sure whether Harry would succeed. However, Eliot came to soften his judgment of Harry which he made in 1950 when in 1956, he saw Paul Scofield (playing the role of Harry) taking the character to such a level that Eliot could not resist a warm praise:

> I am writing to thank you for what you have done to redeem the part of Harry from the obloquy with which I myself (and, alas, many other people) have covered it. You are, in fact, the first to succeed in giving the impression of a *haunted* man—and if Harry isn't haunted then he is insufferable![84]

The character who comes after Harry in the order of the depth of spiritual understanding is Agatha, who plays the role of the priestess by initiating Harry's spiritual journey. She has a better and clearer understanding of the spiritual self when the play begins and is, thus, in a position to perceive better than her sister (and Harry's mother), Amy. Amy deliberately keeps Wishwood unchanged in order to make Harry feel that he was not away for a long time for she feels that in this way she can make him forget his wife and the eight years he spent with her. Agatha observes that "The man who returns will have to meet / The boy who left."[85] She can realize the futility of these materialistic attempts to hold Harry back in Wishwood. She predicts that Harry, after his realization of being the elect of his family, will go in search of the knowledge of 'the hidden':

> When the loop in time comes—and it does not come for everybody—
> The hidden is revealed, and the spectres show themselves.[86]

She is Harry's spiritual mother and she advises him that:

> There is more to understand: hold fast to that
> As the way to freedom.[87]

Like the Charwomen of Canterbury, the other aunts and uncles (who form the chorus) are "watchers and waiters"[88]. Agatha and Mary help Harry in his quest by easing out the way for his departure from Wishwood. Agatha explains their role in Harry's quest:

> At this moment, there is no decision to be made;
> The decision will be made by powers beyond us
> Which now and then emerge. [...][89]

Her enlightening words have inspired Grover Smith to conclude that "Agatha, if not exactly an inhabitant of the world of vital spirituality, is at any rate a guardian of its threshold; and she has looked within."[90] She teaches her spiritual child, Harry, that he has to open up his perspective:

> We must try to penetrate the other private worlds
> Of make-belief and fear. To rest in our own suffering
> In evasion of suffering. We must learn to suffer more.[91]

Intense suffering, following the ideal Suffering of Jesus Christ, is the way of finding the Truth. Harry has to prepare himself for it. He realizes that he must journey alone for Agatha is also a quester. He says:

> I have thought of you as the completely strong,
> The liberated from the human wheel.
> So I looked to you for strength. Now I think it is
> A common pursuit of liberation.[92]

Virendra K. Roy says that Agatha "shares the consciousness of the sin of the Monchenseys with Harry so that both of them may expiate it."[93] The error in his assessment lies in the basic fact that "both" of them will not expiate the sin; it is solely Harry's quest for liberation. Agatha was merely his spiritual mother and this is revealed by what she says to him:

> I felt that you were in some way mine!
> And that in any case I should have no other child.[94]

With her help "he reaches a state of love's communion, which urges him forward from the inferno of hatred and fear to the purgatory of emotional release and love and finally to the discovery of his spiritual mother (Agatha herself)."[95] So it is not an awareness of a sense of crime, but of a sense of sin, which is important. It is not Harry's personal sin, but that of others, which he will have to expiate. However, the suffering will be exclusively his. He will have to burn in the infernal flames of suffering, in humility, in order to expiate the burden of sin that he carries like Christ's Cross.

Agatha had had a flashing glimpse of bliss—symbolized by the rose garden (elaborately used in *The Confidential Clerk*. Like Prufrock's vision of the "mermaids singing, each to each"[96] she had heard "tiny voices" far away. She tries to articulate her experiences:

> I only looked through the little door
> When the sun was shining on the rose-garden:
> And heard in the distance tiny voices.[97]

The "little door" is the way to the possibility and realization of bliss which Eliot came to have a glimpse of in his own life but which had still not been experienced in reality. Agatha, too, could have had a real mature relation with Harry's father if she had settled down in life with him, and she could have been Harry's mother. Spiritually she remained the mother-figure to him. The "tiny voices" symbolize the children she could have borne, signifying the human possibility, just as the "little door" is symbolic of the spiritual life, as in Eliot's case. The "unwinking eye"[98] symbolizes the divine supervision overlooking human life.

The Rose Garden symbolizes the land of divine possibilities—one which Eliot may have come to associate with something related to his personal life—his relationship with Emily Hale. This imagery is associated with Dante, who in the *Divine Comedy* has come to celebrate the idea of Man's fall from the Garden of Eden and, in a sense, the betrayal of God Himself brought about by taking to the fruit of the Forbidden Tree. Man thus, became sinful.

In 'The Garden' Marvell writes about this, "Such was that happy Garden-state, / While Man there walked without a Mate."[99] Marvell was close to Milton, who out of his puritanical zeal, came to hold woman responsible for the fall of Man. Being a Unitarian, Eliot was an extreme kind of Puritan before he contemplated conversion to Anglo-Catholicism. It would, therefore, be natural for him to hold a similar opinion about women. Only once did he have a sense of revival and regeneration, when he looked at Emily Hale emerging from the hyacinth pool, her hair wet and her arms full. This is a variation of the Rose Garden image and it may have had a fleeting moment of the realization of the true love between him and Emily. That love remained unfulfilled. So, the "little door" to that rose garden remained merely a possibility and not something which could be part of the reality.

Real love had the significance of a divine possibility for Eliot. Gordon converted Emily to a Beatrice-figure, attempting to justify Eliot's strange withdrawal from his relationship with her with the explanation that Eliot did not allow the relation to be denigrated. But, this would prevent Gordon from explaining the "little door" to the Rose Garden. Eliot's withdrawal may have been the result of a complexity of reasons, primarily his oppressive Unitarian background, the dominant position of women who took charge of his upbringing, and a continual dilemma in trying to reconcile his inner and outer selves. So, Eliot could never assert himself and Emily was too refined a lady (a College teacher) to thrust herself upon him. Thus, there existed a complex friendship between them, most of which is shrouded in mystery (Eliot's personal correspondences with her have either been destroyed or have been retained from being made public). Mary's role in Harry's life somewhat resembles this friendship.

Harry's relation with his youngest aunt was closer than that with his mother. To Agatha the formation of a curse was like that of a child—unconscious and, possibly, unintentional. She can sense that God's scheme takes the shape of an accidental design (or a designed accident) which will lead Harry towards complete surrender to the Divine Will. This will enable him to restore spiritual fertility in Wishwood, which is the objective correlative of the contemporary fragmented world. Agatha's words hint at the quest of the contemplative when she says to Harry:

> Accident is design
> And design is accident
> In a cloud of unknowing.[100]

She explains to the perplexed Mary that on being forced to remain in Wishwood, Harry will meet with a spiritual death. In order to keep him spiritually alive, he must be allowed to seek for self-realization on his own:

> Here the danger, here the death, here, not elsewhere;
> Elsewhere no doubt is agony, renunciation,
> But birth and life. Harry has crossed the frontier
> Beyond which safety and danger have a different meaning.
> And he cannot return. That is his privilege.[101]

The next character who has a high level of spiritual understanding is Mary, a distant cousin of Harry's, who is carefully prepared by Amy to be his wife. Harry gives this notion no thought. Mary, initially confined to her limited physical and selfish love for him, gets over it when she realizes that his spiritual quest must not be hindered by her. Like the First Tempter in *Murder in the Cathedral* she tempts him with the material and the private. However, unlike him, she realizes her mistake and corrects herself quickly. When Harry is frustrated, thinking that he has lost hope, Mary sympathizes with him. She points out that his actions contradict his words because his return to Wishwood after eight long years indicates that he hoped for something in coming back:

> You hoped for something, in coming back to Wishwood,
> Or you would not have come.[102]

Harry's reply shows that he will leave Wishwood for he sees that he will not find the answer to his quest here. Harry's return to Wishwood was one journey—a physical one. His departure will be a spiritual one, although apparently physical. Mary begins to understand Harry's problem which is "a good that's misdirected."[103] She is certain that he is capable of undertaking his destined journey. It is not what he 'thinks' but what he 'feels'—the urge to seek for his identity—that is important. She encourages him:

> [...] You deceive yourself
> Like the man convinced that he is paralysed
> Or like the man who believes that he is blind
> While he still sees the sunlight. I know that this is true.[104]

Now he becomes sure of himself, feeling that he can find song and light, symbols of joy, when he will open the closed door at the end of the dark corridor—an image which will be repeated in *The Confidential Clerk*. So long, Harry had been thinking that he was groping in a dark labyrinth. Now Mary helps him to clear his perspective. The thrilled Harry says:

> [...] You bring me news
> Of a door that opens at the end of a corridor,
> Sunlight and singing; when I had felt sure
> That every corridor only led to another,
> Or to a blank wall; that I kept moving
> Only so as not to stay still. Singing and light.[105]

But Mary knows that Harry has to undergo intense suffering in order to attain self-realization and rejoice in it. The birth of Jesus Christ, although joyful, was painful, too, because His birth was necessary for His death on the Cross. Suffering is the only way towards salvation; all God's creation has to suffer, says Mary:

> Pain is the opposite of joy
> But joy is a kind of pain
> I believe the moment of birth
> Is when we have knowledge of death
> I believe the season of birth
> Is the season of sacrifice.[106]

She makes Harry's departure easy. When Amy dies on her birthday, without celebrating it and without the family reunion (two of her sons being unable to come), Agatha and Mary walk clockwise round Amy's birthday-cake like a pair of priestesses performing a ritual, while Agatha chants:

> This way the pilgrimage
> Of expiation
> Round and round the circle
> Completing the charm
> So the knot be unknotted
> The crossed be uncrossed
> The crooked be made straight
> And the curse be ended

By intercession
By pilgrimage
By those who depart
In several directions
For their own redemption
And that of the departed—
May they rest in peace.[107]

Agatha's words seem to bear the echoes of Becket's explanation in *Murder in the Cathedral*, when he says:

[...] for the pattern is the action
And the suffering, that the wheel may turn and still
Be forever still.[108]

In a letter to Browne Eliot explains the roles of Agatha and Mary and their relation with Harry:

> The part of Mary, in relation to Harry, was meant to be this. [...] The effect of his married life upon him was one of such horror as to leave him for a time at least in a state that may be called one of being psychologically partially desexed: or rather, it has given him a horror of women as of unclean creatures. The scene with Mary is meant to bring out, as I am aware it fails to, the conflict inside him between the repulsion for Mary as a woman, and the attraction which the *normal* part of him that is still left, feels towards her personally *for the first time*. This is the first time since his marriage ('there is no ecstasy') that he has been attracted towards any woman. This attraction glimmers for a moment in his mind, half-consciously as a possible 'way of escape'; and the Furies (for the Furies are *divine* instruments, not simple hell-hounds) come in the nick of time to warn him from this evasion—though at that moment he misunderstands their function. Now, this attraction towards Mary has stirred him up, but, owing to his mental state, is incapable of developing: therefore, he finds a refuge in an ambiguous relation—the attraction, half of a son and half of a lover, to Agatha, who reciprocates in somewhat the same way."[109]

The depth of Eliot's understanding of these three characters and the precision with which he wanted them to be portrayed could be possible since the dramatist was using his own personal experience.

The character of Amy, on the other hand, is a contrast to that of Agatha. When the play opens Amy is seen craving for warmth and spring. But, in the prime of her youth she had sternly exiled them from Wishwood. Agatha, as a witness and a party to it, reminds her about it. Amy trusts nobody, not even her doctor and friend, Dr Warburton, to whom she says:

> I must see for myself. I do not believe you.[110]

She is spiritually handicapped, obsessed with the institution of the peerage. Her desire to keep the family together is symbolized by the clock. The margins she has created for her world confine her perspective to a clock-like precision where chance has no place. When she says, "Harry is to take command at Wishwood/ And I hope we can contrive his future happiness,"[111] she forgets the vital point that everybody is entitled to his or her freedom, which is encroached upon by 'contriving'. She hated Harry's wife because she did not fit into Amy's scheme for him. She has no grief, regret or remorse for her death. She speaks of remorse because she is aware of a sense of guilt arising out of her elimination of her husband from Wishwood. She allowed her children no freedom. Harry recalls that:

> It's absurd that one's only memory of freedom
> Should be a hollow tree in a wood by the river.[112]

The wood was his private world; the flowing river was the only symbol of spiritual life in the barren Wishwood. When it is time for Harry to leave Wishwood in search of self-realization, his mother, unable to understand the significance of the quest, makes a final attempt to hold him back in her marginalized physical world. It is out of a sense of compassion that he tries to explain to her that:

> Now I know that all my life has been a flight
> And phantoms fed upon me while I fled. Now I know
> That the last apparent refuge, the safe shelter,
> That is where one meets them.
> [.........................................................................]

Now they will lead me. I shall be safe with them;
I am not safe here.[113]

But it is all in vain. She cannot understand him. His departure brings Amy face to face with the reality that her sincere contrivings have ended in failure. She dies broken-hearted crying (off stage):

Agatha ! Mary ! come !
The clock has stopped in the dark![114]

MacCarthy's sympathies for Amy are justified when he says, "The mother turns out to be more sinned against than sinning—except in so far as she is one of those who deny the importance of the spiritual life."[115] Some other critics say that Amy is a clock, implying that she is a machine. But her's is the only life-like character who shows visible signs of change. She is not a clock. Her schemings for the future of her children acquire meticulous precision for which Eliot's objective correlative is the clock.

Another realistic character, not fully developed, is that of Downing, Harry's chauffeur, who is the only witness of his eight-year travel abroad. He closely observes Harry's nervous brooding which lacks in merriment and he draws his own conclusion:

But you know his Lordship was always very quiet:
Very uncommon that I saw him, in high spirits.
For what my judgement's worth, I always said his Lordship
Suffered from what they call a kind of repression.[116]

His conclusions are partial, but he has understood Harry in his own way which is strange considering the fact that the Chorus of aunts and uncles fails to do so. He says:

I've always said, whatever happens to his Lordship
Was just a kind of preparation for something else.
[.........................................................................]
We most of us seem to live according to circumstance,
But with people like him, there's something inside them

That accounts for what happens to them. You get a feeling of it.
[........................................................................]
And that's why I say now, I have a feeling
That he won't want me long, and he won't want anybody.[117]

Although Downing's character occupies very little theatrical-time, his role in the play is important for an understanding of Harry's quest.

The Chorus is at the lowest level of spiritual understanding. It is comprised of Harry's aunts, Ivy and Violet, and uncles, Charles and Gerald, who can sense that something unusual is about to happen as a result of the impact of the past. Like the Charwomen of Canterbury, their role in Harry's quest is that of watchers. They must wait patiently and bear witness to the action of the Divine Will, which is the unfolding of preordained events:

And the past is about to happen, and the future was long since settled.[118]

Their obsession with this idea is emphasized in their reiteration of the same thing in Part II scene i:

And whatever happens began in the past, and presses hard on the future.
The agony in the curtained bedroom, whether of birth or of dying,
Gathers in to itself all the voices of the past, and projects them into the future.[119]

The significance of Eliot's use of the Oresteian myth in *The Family Reunion* is clear from these choric utterances. What was relevant in ancient Greek tragedy is equally applicable in Harry's case, which is the dilemma of the protagonist who is caught between the past and future of his family. The anxiety of the Chorus grows as the play progresses. There seem to be echoes of Sweeney's words, "Death is life and life is death"[120] in their words. Their comprehension is limited to a sense of loss when they fail to prevent Harry's departure. They say:

> We have suffered far more than a personal loss—
> We have lost our way in the dark.[121]

Where Harry, Mary and Agatha "may be described as conscious participants in the drama of sin and expiation," [122] the Chorus has "more psychology, more action and more reality than other persons," [123] says Sarkar. The characters who form the Chorus do not know the world of Harry and they refuse to know it. The closest that they come to this world is expressed in their impersonal statement in the final chorus of the play:

> We do not like what happens when we are awake, because it too closely resembles what happens when we are asleep.
> [...................................................]
> What is happening outside of the circle?
> And what is the meaning of happening?[124]

They represent the common man's plane of spiritual understanding, which is contrasted to Harry's elevated understanding that he has a mission to fulfil. Unger calls Eliot's experiment with the Chorus in this play "a bold one."[125]

In a conversation with Alessandro Pellegrini, Eliot referred to the aesthetic norms of a work of art. Pellegrini records that Eliot "recognized that the protagonist, by wishing to go beyond despair, walked out of the limits of the play, out of its picture and frame,"[126] Eliot said, "in this way the rules of the game are no longer respected,"[127] thereby showing the essential defect of the play. So, it would be natural for him to try to find a solution to this problem in the next play. Eliot had definitely made some progress in using the characters (particularly the protagonist) in his play for his personal quest for self-realization, although the ending of *The Family Reunion* shows that he was dissatisfied with (or even unsure of) Harry's departure for an unknown destination.

## II

The experiment with the form of verse drama continued in *The Family Reunion* in which Eliot desired to mould it to suit the tastes of a modern urban audience. He felt that verse expresses better than the prose of everyday intercourse and adhered to its use in his plays. He wished to shock his audience because he found that:

> People are prepared to put up with verse from the lips of personages dressed in the fashion of some distant age; therefore they should be made to hear it from people dressed like ourselves, living in houses and apartments like ours, and using telephones and motor cars and radio sets. [...] What we have to do is to bring poetry into the world in which the audience live and to which it returns when it leaves the theatre.[128]

Poetic drama would have to "enter into overt competition with prose drama"[129] in order to return to its former glory. It was for the purpose of reinstating poetic drama to this position that he decided to continue with the verse-form in his plays. He says, "I was determined, therefore, in my next play to take a theme of contemporary life, with characters of our own time living in our world. *The Family Reunion* was the result."[130] Peacock lauds this attempt by saying that:

> In taking verse to drama again and drama to verse Eliot made a move of complex significance. It was at once a renovation of verse and a revival of drama. [...] The field of verse is widened again; the form of drama is heightened.[131]

In this play Eliot uses a subtle verse based on iambic blank verse which can either be delivered as prose or stressed rhythmically, according to the requirements of effective expression of feelings, emotions and thoughts. To bring verse drama close to the everyday life of the contemporary times Eliot had to create an elastic verse which would retain its incantatory nature as well as represent the ordinary day-to-day conversation. In his movement towards this end Eliot uses his favourite devices like antithesis, paradox, repetition, the overrunning of sentences from line to line and the use of imagery. For the metrical pattern he goes back to that used in early English poetry, following it closely. He describes his own technique in this play:

> I have continued to employ a line of varying length and varying number of syllables, with a caesura and three stresses; [...] the only rule being that there must be one stress on one side of the caesura and two on the other.[132]

He describes this aim as "ultra-dramatic."[133] Eliot's power rests on the depiction (through sensitive characters) of the reality of the spiritual world and religious experience. He spoke about this in two unpublished talks delivered in 1937, which Gordon came to describe in this way:

> Poetic drama could awaken the audience to a hidden pattern of reality which may supersede what is conventionally dramatic. He believed that an audience would accept this so long as there was something more ordinary to attend to. The characters in such a play have a double existence: they must appear living creatures like ourselves, and at the same time they must make us see through the usual classified emotions into a world of which we are normally unaware, which comes from the depths of the playwright himself.[134]

Eliot admits that "there is a necessary connection between religion and philosophy on the one hand and poetry on the other."[135] He expressed his interest and insight about the significance of poetry as a means of approach to mystical knowledge while responding to Smidt's queries on this function of poetry (in 1948). He said that he did not think it had any direct significance, but that "poetry could help us to approach an understanding of an ultimate reality, and it could give a sensitive reader the assurance that there is this kind of reality."[136] This may be one of the reasons behind his reintegration of drama in the framework of ritual because he found that right from the works of the ancient Greek playwrights, dramatic forms are the development of early liturgies.

In order to run a close parallel between the past and the present so that there is an artistic form rendered to the seggregated and dissipated experiences of the distraught modern civilization, Eliot makes use of the Greek myth which is "a step towards making the modern world possible for art."[137] This is precisely the reason behind his use of Greek myth as backdrop of every subsequent play. In *The Family Reunion*, the use of the myth of Orestes becomes obvious simply because of the presence of the Eumenides. In the later plays, the use of classical myth becomes subtle as the dramatist progresses in his quest for form in drama, experimenting with the methods of knitting various strands of ideas into a fine piece of tapestry.

One significant experiment in form that Eliot undertook was with the varied use of the Chorus in this play—sometimes speaking in unison like the classical chorus, sometimes breaking up into individual voices, as in:

> CHORUS. (IVY, VIOLET, GERALD and CHARLES). Why do we feel embarrassed, impatient, fretful, ill at ease,
> Assembled like amateur actors who have not been assigned their parts?
> Like amateur actors in a dream when the curtain rises, to find themselves dressed for a different play, or having rehearsed the wrong parts,
> Waiting for the rustling in the stalls, the titter in the dress circle, the laughter and the catcalls in the gallery?
>
> CHARLES. I might have been in St. James' Street, in a comfortable chair rather nearer the fire.
>
> IVY. I might have been visiting Cousin Lily at Sidmouth, if I had not had to come to this party.
>
> GERALD. I might have been staying with Compton-Smith, down at his place in Dorset.
>
> VIOLET. I should have been helping Lady Bumpus, at the Vicar's American Tea.
>
> CHORUS. Yet we are here at Amy's command, to play an unreal part in some monstrous farce, ridiculous in some nightmare pantomime.[138]

In *Murder in the Cathedral*, the Chorus of the Charwomen of Canterbury was typically classical in form as well as in the gravity of the utterances. The Chorus of two aunts and two uncles in this play is an advance towards the accommodation of the chorus in a naturalistic play: it is broken up into single voices at times, although the utterances are choric in nature, which Bodkin sums up, saying that:

> [...] the Chorus, which Eliot has constituted from four characters of the play—two aunts, two uncles—who at different points of the drama draw together, and as if hypnotized by some force within the action, speak words presenting not their individual thoughts, but feeling common to them all.[139]

The experiment with the Chorus in *The Family Reunion* was another step towards the accommodation of the chorus in modern realistic drama. Eliot ascribes two types of verse to the Chorus. One being composed of lines having the usual three stressed and any number of unstressed syllables and one caesura. The other consisting of brief lines, which he used thrice in the paly. They appear for the first time at the end of Part I scene i, as in:

> We all of us make the pretension
> To be the uncommon exception
> To the universal bondage.[140]

As they become aware of something unusual taking place in Wishwood (at the end of Part II scene i), they express their inability to gauge its depths in lines like these:

> The making the best of a bad Job
> All twined and tangled together, all are recorded.
> There is no avoiding these things
> And we know nothing of exorcism
> And whether in Argos or England
> There are inflexible laws
> Unalterable, in the nature of music.[141]

Later in the play they feel that they have lost their way in the dark, for they prefer a secure and safe lifestyle. Now that things have gone beyond their ken, they say (as the play draws to a close):

> And what is being done to us?
> And what are we, and what are we doing?
> To each and all of these questions
> There is no conceivable answer.[142]

However, Eliot was not pleased with the Chorus in spite of his experiments with it and he wrote about it in "Poetry and Drama":

> [...] the device of using four of the minor personages, representing the family, sometimes as individual character parts and sometimes collectively as chorus, does not seem to me very satisfactory.[143]

Besides being conscious of the problem of precise articulation on the stage by actors whose lot it is to present a play as convincingly as possible, Eliot was also concerned with "two problems left unsolved: that of idiom and that of the metric (it is really one and the same problem)"[144] and he hoped to remember them when he wrote plays in future.

Structurally, the play is divided into two parts, each having three scenes. (Eliot retained the two-part structure, which he had used in *Murder in the Cathedral*). Part I depicts Harry's return to Wishwood after eight long years and his reception by those members of the family who have already arrived. Part II, which follows the dinner (not represented on the stage) leads to his departure for an unknown destination. This action takes place on the realistic plane which also forms the outer surface of the drama. On the spiritual plane, the action takes place within Harry's being, following the pattern of the ritual of the Mass, when he first comes to recognize his responsibility as the bearer of the burden of sin, which in turn brings a realization of his role in a greater design—that of a quester for liberation. The Eumenides, who appear at crucial moments in the play, serve as agents of spiritual awakening in Harry, and, therefore, as a unifying factor in the play.

Two duologues in the second scenes of the two parts of the play seem to be poised between the first and third scenes, as they help the playwright to expose Harry's inner being. The first, in Part I scene ii, between Harry and Mary, takes stock of Amy's manipulation of their movements and behaviour in order to make them fit into her scheme of affairs in Wishwood (which she has arranged from their infancy). Their frank discussion helps Mary to try to understand Harry better as he gradually leans on her for spiritual support:

MARY. If you think I am incapable of understanding you—
But in any case, I must get ready for dinner.
HARRY. No, no, don't go! Please don't leave me
Just at this moment. I feel it is important.[145]

In the exchange between Harry and Agatha (in Part II scene ii) the discussion centres on the past. This time it is the past of his parents and Agatha—the triangular relationship which developed from Harry's father's affair with Agatha, his sister-in-law. The mist of uncertainty begins to rise as Harry's perspective becomes clear and he can now trace the reason behind his sense of guilt:

Perhaps my life has only been a dream
Dreamt through me by the minds of others. Perhaps
I only dreamt I pushed her.[146]

Agatha initiates Harry into a complete understanding of his spiritual self as a preparation for the quest he will undertake. She performs the role of the priestess in pre-Christian times, who initiated the quester to secret mystical knowledge. When the Eumenides appear in the window embrasure for the last time, Harry is not flustered, for his way has been chosen—he will follow them:

[...] and this time
you cannot think that I am surprised to see you.
And you shall not think that I am afraid to see you.
[.........................................................]
Now I see at last that I am following you,
And I know that there can be only one itinerary
And one destination. Let us lose no time. I will follow.[147]

Agatha's function in the play as that of a priestess, who guides Harry in the initial stages of his quest, becomes clear from her words (which sound like a prophesy) to the Chorus, which form brief lines, conveying a sense of breathlessness, as in Part I scene iii:

Till the knot is unknotted
The crossed is uncrossed
And the crooked is made straight.[148]

There is nearly a repetition of these lines (each consisting of two iambs) in which she says to Harry in Part II scene ii:

O my child, my curse,
You shall be fulfilled:
The knot shall be unknotted
And the crooked made straight.[149]

She reiterates the lines once more in the final speech of the play, on a completely dark stage, which gives her words a quality of mysterious prophesy (in Part II scene iii):

Complete the charm
So the knot be unknotted
The crossed be uncrossed
The crooked be made straight
And the curse be ended.[150]

These lines universalize the necessity for Harry's quest for self-realization and for his identity. The need to straighten out the crooked life of modern men is emphasized by the repetition of Agatha's words; Eliot renders an incantatory tone to them by the device of repeating key phrases. Critics make generous praises of the play. For instance, Ivor Brown says that "there is so much innovation of style and such skilled use of words and rhythms that the play is arresting and important."[151] Much of Eliot's success may be attributed to his knowledge of classical drama from which he imbibed most of the essentials of playwriting. Eliot had in mind not only the plays of the ancient Greek dramatists but those of the Latin playwrights as well. Writing about Seneca's plays, he says that Seneca's maintenance of consistence on one level is an exclusive genre that he created for himself. Seneca's 'form' is "a practical form [...] which might be interesting to attempt in our own time, when the revival of the theatre is obstructed by some of the difficulties which made the stage an impossibility in the age of Seneca."[152] He was aware of the difficulties faced by successful verse-dramatists in preceding ages.

Eliot's concern with the right presentation of plays which, it must not be forgotten, are works of art, rests largely on the limits that the playwright must create for himself. In 'Four Elizabethan Dramatists' he says that:

> It is essential that a work of art should be self-consistent, that an artist should consciously or unconsciously draw a circle beyond which he does not trespass: on the one hand actual life is always the material, and on the other hand an abstraction from actual life is a necessary condition to the creation of the work of art.[153]

The desire to attain a better integration of ideas and a greater precision of expression was the driving force behind Eliot's experiment with the verse-form in each succeeding play. Williams, talking of the verse-form, says, "It is a form designed to express the interpenetration of different levels of reality; not merely as a dramatic device, but because this interpenetration is the condition of experience of the play as a whole."[154] The only element in the play which turned out to be thorny for the director was the presentation of the Eumenides, about which the dramatist was also aware, for he wrote in a letter dated 13 September 1939 to his first cousin, Eleanor Hinkley:

> The Furies did not work out very well. It would have been better to have had them invisible to the audience, but in any case this is a piece of machinery which I do not intend to employ again.[155]

Browne, in a letter to Coghill (dated 25 March 1967), points out that the main flaw in the presentation of the Eumenides at two climactic points of the play lies in the lack of speech, which he says, is catastrophic.[156] Even after nearly thirty years since the first presentation of the play, the use of the Eumenides in *The Family Reunion* seemed "catastrophic" to the director. Barring this and Harry's journey for an unknown destination (where an element of uncertainty creeps in), the play is a stepping stone in Eliot's quest for an adequate form of expression.

## III

Harry finds it extremely hazardous to convey, linguistically, the processes going on within his inner being. His quest for self-realization is, therefore, associated with the quest for articulation. Leeming notices this when she comments that "he struggles hard to overcome the problem of communication, realizing the incomprehension of the other characters."[157] The other side of this problem of articulation that Harry experiences is seen by some critics as the dramatist's wish to express many things within the limited span of the drama, as a result of which the play is better read than seen performed. One such critic, Frederick Lumley, opines that the play is "a vehicle for personal experience."[158] Harry, who in a sense represents Eliot himself, is unable to communicate with the other characters in a satisfactory manner. His concern is with his inner self. His family, except Agatha and Mary, is concerned with his outer self—the peer of Wishwood. This is the source of the tension in the play. Jones detects Eliot's technique of resolving this tension:

> But the fact that he cannot communicate with them tends to lead to baffled inaction. Eliot solves this problem by having intermediary characters to whom Harry can talk effectively and who can help him to understand his predicament and thus to develop.[159]

This is what happens when he tries an explanation before his uncles, Charles and Gerald, who cannot understand him in their state of ignorance:

> But how can I explain, how can I explain to *you*?
> You will understand less after I have explained it.
> All that I could hope to make you understand
> Is only events: not what has happened.
>
> And people to whom nothing has ever happened
> Cannot understand the unimportance of events.[160]

He experiences extreme difficulties in communicating his inmost feelings. Eliot's achievement lies in what he does with his theme, giving it an order or form, thereby converting the commonplace into a work of art. Dobree says:

> But what in a play makes a commonplace theme into a universal one is the power with which it is driven home, how far it is thrown into relief against the whiffling activity, or the pompous pretensions, of everyday life.[161]

This is possible because of Eliot's experiment in articulation which is one of his major contributions to poetic drama.

His awareness of "the intolerable wrestle with words and meanings"[162] is reflected in 'East Coker':

> Trying to learn to use words, and every attempt
> Is a wholly new start, and a different kind of failure
> Because one has only learnt to get the better of words.[163]

Eliot strove persistently towards precision in articulation. This is expressed in his writings from time to time. Experience and knowledge change with the passage of time and:

> [...] There is, it seems to us,
> At best, only a limited value
> In the knowledge derived from experience.[164]

So Harry has a feeling that his mother is forcing him to remain in Wishwood. He feels cornered and uneasy—a stage preceding his epiphanic realization of the purpose of his quest. He cannot express himself in cognitive terms. So, he uses negatives to assert the positive:

> You do not know what hope is, until you have lost it.
> You only know what it is not to hope:
> You do not know what it is to have hope taken from you,
> Or to fling it away, to join the legion of the hopeless
> Unrecognized by other men, though sometimes by each other.[165]

Harry's sense of guilt for a crime he may not have committed stems from his awareness of tradition and of the modern man's spiritual infertility. The awareness of sin is the beginning of the quest for salvation. He also understands that it is a lonely journey. However, the disparity between the levels of understanding of the different characters in the play is brought out when attempts at communicating these complex feelings fall through. But Leeming, unable to sense the different levels of understanding that Eliot wishes to depict, interprets the inability of the characters to communicate their inmost feelings, if any, as that of the dramatist himself and says, "Because the characters sound embarrassed at what the playwright has made them do, Eliot falls as it were between two stools and neither jolts the audience positively nor retains the illusion of reality."[166] The error in Leeming's judgement is proved when Amy interprets to the Chorus Harry's desire to leave Wishwood as his decision to become a missionary. He objects to this piece of wrong information saying:

> I never said that I was going to be a missionary.
> I would explain, but you would none of you believe it;
> If you believe it, still you would not understand.
> You can't know why I am going. You have not seen
> What I have seen.[167]

He refuses to talk in a way that will please his mother:

> [...] Only that's not the language
> That I choose to be talking. I will not talk yours.[168]

Even the best efforts on his part get him nowhere near communicating his experiences to his family. However, his desire to articulate in cognitive terms can be recognized in his frustrated ejaculation:

> Oh, there must be another way of talking
> That would get us somewhere. [...][169]

which is one way of articulating his inability to express his personal experience in concrete terms.

The use of images and symbols is another way of articulating ideas which would otherwise be impossible. "Images in verse are not mere decoration, but the very essence of an intuitive language,"[170] says Hulme and Eliot makes use of images like those of the Rose Garden and the corridor to convey Harry's psychological state. Eliot clearly admits in 'The Three Voices of Poetry' that his early dramatic endeavours (*Sweeney Agonistes, The Rock*, and even *Murder in the Cathedral*) did not make conscious use of the third voice (or, the dramatic voice). He writes:

> The third, or dramatic voice, did not make itself audible to me until I first attacked the problem of presenting two (or more) characters, in some sort of conflict, misunderstanding, or attempt to understand each other, characters with each of whom I had to try to identify myself while writing the

> words for him or her to speak. [...] It was in 1938, then that the third voice began to force itself upon my ear.[171]

One significant facet of the use of the third voice was the chorus with which Eliot experimented widely. In *The Family Reunion* for the first time, Eliot splits up the Chorus and they speak as individuals more often than they do so in unison. Obviously, his aim was at a better communication with the twentieth century auditors. Browne, the director of Eliot's plays, finds that:

> The Chorus' speech does not necessarily have to be begun in unison, and the lines are meant to be split up among the individual speakers, so that at moments of strong common emotion do all four speak together.[172]

The splitting up of the Chorus is one way of shouldering the poet's "responsibility of preserving, developing, and revitalizing his native language"[173] in a naturalistic play intended for a modern audience, about which Headings says that "Their concerted speeches, in which they express their unenlightened condition and the emotions that go along with it, are punctuated by individual lines in which they characterize themselves or one another."[174] This shows that Eliot was experimenting with the expression of the inexpressible because the ideal of the precise statement of ideas and emotions fascinated him. Matthews feels that this tendency in Eliot was nourished by his study of Sanskrit literature for about two years during his days in Harvard:

> And in the Sutras of Patanjali he discovered that only essential words are necessary, and that a complete sentence structure is not always needed.[175]

The result was a polyphony of voices which created a music of poetry. Peacock calls this "a new music of dramatic language"[176] which creates an effect chiefly through suppleness and variety of cadence. Eliot's aim was to bring to the understanding of his auditors the complex spiritual condition of the protagonist for which he used the speech-rhythm and idiom of the contemporary urban Englishmen.

*The Family Reunion* occupies a key position in Eliot's quest for self-realization, as well as for form and articulation. He continued to merge the formalist and realistic elements in this play, but unlike *Murder in the Cathedral* it was written for the commercial theatre. This innovative technique differentiated Eliot's play from other plays in performance at that time. It was clear that Eliot had a definite purpose in using the form of verse drama as the medium of his play. However he reviewed the play with his critical insight and pointed out the deficiencies of *The Family Reunion* which he hoped to do away within the next one where there would be no chorus, no supernatural beings and no uncertainty regarding what happens to the protagonist. So the next play would be another experiment, but of a different kind.

## NOTES AND REFERENCES

1. Sarkar, *T.S. Eliot the Dramatist* 3.
2. Coghill, Introduction, *The Family Reunion*, by Eliot (Oxford: Oxford UP, 1963) 13.
3. Coghill, Introduction, *The Family Reunion*, by Eliot 41.
4. Sarkar, *T.S. Eliot the Dramatist* 120.
5. Maud Bodkin, "The Eumenides and T.S. Eliot: Critical Present-Day Consciousness," in Clarke, Vol. 3: 338.
6. Eliot, *The Family Reunion*, CPP 291.
7. Bodkin, *The Quest for Salvation in an Ancient and a Modern Play* (London: Oxford UP, 1941) 15.
8. John Middleton Murry, "The Plays of T.S. Eliot," in Clarke, Vol. 3: 549-50.
9. Eliot, "'Ulysses', Order, and Myth," *Selected Prose of T.S. Eliot*, ed. Frank Kermode (London: Faber, 1975) 177.
10. William V. Spanos, *The Christian Tradition in Modern British Verse Drama* (New Brunswick: Rutgers UP, 1967) 209-10.
11. Eliot, *After Strange Gods* 48.
12. Eliot, *After Strange Gods* 46.
13. Eliot, "Religion and Literature," *Selected Prose*, ed. John Hayward (Hammondsworth: Penguin, 1953) 42.
14. Eliot, *Sweeney Agonistes*, CPP 124.
15. Eliot, *The Family Reunion*, CPP 322.

16. Kristian Smidt, *Poetry and Belief in the Works of T.S. Eliot* (London: Routledge and Kegan Paul, 1949) 202.
17. Eliot, "John Marston," *Selected Essays* 232.
18. Eliot, *The Family Reunion*, CPP 309.
19. Eliot, *The Family Reunion*, CPP 310.
20. Eliot, "East Coker," *Four Quartets*, CPP 182.
21. C.H. Smith 135.
22. Frederick A. Pottle, "A Modern Verse Play," in Clarke, Vol. 3: 341-42.
23. C.L. Barber, "Strange Gods at T.S. Eliot's 'The Family Reunion'," in Clarke, Vol. 3: 460.
24. Sarkar, *T.S. Eliot the Dramatist* 120.
25. Eliot, "East Coker," CPP 181.
26. Eliot, "East Coker," CPP 180.
27. Jones 103.
28. Leeming 107.
29. Leeming 107.
30. Eliot, *The Family Reunion*, CPP 309.
31. Eliot, *The Family Reunion*, CPP 317.
32. Eliot, *The Family Reunion*, CPP 317.
33. Eliot, "Tradition and the Individual Talent," *The Sacred Wood* 59.
34. Eliot, *The Family Reunion*, CPP 324.
35. Eliot, *The Family Reunion*, CPP 326.
36. Eliot, *The Family Reunion*, CPP 332.
37. Eliot, The Family Reunion, CPP 338.
38. Eliot, *The Family Reunion*, CPP 338.
39. Eliot, *The Family Reunion*, CPP 343.
40. Weales 195.
41. Matthews 179.
42. Gordon, *Eliot's New Life* 280.
43. Matthews 22-23.
44. Matthews 83.
45. Matthews 44.
46. Matthews 68.
47. Eliot, *The Family Reunion*, CPP 334.
48. Gordon, *Eliot's New Life* 82.

49. Gordon, *Eliot's New Life* 83.
50. Gordon, *Eliot's New Life* 83.
51. Matthews 46-47.
52. Ackroyd 236-37.
53. Matthews 148.
54. Matthews 138.
55. Gordon, *Eliot's New Life* 86-87.
56. Gordon, *Eliot's New Life* 89.
57. Eliot, *The Family Reunion,* CPP 293.
58. Anon., "Mr. Eliot in Search of the Present," in Clarke, Vol. 3: 322.
59. Desmond MacCarthy, "Same Notes on Mr. Eliot's New Play," Clarke, Vol. 3: 323.
60. Eliot, *The Family Reunion*, CPP 294.
61. Eliot, *The Family Reunion*, CPP 318.
62. Eliot, "Tradition and the Individual Talent," *The Sacred Wood* 50.
63. Eliot, *The Family Reunion*, CPP 294.
64. Eliot, *The Family Reunion*, CPP 331.
65. Coghill, in Matthews 127.
66. Eliot, "Poetry and Drama," *On Poetry and Poets* 84.
67. Browne 117.
68. Browne, in Matthews 127.
69. Coghill, in Matthews 127.
70. Matthews 127.
71. Eliot, *The Family Reunion*, CPP 334.
72. Eliot, *The Family Reunion*, CPP 334.
73. Eliot, "East Coker," CPP 177.
74. Eliot, "East Coker," CPP 183.
75. Eliot, "East Coker," CPP 179.
76. Eliot, *The Family Reunion*, CPP 335.
77. Marvell, "To His Coy Mistress," in Gardner, ed. 251.
78. Ackroyd 281.
79. Robert J. Andreach, *Studies in Structure* (Fordham: Fordham UP, 1964) 89.
80. Andreach 89.
81. Eliot, *The Family Reunion*, CPP 338.
82. Eliot, *The Family Reunion*, CPP 338.

83. Eliot, "Milton I," *On Poetry and Poets* 145.
84. Coghill, Introduction, *The Family Reunion* 51.
85. Eliot, *The Family Reunion*, CPP 288.
86. Eliot, *The Family Reunion*, CPP 289.
87. Eliot, *The Family Reunion*, CPP 296.
88. Eliot, *The Family Reunion*, CPP 305.
89. Eliot, *The Family Reunion*, CPP 305.
90. Grover Smith 198.
91. Eliot, *The Family Reunion*, CPP 327.
92. Eliot, *The Family Reunion*, CPP 331.
93. Virendra K. Roy, *T.S. Eliot: Quest for Belief* (Delhi: Ajanta Publications, 1979) 316.
94. Eliot, *The Family Reunion*, CPP 333.
95. Sarkar, *T.S. Eliot the Dramatist* 143-44.
96. Eliot, "The Love Song of J. Alfred Prufrock," CPP 16.
97. Eliot, *The Family Reunion*, CPP 334-35.
98. Eliot, *The Family Reunion*, CPP 335.
99. Marvell, "The Garden," in Gardner ed. 257.
100. Eliot, *The Family Reunion*, CPP 336-37.
101. Eliot, *The Family Reunion*, CPP 342.
102. Eliot, *The Family Reunion*, CPP 308.
103. Eliot, *The Family Reunion*, CPP 309.
104. Eliot, *The Family Reunion*, CPP 309.
105. Eliot, *The Family Reunion*, CPP 310.
106. Eliot, *The Family Reunion*, CPP 310.
107. Eliot, *The Family Reunion*, CPP 350.
108. Eliot, *Murder in the Cathedral*, CPP 245.
109. Eliot, letter dt. 19 March 1938, in Browne 107.
110. Eliot, *The Family Reunion*, CPP 323.
111. Eliot, *The Family Reunion*, CPP 290.
112. Eliot, *The Family Reunion*, CPP 307.
113. Eliot, *The Family Reunion*, CPP 338.
114. Eliot, *The Family Reunion*, CPP 347.
115. MacCarthy, in Clarke, Vol. 3: 326.
116. Eliot, *The Family Reunion*, CPP 299.
117. Eliot, *The Family Reunion*, CPP 346.

118. Eliot, *The Family Reunion*, CPP 315.
119. Eliot, *The Family Reunion*, CPP 329.
120. Eliot, *Sweeney Agonistes*, CPP 125.
121. Eliot, *The Family Reunion*, CPP 349.
122. Sarkar, *The Chorus in Eliot's Plays and Other Essays* (Calcutta: Rupa, 1993) 15.
123. Sarkar, *The Chorus in Eliot's Plays and Other Essays* 15.
124. Eliot, *The Family Reunion*, CPP 348.
125. Leonard Unger, *T.S. Eliot: Moments and Patterns* (Minneapolis: University of Minnesota P, 1958) 86.
126. Alessandro Pellegrini, "A London Conversation with T.S. Eliot," trans. Joseph Frank, *Sewanee Review* Spring 1949, 57: 289.
127. Pellegrini, in *Sewanee Review*, Spring 1949, 289.
128. Eliot, "Poetry and Drama," *On Poetry and Poets* 81-82.
129. Eliot, "Poetry and Drama," *On Poetry and Poets* 81.
130. Eliot, "Poetry and Drama," *On Poetry and Poets* 82.
131. Peacock 3.
132. Eliot, "Poetry and Drama," *On Poetry and Poets* 82.
133. Eliot, qtd. in Gordon, *Eliot's New Life* 91.
134. Gordon, *Eliot's New Life* 91.
135. Eliot, in Smidt 51.
136. Eliot, in Smidt 57.
137. Eliot, "'Ulysses,' Order, and Myth," *Selected Prose of T.S. Eliot* 177.
138. Eliot, *The Family Reunion, The Complete Poems and Plays* 290-91.
139. Bodkin, *The Quest for Salvation in an Ancient and a Modern Play* 12.
140. Eliot, *The Family Reunion*, CPP 301.
141. Eliot, *The Family Reunion*, CPP 329.
142. Eliot, *The Family Reunion*, CPP 349.
143. Eliot, "Poetry and Drama," *On Poetry and Poets* 82.
144. Eliot, "Poetry and Drama," *On Poetry and Poets* 80.
145. Eliot, *The Family Reunion*, CPP 309.
146. Eliot, *The Family Reunion*, CPP 333.
147. Eliot, *The Family Reunion*, CPP 336.
148. Eliot, *The Family Reunion*, CPP 316.
149. Eliot, *The Family Reunion*, CPP 337.
150. Eliot, *The Family Reunion*, CPP 350.

151. Ivor Brown, "The Family Reunion," in Clarke, Vol. 3: 328.
152. Eliot, "Seneca in Elizabethan Translations," *Selected Essays* 76.
153. Eliot, "Four Elizabethan Dramatists," *Selected Essays* 111.
154. Williams 256.
155. Eliot, letter dt. 13 September 1939, in Coghill 47.
156. Browne, letter dt. 25 March 1967, in Coghill 47-48.
157. Leeming 110.
158. Frederick Lumley, *Trends in Twentieth Century Drama* (London: Rockliff, 1956) 85, qtd. in Sarkar, *T.S. Eliot the Dramatist* 141.
159. Jones 110.
160. Eliot, *The Family Reunion*, CPP 293.
161. Bonamy Dobree, *The Lamp and the Lute* (New York: Barnes and Noble, 1929) 145.
162. Eliot, "East Coker," CPP 179.
163. Eliot, "East Coker," CPP 182.
164. Eliot, "East Coker," CPP 179.
165. Eliot, *The Family Reunion*, CPP 307.
166. Leeming 115.
167. Eliot, *The Family Reunion*, CPP 344.
168. Eliot, *The Family Reunion*, CPP 324.
169. Eliot, *The Family Reunion*, CPP 327.
170. Hulme 135.
171. Eliot, "The Three Voices of Poetry," *On Poetry and Poets* 91-92.
172. Browne 127.
173. Matthews 174.
174. Philip R. Headings, *T.S. Eliot* (1964; New York: Twayne, 1982) 153-54.
175. Matthews 35.
176. Peacock 24.

# 4 Quest for Meaning in Social Life and Beyond and for a Successful Verse Medium

Nearly ten years separated *The Family Reunion* and *The Cocktail Party*, which came to be presented for the first time at the Lyceum Theatre, Edinburgh, on 22 August 1949 (exactly two years and seven months after Vivienne's death). By this time Europe had experienced the horrors of the Second World War which included the German 'blitz' and the nuclear holocaust. During the war Eliot had moved out to Shamley Green, in order to avoid the constant threat of aerial bombings that prevailed upon the metropolis of London. All social, cultural, traditional and ethical values crumbled down in the aftermath of the war, leaving a huge void in front of the Western civilization. Eliot's deep concern with the effects of the war could be felt from what he said, in an interview, to Lehmann: "[...] the conditions of one's life changed, and one was thrown in on oneself."[1] He had already experienced the First World War and its impact on Europe. This enabled him to comment, in 1934, on the relation between war and mankind, which proved to be equally relevant in the wake of the Second World War. He had written:

> In face of any naturally horrifying phenomenon like war we must measure the suffering, direct and indirect, against the spiritual goods which may come of suffering. We may find that the proportion of futile suffering, and of that kind of suffering which makes men worse rather than better, which abates their human dignity and deadens their sense of responsibility, is far too high; and that the total effect is at best one of futility. What we have to concern ourselves with primarily is the causes in modern society, in our industrial

> and financial machinery it may be, which bring about the *kind* of war which we have experienced; and to give our adherence to all alterations in that machinery which tend to remove the motives. We do not, I suppose, deny that society is very deeply affected morally and spiritually by material conditions, even by a machinery which it has constructed piecemeal and with short sighted aims. This is not to accept any doctrine of determinism, for it means no more than that society, and the majority of individuals composing it, are only imperfectly conscious of what they are doing, directed by impure motives and aiming at false goods.[2]

This shows his concern for the spiritual future of mankind. The war brought Eliot face to face with the question of the survival of the European civilization. He had become an expatriate in Europe very early in the twentieth century when he realized that his own roots lay in the rich cultural tradition of Europe. However, in January 1946 he found that the public world was more incredible and the private world more intolerable.

Although he tried a number of times, Eliot could not bring himself to write another play for as long as the war lasted. Eventually he wrote a play in which he wished to depict that selfless love could empower man to reinstate the spiritual equilibrium which was disturbed by the war. *The Cocktail Party* shows how human suffering can be reduced by the practice of tolerance, love and compassion, which are the basic tenets of Christianity, Buddhism and Hinduism. His Holiness the fourteenth Dalai Lama explained in a 1981 interview that:

> [...] it is quite possible that a person who is basically a Christian, who accepts the idea of God, who believes in God, could at the same time incorporate certain Buddhist ideas and techniques into his/her practice. The teachings of love, compassion, and kindness are present in Christianity and also in Buddhism.[3]

These words of the Dalai Lama explain, in a way, Eliot's own experiences when he came across the teachings of the Buddha. As a child, Eliot had read Edwin Arnold's *The Light of Asia*, in which Arnold depicted the life and character and indicated the philosophy of Gautama Buddha, the founder of Buddhism. This religion offers a concrete example of the best that can be had through disciplined life and ascetic renunciation. Since Eliot took an avid interest in the Buddhistic doctrines during his studies at Harvard under Charles Lanman, his works bear testimony to the extent of their influence on his spiritual development. It was the Buddhism of the Pali canon which drew Eliot's attention when he read the Buddhist literature, both in the original and the translations of Henry Clarke Warren. He was further exposed to a more sympathetic understanding of Mahayana Buddhism through the teachings of James Woods and the lectures of Masaharu Anesaki at Harvard. Eliot was particularly attracted by the denial of the substantive reality in Buddhism (which Warren calls the *Ego*) that leads towards *Nirvana* which involves the extinction of the fires of lust, hatred, infatuation, pride, false belief and all the other passions. Buddhism shows the way towards *Nirvana* (which implies a detachment from the material world) with the help of Dependent Origination. According to Dependent Origination (*Pratityasamutpada*), which might be described as the 'postulate of morality', a real thing must make itself felt; it must affect or be affected by other things. In order to be causally effective a thing must enter into a causal sequence becoming a link in a causal chain. Causation is simply the law that the succeeding moment continues the series initiated by the previous one. Causation is not substantial, but serial. Therefore, every moment is a kind of death, to be succeeded by a new birth. Nothing binds these moments together; it is their very nature to succeed each other in an endless change. If this is the nature of life, it is a great mystery.

The structural pattern of *The Cocktail Party* follows the Buddhist doctrine of the *Parinirvana Sutra* which expounds the two-fold way of life—the *nivritti-marga* (path of renunciation) which Eliot calls "the way of illumination"[4] and the *pravritti-marga* (path of active social life) which Eliot calls "the common routine"[5]. In his sermons, Lord Buddha spoke of a golden mean between these two ways. For the ascetics, who were meant to lead a life of mortification, he prescribed meditation and self-renunciation. For those who wished to lead a social life and yet sought *Nirvana*, he recommended the 'Noble Eightfold Path'. He also spoke of a middle way between these two which each individual could chalk out for himself in order to reach self-realization, which is the ultimate goal of being.

*The Cocktail Party* is a play about the modern quest for understanding and analysis of the inevitable disease of loneliness and isolation arising out of the individual's failure to respond to others by going beyond one's delimited world of ego or self-centredness. Eliot chooses the *Parinirvana Sutra* as the essential platform of this play because it speaks of a middle way which is a kind of solution for the spiritual crisis which the European civilization was experiencing after the Second World War. In order to show his auditors how the *Sutra* becomes relevant to their own existence in the post-war situation, Eliot created the character of Celia Coplestone who will follow the *nivritti-marga* (which may be considered as similar to the Contemplative Way in Christian mysticism) and the characters of Edward and Lavinia Chamberlayne, the couple who will follow the *pravritti-marga* (which is somewhat similar to the Affirmative Way).

By the time *The Cocktail Party* was staged, Eliot had received two prestigious awards—the Nobel Prize for Literature and the Order of Merit. These honours increased his sense of responsibility towards his auditors and he expressed an awareness of this responsibility in a comment on the process of writing *The Cocktail Party*: "I had always believed a Nobel Prize to be a sort of advance death notice, and I was putting everything I had into the play in the effort to keep it alive."[6]

In order to make the audience feel at home Eliot continued with the use of the drawing-room setting in his new play. This time it belongs to the affluent lawyer, Edward Chamberlayne, whose flat is in London. While the world of the play is close to that of the auditors, the play itself has a number of layers. Its infrastructure is provided by the *Parinirvana Sutra* on which rests the superstructure of the quest for self-realization. The ideas of the Incarnation and the symbolic Quest of the Holy Grail support this superstructure. All these contribute towards making the play realistic on one hand and symbolic on the other.

When the play begins it is discovered that Edward is compelled to entertain a few guests whom he could not inform about the cancellation of a cocktail party which his wife, Lavinia, had decided to host, since she had left (apparently) without informing him. After Lavinia leaves him Edward realizes that he must have her back if he is to have an understanding of his own self. However, at this stage he is not humble enough to disclose this truth before his acquaintances. He wards off any possibility of love shared between him and Lavinia. Simultaneously, he contemplates on his inability to understand his sense of a loss of desire for the material world. He says:

> That is the worst moment, when you feel that you have lost
> The desire for all that was most desirable,
> Before you are contented with what you can desire;
> Before you know what is left to be desired;
> And you go on wishing that you could desire
> What desire has left behind. [...][7]

He finds that he is facing a strange problem. The next day the Unidentified Guest returns to Edward's flat and speaks in riddles to Edward. He is a psycho-analyst (playing the role of a Guardian) who knows that Edward has to realize the necessity of his wife before he can arrange for Lavinia's return to her husband. He had said to Edward in the opening scene that:

> There is certainly no purpose in remaining in the dark
> Except long enough to clear from the mind
> The illusion of having ever been in the light.[8]

So, Edward decides to have Lavinia back. Like Edward, Lavinia makes a choice, setting in motion a chain of events in which she also becomes a participant. The other Guardians, Julia Shuttlethwaite and Alexander MacColgie Gibbs, make no attempt to reduce her perplexity, for she must quest for self-realization. That is her burden and her action. They discuss about this:

> JULIA. Alex, do you think we could explain *anything*?
> ALEX. I think not, Julia. She must find out for herself:
> That's the only way.[9]

So, Lavinia gradually learns to be humble and trustworthy. After she returns to Edward in Act I scene iii, she says that she has decided to tell the truth always in future for she has realized that she and the others have wasted a lot of time in lying to each other. On analyzing her behaviour with her husband she discovers that she had presumed him to be a different man whom she had taken for granted. She admits that this is "a very important discovery."[10] The Chamberlaynes realize that their quest will not be an easy one. They lack the virtue of selfless love for each other. It is the best of a bad job that they will have to make out of a situation which is their own creation. Although they sense a compulsion that forces them to stay with each other, they do not possess the ability to understand it as yet. They will have to search for this superior force which is actually the quest for self-realization and meaning of life. Like Lavinia, Edward learns to see himself as he actually is and he admits that "The change that comes / From seeing oneself through the eyes of other people"[11] is remarkable. In the course of their introspective discussion the Chamberlaynes wonder why they married each other. Lavinia explains that she married Edward because he "kept on *saying*"[12] that he was in love with her. Now she realizes that during their courtship he was trying to persuade himself that he was in love with her, which he admits, adding that others told him so. She comments on this dryly, saying, "It's a pity that you had no opinion of your own."[13] Here, Eliot draws from the image of the rose garden when Edward tries to articulate his loneliness in spite of being in the company of other persons. It is his spiritual loneliness that he is trying to explain when he says:

> There was a door
> And I could not open it. I could not touch the handle.
> Why could I not walk out of my prison?
> What is hell? Hell is oneself,
> Hell is alone, the other figures in it
> Merely projections. There is nothing to escape from
> And nothing to escape to. One is always alone.[14]

This inner suffering is an indication of his growing awareness of himself as a quester for self-realization. He knows that this spiritual malaise cannot be cured by any doctor in a "professional capacity."[15] Even after Lavinia returns to him, Edward is unprepared for a conjugal life with her. Lavinia complacently believes that she can bully her husband as she did in the past. But she is surprised to find that he has become assertive when he makes it out to her that:

> You don't understand me. Have I not made it clear
> That in future you will find me a different person?[16]

He is not going to allow his wife to push him around any more. He rather feels that there is not much to expect from the marriage, but is prepared to search for an acceptable relationship. The complex nature of his relation with his wife began to dawn on him in her absence, as he confesses to Reilly, later in the play:

> I cannot live with her—that is now intolerable;
> I cannot live without her, for she has made me incapable
> Of having any existence of my own.[17]

To him Lavinia is an image of temptation (like that of Eve) towards damnation. So, he addresses her as "The python. The octopus."[18] He fears that she will destroy his inner self under the pressure of her domineering personality. However, he has to accept his wife because both of them are part of an unchanging design. After his choice is made he has no other alternative and he has to comply with the chain of events he has already set in motion. The Unidentified Guest had warned him that his "moment of freedom was yesterday."[19] When he arrives at the psychiatrist's consulting room he discovers that Sir Henry Harcourt-Reilly is the Unidentified Guest who made frequent visits to his flat. Edward is very annoyed because he feels that his decision was actually forced on him by Reilly. While he still struggles for a better understanding of himself, Reilly admonishes him saying that he was on the verge of ruining three lives (those of Celia, Lavinia and himself) by his inability to make the right choice. Now he can save his wife's and his own lives from being destroyed. Reilly is talking about the Chamberlaynes here because Celia is destined to follow a different path. Edward needs to be reassured that he is capable of action Reilly helps him to have a spiritual awareness: an experience of spiritual suffering will lead him in his quest for salvation. He is afraid of a spiritual death which he expresses before Reilly, saying:

I am not afraid of the death of the body,
But this death is terrifying. The death of the spirit—
Can you understand what I suffer?[20]

This is a way of articulating the growing awareness of his inner being. However, Edward is still unsure of himself and is displeased with Reilly's uninvited interference in his private life but Reilly puts him in his place very firmly saying that Edward should be honest with himself and others. It is a joint quest for the Chamberlayne couple who need to retain their wedlock in order to seek for meaning of life. The only way to put the couple together is by laying bare their real selves before each other. Reilly undertakes this job with the ease of a professional psychiatrist. He admits Lavinia into his consulting room when Edward is still there so that he can handle them together. They are surprised to see each other there. When he talks about one of them having an honest mind, they burst out together:

LAVINIA. No one can say my husband has an honest mind.
EDWARD. And I could not honestly say that of you, Lavinia.[21]

Congratulating them on their perspicacity, Reilly clamps the couple together, making them realize that they can have a better life together if they discard the web of illusions and falsities which they have woven around themselves. He sums up the couple very neatly when he says:

And now you begin to see, I hope,
How much you have in common. The same isolation.
A man who finds himself incapable of loving
And a woman who finds that no man can love her.[22]

He points out to them that they will have to accept the situation gladly as part of the Divine Design in order to succeed in their search for meaning of life. They represent the spiritual barrenness of the twentieth century European civilization. Reilly tells them that whether they like it or not, they will have to make "the best of a bad job."[23] They must suffer in faith and perseverance for atonement in order to achieve salvation.

Philip Rahv says that the Chamberlaynes are "a couple without any life of their own: they have no motive power except that of illustrating as neatly as possible the Weltanschung which the author imposes upon them by main force."[24] It is not Eliot's philosophy with an interpretation of world history or civilization that Edward and Lavinia are working out. They are questers for self-realization along the Affirmative Way or *pravritti-marga*. It is from *The Cocktail Party* that Eliot begins to experiment with the possibility of a successful culmination of a quest along this path. The words spoken by Reilly as the Chamberlaynes prepare to leave his consulting room echo the final words of the Buddha to his favourite disciple, Ananda. Reilly says: "Go in peace. And work out your salvation with diligence."[25]

As the play draws to a close, The Chamberlaynes are found in their flat, making preparations for another cocktail party. Their earnestness in trying to make the best of a bad job is revealed in their duologue. Edward compliments Lavinia on her dress and she says to him:

> Do you know it's the first time you've paid me a compliment
> *Before* a party? And that's when one needs them.[26]

Towards the end of the play their relation has become stable and they have learnt to respect and trust each other. In spite of their satisfaction in making a steady progress towards enlightenment, they cannot forget their shabby behaviour with Celia. Reilly points out to them that:

> You will have to live with these memories and make them
> Into something new. Only by acceptance
> Of the past will you alter its meaning.[27]

The pastness of the past is unimportant, but its presence is, because the past has a bearing on the present. The Chamberlaynes will have to accept the past in order to proceed towards *Nirvana* (the extinction of desires), which is the aim of their quest. They have been prepared by the Guardians to search for self-realization together. However, Edward is still struggling for an understanding when he tries to explain to Lavinia what Reilly and Julia meant:

> Oh, it isn't much
> That I understand yet! But Sir Henry has been saying,
> I think, that every moment is a fresh beginning;

And Julia, that life is only keeping on;
And somehow, the two ideas seem to fit together.[28]

This is the Buddhist idea of Dependent Origination. The playwright's deliberate portrayal of the Chamberlaynes as they are found in *The Cocktail Party* shows that he had a definite purpose behind this scheme. In a letter to Browne dated 2 July 1949 Eliot wrote, "E. and L. didn't want to be left alone together—which would spoil the relation I had so laboriously built up between them."[29] Browne adds that the dramatist's opinion rested on the last half-line of the play, in which Lavinia says, "Oh, I'm glad. It's begun."[30] Eliot called this line "the trickiest bit of all."[31] It is clear from the ending of the play that Eliot's lack of any first-hand knowledge of a couple's behaviour in such circumstances formed a sort of impediment to a precise expression of their feelings. However, he picked up the strands from here and moved onward in the next play because he realized that "self-confidence is very important. [...] On that basis human beings can transform themselves by increasing the good qualities and reducing the negative qualities,"[32] as the Dalai Lama explains.

The character who will search for self-realization along the path of asceticism is Celia. Her name derives from Saint Cecilia, a Roman martyr who died in century 230 A.D. Although Celia's name bears symbolic implications, the demands of naturalistic drama do not allow Eliot to dress her with the trappings of the supernatural. In the initial stages of the play, she is Edward's mistress and is in love with him. She thinks that Edward will marry her since Lavinia has left him. Edward, however, has advanced to a higher level of spiritual understanding after his conversation with the Unidentified Guest. He is trying to come to terms with the fact that his wife has left him. While Edward slowly becomes aware of his true self as the darkness of his illusion about himself gradually disappears, Celia remains in her world of illusions. When she realizes that the real Edward is a very different man from the image of Edward which she had constructed in her illusory world, she begins to recoil from an uninhibited dependence on him. Simultaneously, she senses the power which the Unidentified Guest exerts over them, feeling "rather afraid of him."[33] Edward informs Celia that Reilly has a hand in Lavinia's disappearance. What surprises her is Edward's preference to conform to social approval by retaining his marriage with Lavinia. Eliot gradually develops his characters in consistency with their roles in the play. Celia makes one last desperate attempt to have Edward, but her confidence becomes shaky when she is compelled to face the reality that Edward has made up his mind about Lavinia. She feels let down, calling it "humiliation."[34] It is hard for her to accept her own shortcoming for which she failed to recognize Edward's true nature, which is an inability to love anyone. Instead of accusing Edward, she expresses her compassion for him. This unexpected behaviour surprises Edward who makes a hollow declaration of love for her. By this time she has detached herself from him as she becomes aware of her spiritual self. Celia says to Edward, "I shall not loathe you. I shall only feel sorry for you."[35] in the duologue in Act I Scene ii, Edward explains to Celia his awareness of the quest for self-realization. He says to her:

> I see that my life was determined long ago
> And that the struggle to escape from it
> Is only a make-believe, a pretence
> That what is, is not, or could be changed.
> The self that can say 'I want this—or want that'—
> The self that wills—he is a feeble creature;
> He has to come to terms in the end
> With the obstinate, the tougher self; who does not speak,
> Who never talks, who cannot argue.[36]

According to the Buddhist scriptures, *Self* is the universal principle of life, over and above the *self* or ego. The cessation of the fires of desire may free the *Self* from the bondage of the *self*. Eliot names the *Self* "the tougher self" and *self* "The self that wills". The willing self "can only flourish / In submission to the rule of the stronger partner."[37] This is the way of reconciliation and adjustment which the Chamberlaynes follow.

Eliot was concerned about the impact of the saint's sacrifice on the lives of ordinary men and women. When J.P. Hodkin asked him, "How would you, out of the bitter experience of the present time, wish mankind to develop?" Eliot answered:

> I should speak of a greater spiritual consciousness, which is not asking that everybody should rise to the same conscious level, but that everybody should have some awareness of the depths of spiritual development and some appreciation and respect for those more exceptional people who can proceed further in spiritual knowledge than most of us can.[38]

He is referring to persons like Celia who proceed along the path of sacrifice, renunciation and suffering on the way to enlightenment. In her interview with Reilly in his consulting room, Celia expresses her humility and says that she has no illusions except that the material world "seems all a delusion."[39] Her inherent honesty enables her to work out the path she wishes to take, with only hints from Reilly who can discern her rare qualities but cannot reach up to her level of spiritual understanding. She suffers from a sense of sin which Reilly finds unusual. Celia realizes that the lack of selfless love alienates human beings from each other. Unlike Becket and Harry, who had to achieve humility, Celia already possesses this virtue when she is interviewed by Reilly because Edward's rejection of her hinted offers of physical love enabled her to recognize the futility and unenduring nature of such a relationship. She struggles for clarity when she expresses her inner experiences, and like Harry, uses negatives to explain her sense of sin. She says to Reilly that "it's much easier to tell you what I don't mean: / I don't mean sin in the ordinary sense."[40] She is aware of the spiritual aridity of the post-Second World War civilization for which she must atone, suffering in penance for the salvation of mankind. Celia knows that she will take the *nivritti-marga* for self-realization. So, she says to Reilly:

> I shall be left with the inconsolable memory
> Of the treasure I went into the forest to find
> And never found, and which was not there
> And perhaps is not anywhere? But if not anywhere
> Why do I feel guilty at not having found it?[41]

The forest symbolizes the darkness of unknowing which must be penetrated by the aspirant. Celia knows that the quest will be hazardous, so she tries to break the shackles of human bonds. The love she aspires after is Divine Love which should be experienced "In the spirit, a vibration of delight / without desire."[42] Since Celia has not crossed the frontier of social existence, Reilly allows her a final chance to retrace her steps from the way of the ascetic. He describes the two ways to her:

> The first I could describe in familiar terms
> Because you have seen it, as we all have seen it,
> Illustrated, more or less, in lives of those about us.
> The second is unknown, and so requires faith—
> The kind of faith that issues from despair.[43]

Since those who follow the second path cross the frontier of the physical existence, Reilly has no first hand information about this tough way towards self-realization. Here comes the relevance of the Buddha's parting message to Ananda on the eve of his *Parinirvana*. Reilly repeats the words of the Buddha once more when he says to Celia, "Go in peace, my daughter. / Work out your salvation with diligence."[44]

Two years later, in Act III, Alex (the globetrotting Guardian) brings news of Celia's horrible death in Kinkanja, an island in the East inhabited by barbarian tribes. It is noticeable that there is a gradual shift in Eliot's naturalistic plays from the overtly ritualistic elements found in the first two plays; this involves a sort of distancing from the essence of the Christian rituals. This phenomenon can be traced back to an awareness of the lack of spirituality in most modern men, particularly after the Second World War. Here, Eliot appears to use the idea of Celia's martyrdom near an anthill as an indirect parody of Christ's Crucifixion because modern men are incapable of recognizing the meaning of the commitment of the Son of God. Her martyrdom seems to symbolize the culmination of her quest for self-realization because it follows, in a way, the pattern of Jesus' Sacrifice. Her recognition of the impermanence of the material existence may be explained with the help of the Dalai Lama's discourses on how to deal with death, where he says:

> By reflecting on the coarser levels of impermanence one will be able to confront and counteract grasping at permanence or eternal existence of one's own identity or self, because it is grasping at permanence that forces us to cling onto this very 'now-ness' or matters of one's lifetime alone.[45]

The other aspect of Celia's martyrdom is the reception of the news of her death by the aristocratic Londoners. They seem to undergo, in a subtly refined manner, the same experiences which the charwomen of Canterbury had on witnessing Becket's martyrdom in *Murder in the Cathedral.* In this naturalistic play the martyrdom is reported in order to accommodate the crucifixion on the realistic stage. Eliot brings the important characters together to hear about Celia's death because he wants to uphold the Buddhist idea of the *Parinirvana Sutra* where a golden mean is struck between the *pravritti-marga* and the *nivritti-marga.* In order to bring the golden mean within the comprehension of his auditors, Eliot makes use of the character of Peter Quilpe. The news of Celia's death has an immediate personal relevance for him. He reflects that he had created an illusion of a life with her (or at least, for her) which becomes worthless in her absence. The Chamberlaynes have undergone similar experiences of emptiness and futility. Now they are trying to "make the best of a bad job."[46] So, they are in a position to give Peter a hint at their chosen way towards self-realization. Lavinia points out to him that he has been living in an illusory world which he has created for his selfish needs. Edward encourages him to undertake his own quest, saying:

> [...] some men have to learn much worse things
> About themselves, and learn them later
> When it's harder to recover, and make a new beginning.
> It's not so hard for you. You're naturally good.[47]

Edward's words appear to express Eliot's own regret for deciding to marry Vivienne. While the Chamberlaynes explain their understanding of the way of reconciliation and adjustment which they have taken in their quest for meaning of life, Julia tries to point out to Peter that he could be reconciled to the reality of Celia's death. Julia says that he must detach himself from all selfish desires for Celia. She uses an image from cinematography in order to explain herself to Peter who is a film-script writer:

> You must have learned how to look at people, Peter,
> When you look at them with an eye for the films:
> That is, when you're not concerned with yourself
> But just being an eye. [...][48]

Eliot brings the two observations together so that Peter can see for himself that there is another way towards self-realization besides those taken by the Chamberlaynes and Celia, which is the way of the golden mean. Detachment from the world of illusions (which Buddhism calls *Maya*) is a prerequisite for the cessation of the fires of desire that burn the human beings, forcing them to remain within the limits of a material existence. The dramatist makes use of the 'third voice' here in order to point out a way towards spiritual fertility to his auditors.

All the important characters, Edward, Lavinia, Celia and Peter, live in their egocentric milieu, their vision circumscribed by their narrow and subjective attitude to life. They badly need a kind of liberation from the narrow and egocentric vision. What Eliot has tried to highlight in *The Cocktail Party* is the modern man's delusion of being overwhelmed by another individual's influence or unwanted sway, whereas he himself is utterly ignorant of his own obduracy or failure to respond to others. That a modern man or woman suffers from the selfish urge of self-deception which lies at the root of most complications in human relations is made more than aptly clear by Sir Henry Harcourt-Reilly in Act II of the play, where he appears as a psychiatrist. Introduction of psychiatry or psychoanalysis in modern drama is a significant contribution by Eliot in the context of investigation into the spiritual malaise of the modern society. In fact, one of the most significant developments in the twentieth century social set-up is the recognition of the role of psychiatry in loosening the knots of the self-centred modern man's mental complications which pass in the name of 'nervous breakdown.' Both the Chamberlaynes suffer from this malaise. Reilly is able to loosen the knots of their mental complications by making them confess their deceitfulness and self-deception. This leads both of them to the path of adjustment and reconciliation. This is what, Reilly says, all modern people do, except those who are saints or choose the extreme path of self-sacrifice, like Celia. His role in the lives of the Chamberlaynes and Celia was to make them aware of the illusion of a materialistic existence that is spiritually barren, so that they may seek for meaning of life. Stephen Spender's allegation that Reilly reviews the news of Celia's martyrdom with "self-congratulatory self-complacency"[49] is refuted by what Reilly says in Act III:

> I'd say she suffered more, because more conscious
> Than the rest of us. She paid the highest price
> In suffering. That is part of the design.[50]

These words express his humble acknowledgement of the Divine Design in which his role is that of an advisor, or the father-confessor. Sir Henry combines in his role in *The Cocktail Party* the functions of the priest (both classical and Christian) and psychiatrist, which is yet another example of Eliot's synthesis of the formalist and realist elements in his naturalistic plays. In the opening scene, Edward thinks that a disclosure of his personal problems before a stranger is safe. Little does he know that this man is the modern naturalistic version of the priest-figure who has come to him with the intention of guiding him in his search for self-realization. When E.M. Forster said to Eliot that as a reader of *The Cocktail Party,* he found that he was in the presence of the Church which directs, through its priests, men (children of the Church) on their appropriate paths, Eliot explained to him saying, "Religion is the most important element in life and it is in the light of religion that one understands anything."[51] As part of his role as priest, Reilly resorts to the technique of observing his "clients"[52] (not patients) when they are unaware that they are being studied: this method enables him to get more information than he would if he interviewed them. Reilly gradually prepares Edward for his quest and makes him wait before he is allowed an appointment with the psychiatrist. This deliberate measure teaches Edward a lesson in patience, so that he learns to be humble because humility is essential for his quest. In Act I Reilly observes his clients (Edward, Lavinia and Celia) under the guise of the Unidentified Guest, so that he can advise them in Act II when they visit his consulting room, and in Act III he arrives at Edward's flat in order to see how the Chamberlaynes are progressing in their quest for self-realization. Eliot had a deliberate aim when he created the character of the psychiatrist because he wanted to use this modern professional's analytical nature to convey religious ideas so that the auditors could easily accept his remedial suggestions. Eliot's interest in the subject of psycho-analysis can be gauged from a radio talk broadcast in 1932, in which he discussed the benefits and limitations of psychology:

> Psychology has very great utility in two ways. It can revive and has already to some extent revived, truths long since known to Christianity, but mostly forgotten and ignored, and it can put them in a form and language understandable by modern people to whom the language of Christianity is not only dead but undecipherable.[53]

Thus, the modern clients arrive one by one, at the psychologist's consulting room, to be treated for what they think is a sort of nervous breakdown. Reilly offers them remedies for their actual malady, which has more to do with the spiritual self. He points out to Edward that:

> Half of the harm that is done in this world
> Is due to people who want to feel important.
> They don't mean to do harm—but the harm does not interest them.[54]

They fail to realize that an acknowledgement of their role in the Divine scheme of things is the key to humility which is an important stepping stone in the spiritual quest.

Celia's quest appears to terminate with her martyrdom, which is a kind of culmination from the layman's perspective. The spiritual quest undertaken by the Chamberlaynes continues when the play ends. The playwright was aware of the curiosity of the auditors about the success of the Chamberlaynes in making "the best of a bad job,"[54] about which he remarked in an interview: "some people want to get a general statement on marriage out of the relations of Edward and Lavinia. You can't depict all your views about life. You are limited by time."[55]

The Guardians' concern about the well-being of their clients is clear from the care with which they handle each case. When Julia informs Reilly that Celia has said that she cannot believe that she deserves to be taken seriously, all that he can articulate is: "That is most uncommon."[56] He discusses with Julia about Celia after she has left his consulting room:

> JULIA. She is too humble. She will pass between the scolding hills,
> Through the valley of derision, like a child sent on an errand
> In eagerness and patience. Yet she must suffer.
> [.....................................................................]
>
> REILLY. And when I say to one like her
> 'Work out your salvation with diligence,' I do not understand
> What I myself am saying.[57]

They ponder over her future because they do not have a complete understanding of the quest of the ascetic, although they have helped Celia to make her choice of the *nivritti-marga*. However, the Guardians express a kind of satisfaction with the role they have been able to play in the lives of the Chamberlaynes and Celia. In keeping with the role of the priest and his associates in classical drama (and fertility rites), they proceed to the libation and Julia says:

> May the holy ones watch over the roof,
> May the moon herself influence the bed.[58]

A libation is an ancient ritual (stemming from the fertility cults) in which unmixed wine, or milk, honey, other fluids, and even pure water, is poured on the ground as an offering to the Gods. Thus, the libation, complemented by the symbolic function of the life-giving waters of the Legend of the Holy Grail, indicates the necessity of the spiritual fertility of modern man. In accordance with this idea, Reilly functions in *The Cocktail Party* as the priest who initiates the Chamberlaynes into a quest for self-realization through love on the human plane, and Celia into a quest for enlightenment on the higher spiritual level of renunciation and asceticism. Julia's invocation of the moon to "influence the bed" draws upon the cult of Artemis, who was thought of as a Moon-Goddess who brought fertility to mankind and animals. Eliot makes use of the ancient concept of the fertilizing power of Artemis to convey symbolically the necessity of the spiritual fertility of the barren post-Second World War Western civilization, which is represented in this play by the apparently barren marriage of the Chamberlaynes.

Eliot studied the weaknesses of each play he wrote and tried to do away with them in the next play. So, after studying *The Family Reunion* he decided that the new play would have no chorus and no ghosts, although he wished to continue with the use of a Greek play as it's source. He wrote about his aims in 'Poetry and Drama':

> I was determined to do so merely as a point of departure, and to conceal the origins so well that nobody would identify them until I pointed them out myself.[59]

The myth has been woven into the texture of *The Cocktail Party* in such a way that it cannot be discerned easily. Eliot had reviewed, for the *Criterion*, a translation of Euripedes's *Alcestis* by Dudley Fitts and Robert Fitzgerald. Euripedes drew upon the myth of Alcestis, daughter of Pelias and Anaxibia. Pelias would let her marry only a suitor who could yoke a lion and a boar to a chariot and drive it—a condition which was fulfilled by Admetus, with the help of Apollo. Alcestis became his wife and, in the course of events, accepted as natural the duty of dying in his stead because she was a virtuous woman. Heracles rescues her from Death and restores her to Admetus. Euripedes's *Alcestis*, produced in 438 B.C., is a tragedy which contains a certain burlesque element provided by the genial and drunken Heracles, who is an attractive character in the play, relaxing between the Labours that form the main business of his life, to enjoy himself and do a good turn for a friend. Eliot's dexterity enabled him to convert the elements of Euripedes's tragedy into those of his drawing-room comedy. Of the characters in the two plays, Admetus has a likeness to Edward and Alcestis is split up to form the characters of Lavinia, the wife, and Celia, the lover who is willing to sacrifice herself, with some obvious differences in her motive. The similarities between Heracles and Reilly can be easily discerned. However, some critics misinterpreted Reilly's character for which Eliot had to explain:

> But those who were at first disturbed by the eccentric behaviour of my unknown guest, and his apparently intemperate habits and tendency to burst into song, have found some consolation in having their attention called to the behaviour of Heracles in Euripedes' play.[60]

In *The Cocktail Party*, it is Reilly who brings Lavinia back to Edward. The myth of Alcestis served "merely as a point of departure"[61] from where Eliot embarked, as usual, upon his personal quest for meaning of life behind the facade of *The Cocktail Party*. For the first time in his drama, Eliot adopted the loving and compassionate aspect of the Incarnation while creating the characters of the Chamberlaynes and the Guardians. At the same time he continued to show, through Celia's choice of the way of asceticism, how Christ's selfless Suffering helps to redeem mankind. The symbolic Quest of the Holy Grail is hinted at in the quest for enlightenment which is the fulfillment of spiritual fertility.

Eliot divorced Vivienne in 1933 thinking that this would solve the problem of an unhappy marriage. However, he could not overcome a sense of responsibility towards her and he kept in touch with Northumberland House, the asylum in north London where Vivienne was resident patient till she passed away on 22 January 1947. After she died, instead of being relieved, Eliot experienced an intense grief which showed signs of remorse. He said, through tears, to Hayward that he had "not a single second of happiness to look back on, and that makes it worse."[62] Vivienne had "fastened her emotional needs"[63] on a man whom she did not understand properly and who shrinked from her obsessive possessiveness over him. Eliot referred to the incompatibility between husband and wife, by way of analogy, while discussing the misunderstandings among cultures in *Notes Towards the Definition of Culture* where he wrote: "It is human, when we cannot understand another human being, and cannot ignore him, to exert an unconscious pressure on that person to turn him into something that we *can* understand: many husbands and wives exert this pressure on each other."[64] During this phase of his life Eliot was like "a snow-covered volcano, as symmetrical as Fujiyama."[65] During the rehearsals of *The Cocktail Party*, Eliot's first-hand experience of a tempestuous conjugal life got expressed when he emphasized precision while articulating their speeches to renowned performers like Alec Guiness and Irene Worth who were being directed by Browne himself. Worth recalls Eliot's behaviour on one occasion, when he intervened in the rehearsal:

> Lavinia and Edward, the only married couple in the play, are quarrelling (he had once again delineated the woes of marriage): 'Eliot bolted up to the stage looking quite unsettled. "The wife," he insisted, "must be fierce. *Much more fierce*. The audience must understand that she is impossible."[66]

Although Vivienne had expired, Eliot could not get over the nightmarish relationship with her, which got expressed unconsciously whenever Edward and Lavinia came face to face in the First and Second Acts of the play.

During the years which followed his separation from Vivienne, Eliot turned to Emily Hale for emotional support and she responded accordingly. Eliot's family in America and Emily felt that some day he would marry her. When Vivienne died, Emily expected that Eliot would propose to her, about which she wrote on 7 August 1947 to her close friend, Lorraine Havens:

> [...] a mutual affection he and I have had for each other has come to a strange impasse whether permanent or not, I do not know. Tom's wife died last winter very suddenly. I suppose he would then feel free to marry me as I believed he always intended to do.[67]

However, he maintained a strange silence in this matter. At this time Eliot was sixty and Emily fifty-six and there was no logical explanation for this behaviour. Eliot's personal correspondences during this phase of his life have been withheld from publication till about 2018, so it is difficult to justify this queer behaviour with Emily. It must be kept in mind that he maintained a close relationship with her when Vivienne lived and there could be no reason for its being terminated after her death, unless the Puritan restraint which formed an intrinsic part of his very being impeded him from proposing marriage to Emily. There was no other woman whom he considered marrying during this period. Gordon's explanation that "In so far as Emily Hale was the source for Celia, it was Eliot's imaginative farewell,"[68] cannot be accepted because such simple parallels cannot be constructed between Celia and Emily.

The structure of *The Cocktail Party* follows the Buddhist doctrine of the *Parinirvana Sutra,* which refers to the golden mean between the two ways of life prescribed by the Buddha to his two types of disciples. In his personal quest, Eliot seems to prefer this middle path (which is absent in Christian doctrine) which combines the way of asceticism and renunciation with that of reconciliation and adjustment. The centrality of the idea of the Incarnation in Eliot's personal life enabled him to complement the idea of the *Parinirvana Sutra* by Christ's Suffering on one hand and His Love and Compassion for mankind on the other. However, Eliot's inherent Puritanical restraint appears to make it difficult for him to propose to Emily although she discerned his desire to marry her and expected him to recover from the "abnormal reaction"[69] to Vivienne's death. Under such circumstances, the middle path of Buddhism appears to be commensurate with Eliot's inner crisis. In *Murder in the Cathedral* and *The Family Reunion*, Eliot drew on Christ's Suffering for mankind and emphasized the way of the Contemplative for the attainment of an understanding of the meaning of life. There is a shift in emphasis in *The Cocktail Party* where he upholds the golden mean prescribed by the Buddha in the *Parinirvana Sutra* because Christianity does not offer a middle way between the Contemplative and Affirmative Ways. At this stage of his development as a dramatist, Eliot was not prepared to give up completely his experiment with the way of the ascetic. So, he turned to the middle path between the way of the saint and that of social being. At the same time, Eliot emphasized the loving and compassionate aspect of the Incarnation in order to point out to his auditors that these virtues could bring back spiritual fertility to the barren inner selves of those people who experienced a sense of desolation in the wake of the Second World War. When it was suggested to him in an interview by the *Glasgow Herald* (27 August 1947) that the Festival audiences had not found his meaning in *The Cocktail Party* very plain when the play was performed the previous evening, Eliot replied gently: "Perhaps I did not intend that they should. [...] I would not want to say to anyone that this or that is the meaning (of the play), because the whole interest of the process is in getting your own meaning out of it."[70] Eliot would like his audience to undertake their personal quest for self-realization by drawing inspiration from the play. His preference of the *Parinirvana Sutra* as the structural basis of this play may be understood from the essay 'Shelley and Keats' in which he wrote, "I am not a Buddhist, but some of the early Buddhist scriptures affect me as parts of the Old Testament do."[71] Like Christianity, Buddhism is a living religion which can be practised by persons of every level of understanding and sensibility. When Lawrence Durrell once suggested to Eliot that he was not a Christian but more like a Buddhist, his reply was interrogative: "Perhaps they haven't found me out yet?"[72]

## II

Eliot continued with his experiment with verse drama in *The Cocktail Party* in order to harmonize it with the temperament of the audience. In the interview Eliot gave to the *Glasgow Herald* (27 August 1949), he explained his objectives, saying:

> All that one can aim at in a play of this type, which endeavours to combine the dramatic and the poetic in a somewhat new way, is to provide a plot and characters and action which are on the immediate theatrical level intelligible. That is, the immediate situation and the troubles and conflicts which agitate people should be obvious, the characters should not be on the surface unusual or different

> from ordinary human nature, and there should be perfectly intelligible things going on, with a reasonably intelligible conclusion.[73]

In the same interview, Eliot states that the first and only law of drama is to sustain the attention and interest of the audience till the end. He believed that good poetry cannot be adequately explained in the ordinary sense because "One of the things about poetry is that it does excite different reactions from different people."[74] What is most important is that they should enjoy it. As far as he was concerned, Eliot was against imposing his personal views on his audience or readers because he felt that "if you read an explanation by a literary critic and entirely agree, the thing is finished. One should never entirely agree with any literary critic."[75] He knew that the presentation of *The Cocktail Party* on the stage was not an easy matter, possibly because it involved the structural pattern of the *Parinirvana Sutra* on one hand and a simplified communication of the theme of quest in the naturalistic setting of the drawing-room on the other. In a letter to Henzie Browne, dated 28 August 1949, Eliot praised her husband's direction of the play for he believed that no one but Martin Browne could have got the actors to "see what it was all about."[76] The actor Robert Speaight praises Browne's direction saying, "Author, actor and audience should be grateful that he has assisted into life a play which is among the rare masterpieces of the modern stage."[77]

*The Cocktail Party* is a comedy which conveys a serious message to the contemporary auditors under the cover of the comic devices that are employed to evoke uninhibited laughter in the audience. The comic devices which Eliot uses in this play are mainly borrowed from the music-hall performances, besides some traits from the Comedy of Manners. Julia and Reilly subscribe to the behavioral pattern of the music-hall performers. Julia adopts an air of innocence in order to play her role as Guardian; for example, she creates a comic situation when she suddenly enters Edward's drawing-room just when he is saying to the Unidentified Guest that "she always turns up when she's least wanted."[78] She immediately bursts into speech, saying:

Edward! How lucky that it's raining!
It made me remember my umbrella!
And there it is! Now what are you two plotting?
How very lucky it was my umbrella,
And not Alexander's—he's so inquisitive!
But I never poke into other people's business.[79]

Although she leaves promptly, her sudden arrival provokes Edward's realization that he does not want to be alone. This triggers off the duologue between him and the Unidentified Guest which is a very important groundwork for the psychological treatment Edward will receive in the Second Act. Bethell points out that in this play, Eliot "exploits music-hall devices in the service of the highest dramatic aims."[80] Bethell's observation rests on Eliot's sustained interest in music-hall performances, from some of which he could quote entire songs. The song which Reilly sings in Act I scene i may be said to bear the influence of music-hall comedies. The first stanza of the lyric goes thus:

*As I was drinkin' gin and water,*
*And me being the One Eyed Riley,*
*Who came in but the landlord's daughter*
*And she took my heart entirely.*[81]

The initial title of the play, *One-Eyed Riley*, shows Eliot's affection for the music-hall. However, he was doubtful about the success of the idea of the false teeth which he used in the play. He expressed his apprehension in a letter to Browne, dated 13 June 1948, saying, "Perhaps that is too near a stale music-hall joke."[82] Even the small talk when the play opens is reminiscent of the stylized repetition of the same words, (a stock device of the music-hall performances) which Eliot had adopted in *Sweeney Agonistes*. When Celia asks Julia to tell the story about Lady Klootz and the wedding cake, the conversation takes a turn towards the rhythmic exchanges in music-hall shows:

PETER. I like that story.
CELIA. I love that story.
ALEX. I'm never tired of hearing that story.[83]

This technique sets apart the light portions of the play from the more serious dialogue.

From the Comedy of Manners Eliot borrows the love intrigue, which was the principal theme in the Restoration Comedy. In the post-Second World War situation, accepted social norms were disregarded by most men and women. Their supercilious intrigues found adequate expression in the Restoration Comedy of Manners. So, there was a considerable revival of interest in these seventeenth-century plays. Eliot shows in *The Cocktail Party* how Celia's relationship with Edward verges on licentiousness. She avoids Peter's company but is eager to speak to Edward in private, for quite obvious reasons. Although Edward is unsure of having a worthwhile relationship with Celia, he has no inhibitions about an extra-marital affair with her. In the First Act, when Reilly is still the Unidentified Guest at Edward's cocktail party, he makes some pertinent observations on this issue. On asking Edward whether Lavinia had any reason for leaving him, Reilly receives the reply that Lavinia had "nothing to complain of"[84] in Edward's behaviour. Reilly points out to Edward:

> If another man, then you'd want to remarry
> To prove to the world that somebody wanted you;
> If another woman, you might have to marry her—
> You might even imagine that you wanted to marry her.[85]

It is in his consulting room, when he emerges as the psychiatrist, that Reilly admonishes the Chamberlaynes by disclosing the truth about their extra-marital affairs. He scolds them, saying that they are "exceptionally well-suited to each other."[86] Eliot used the device of the love-intrigue in order to convey the hollow nature of such relationships that have nothing to do with selfless love which alone can redeem mankind.

Unlike the two-part structure of the previous plays, *The Cocktail Party* has three Acts of which only the First Act is divided into three scenes. Act I scene i serves as the exposition by introducing all the important characters, except Lavinia (who has apparently left her husband), and revealing their relations to each other. Sir Henry remains the Unidentified

Guest throughout Act I because it is necessary for his role as priest-cum-psychiatrist. The long second scene unfolds Edward's affair with Celia, in which she is completely involved while Edward shows signs of lacking a commitment towards her. Julia's brief entry to cook some food for Edward seems to be an excuse for intervening in his conversation with Celia because this is part of her role as a Guardian. In the third scene, the Unidentified Guest prepares Edward for Lavinia's return and when Celia turns up instead of Lavinia, Edward is noticeably uneasy. Thoroughly amused by his discomfiture, Celia says to Edward:

> Just looking at you. Edward, forgive my laughing.
> You look like a little boy who's been sent for
> To the headmaster's study; and is not quite sure
> What he's been found out in. I never saw you so before.
> This is really a ludicrous situation.[87]

Celia gets completely absorbed in her relationship with Edward, but when she discovers his lack of commitment, she withdraws herself. The past twenty-four hours have taught her a lot and Eliot is able to show how the principle of Dependent Origination, or Law of Causation, comes to operate in her quest for meaning of life. Edward's anxiety gets expressed through brief ejaculations like "There's Lavinia"[88] and "What aunt?"[89] Peter arrives to inform them about his departure for California and he is followed by Lavinia, who uses a latch-key to let herself in (showing that she is the mistress of the place). Here, it is discovered that the Guardians had arranged to bring these four characters together, and after a brief stay the others depart, leaving Edward and Lavinia to themselves.

Several weeks pass between the First and Second Acts. It is in the Second Act of the play that Reilly points out the twofold path to the Chamberlaynes and Celia. It may be said that this central Act serves the same purpose as the Interlude in *Murder in the Cathedral*. However, the message of the priest-figure is modified in order to adjust itself with the naturalistic setting of the play. It is in this Act that Reilly emerges as the priest-cum-psychiatrist, playing a very significant role in the spiritual lives of the three characters who will follow the twofold path. His advice to them may be said to be a modified version of the sermon. In *Murder in the Cathedral* it was Becket himself who spoke of the way towards self-realization, in *The Family Reunion* Agatha played the role of the priestess initiating Harry's quest for meaning of life and here, in *The Cocktail Party*, Sir Henry exposes the twofold way before the questers.

Two years pass between the Second and Third Acts. Celia's martyrdom, which is reported by Alex, is the last of such martyrdoms in Eliot's plays where the quester gives up his or her life in order to be "possessed of the divine union."[90] On the other hand, the Chamberlaynes show positive signs of success in their quest for self-realization by following the way of adjustment and reconciliation.

The play has a symmetrical structure that helps to reveal the progress of the questers from a state of spiritual barrenness towards understanding of the meaning of life. The role of the Guardians is not only to help the questers in choosing the right way towards spiritual fertility; they help the modern auditors to have a grip on the course of events in the play with their discussions and comments, which perform the same function as the commentaries of the Greek Chorus.

The experiment with the verse-medium continues in this play. In order to show his own progress towards forging an appropriate verse-form for the contemporary naturalistic stage, Eliot used the Zoroaster line from Shelley's *Prometheus Unbound* on the lips of Sir Henry in the Third Act of *The Cocktail Party*, where he says:

*Ere Babylon was dust*
*The magus Zoroaster, my dead child,*
*Met his own image walking in the garden.*
*That apparition, sole of men, he saw.*
*For know there are two worlds of life and death:*
*One that which thou beholdest; but the other*
*Is underneath the grave, where do inhabit*
*The shadows of all forms that think and live*
*Till death unite them and they part no more!*[91]

Eliot's purpose was to contrast these lines from the only verse play Shelley wrote, with his own lines. He quotes Shelley with a careless ease, passing on to his own mode of verse dialogue in order to point out, by way of contrast, the subtle shades of difference between the conventional form of verse used by Shelley, the Romantic poet, and the modern speech-oriented verse-form he forged for articulation in the naturalistic plays. In the essay 'Shelley and Keats' Eliot had commented that "the ideas of Shelley seems to me always to be ideas of adolescence—as there is every reason why they should be"[92] and he quotes the Zoroaster lines in *The Cocktail Party* to show the maturity of his own verse. Eliot had come a long way, in 1949, towards his goal of bringing the cadences of the verse dialogue in his plays close to the rhythms of the everyday speech of the contemporary urban English-speaking world. This resulted from his experiment with each play where he tried to forge an appropriate verse-medium which could communicate the complexity of expressions he wanted to share with the modern audience. However, poetry had to he modulated if poetic naturalism was to triumph on the commercial stage. Eliot was aware of this requirement, so he made "a great sacrifice of the rich contents of the poetry of his earlier creations,"[93] according to Sarkar. The playwright's own comments on his quest for an appropriate verse-medium throws a great deal of light on his progress towards that end:

> [...] and I had—the one thing of which I felt sure—made good deal of progress in finding a form of versification and an idiom which would serve all my purposes without recourse to prose, and be capable of unbroken transition between the most intense speech and the most relaxed dialogue.[94]

Eliot's persistent efforts to bring poetry back to the theatre were guided by his belief that poetry alone can convey the multiple facets of reality, making drama (which is the most impressive form of literature) meaningful in the context of the post-war situation. In order to make the new play relevant to the contemporary auditors, he used the structure of the Buddhist doctrine of the *Parinirvana Sutra* to prescribe two ways of attaining self-realization—one for those who wished to remain within the society and the other for those who wished to follow the lonely path of asceticism. The best representative of the former would be a married couple, for which Eliot has the Chamberlaynes in *The Cocktail Party*, and Celia represents the latter type. It is noteworthy that in this play a woman proceeds towards martyrdom, possibly because Eliot had the myth of Alcestis in mind.

There are a number of concentric patterns in this play (as in all his plays) which could be expressed only through the medium of verse-drama. However, in *The Cocktail Party* Eliot abandoned the use of choral passages, lyric duets and runes, although he retained the three-stress metre. All this was done to accommodate the verse-dialogue in the naturalistic theatre.

In order to cater to the tastes of the audience and to make them feel at par with the events in the play, Eliot used the cocktail party as the background of the first scene and ended the play when another cocktail party was about to begin. The significance of the title of the play is brought out clearly by what Eliot writes in a letter to Browne, dated 15 March 1949, explaining why the play ends with a cocktail party:

> It seems to me to add to the point of the scene for the audience to have in mind that my people have got to go on with their party in spite of everything; and this ending also seems to provide an effective exit for the other three.[95]

The term 'cocktail' could have another meaning in this play. Since a good cocktail implies a proportionate admixture of wines, the term may symbolize the golden mean between the two ways of the *Parinirvana Sutra*. Therefore, the title of play seems to have symbolic connotations which introduce the post-Second World War auditors to the twofold way of life through the medium of naturalistic drama.

## III

Eliot's quest for articulation continues in *The Cocktail Party*, a play in which all the characters belong to the aristocracy of London. Their polished conversation reveals the complexity of the situation in which they find themselves. The Chamberlaynes and Celia have sought for self-realization in the wrong places, making their own lives miserable. Reilly, the priest-figure, who occupies a central position in the hierarchical arrangement of the dramatis personae in terms of spiritual understanding, mediates between those on the highest levels of understanding and those below his own level. His role as mediator becomes obvious when the news of Celia's death is broken and Peter utters, "I suppose I didn't know her, / I didn't understand her. I understand nothing."[96] Reilly encourages him, saying:

> You understand your *metier* Mr. Quilpe—
> Which is the most that any of us can ask for.[97]

Whatever remains unstated in *The Cocktail Party* is the wordless experience of which a Buddhist monk had spoken to Anne Gage in Bangkok. During the interview he said:

> If a man realizes God and is among other men who do not, it is useless to speak about Him for they would not understand. It is better to indicate how they can come to know Him themselves. Man must discover God and his True Self or Ego following the Path of Enlightenment.[98]

Peter's experience of happiness in Celia's company is a rudimentary form of what the monk explains. He is unable to articulate his happiness in the moments he shared with Celia when he says:

> And I was so happy when we were together—
> So ... contented, so ... at peace: I can't express it;
> I had never imagined such quiet happiness.
> [..............................................................]
> It was something very strange. There was such ... tranquility...[99]

Even Celia tries and fails to articulate her spiritual experiences to Reilly, but she has the ability to recognize the incapacity of most modern men to communicate with each other in intelligible terms. She discusses this with Reilly in his consulting room:

> No ... it isn't that I *want* to be alone,
> But that everyone's alone—or so it seems to me.
> They make noises, and think they are talking to each other;
> They make faces, and think they understand each other.
> And I'm sure that they don't. [...][100]

When Alex brings the news of Celia's crucifixion in Kinkanja, Reilly quotes the Zoroaster lines from Shelley's *Prometheus Unbound* to explain the deep philosophy of existence. Eliot found that "abstractions could excite in [Shelley] strong emotion"[101] and he used Shelley's lines as a device of irony. Romantic poetry could have been the last possible device which Eliot wished to employ in his own work unless he wanted to be ironical. The last line in the quotation from Shelley's play, which Reilly utters ("*Till death unite them and they part no more*!"[102]), is an ironical inversion of the marriage vow. By using the device of irony Eliot explains, in a way, the state of *Nirvana* which does not mean annihilation and the death of the soul (as most people commonly believe) but the extinction of ignorance and separation. This Buddhist doctrine, founded on an acute and objective analysis of the world and man, leads to a way of life that is full of tolerance, compassion and selfless love. A passage in the *Parinirvana Sutra* states that:

> It is only when all outward appearances are gone that there is left that one principle of life which exists independently of all external phenomena. It is the fire which burns in the eternal light, when the fuel is expended and the flame is extinguished; for that fire is neither in the flame nor in the fuel, nor yet inside either of the two, but above, beneath, and everywhere.[103]

This eternal light is the highest conceivable symbolic representation of the Absolute Reality. In *The Cocktail Party* the chief imagery is that of darkness and light which represent illusion and reality, or maybe, self-deception and knowledge. For instance, in the Second Act, Sir Henry says to Celia, "compassion may be already a clue / Towards finding your own way out of the forest."[104] Obviously, the forest symbolizes darkness which is the unknown, the impenetrable, the primitive, the evil and, of course, night. Eliot's symbolic use of the forest is similar to Conrad's use of the African forest in his novella, *Heart of Darkness*, where the forest symbolizes the darkness in the spiritual being of civilized Europeans, and gives Marlow's journey into the heart of darkness "a mythical quality and makes it an objective correlative for Marlow's spiritual-emotional development."[105] It may be seen that Conrad's description of the forest of the Congo basin, "[...] the forest, the creek, the mud, the river—seemed to beckon with a dishonouring flourish before the sunlit face of the land a treacherous appeal to the lurking death, to the hidden evil, to the profound darkness of its heart,"[106] came to serve as the same objective correlative for Eliot who was an ardent admirer of Conrad.

The warm response of the auditors to *The Cocktail Party* indicates Eliot's success in communicating, though the medium of his verse-drama, the theme of quest for self-realization. He was trying to mould a verse representing everyday reality and reaching out to something metaphysical at the same time.

Eliot's personal quest for self-realization and for form and articulation continue in this play, in which he initiates his experiment with the Affirmative Way towards self-realization. So, it may be said that *The Cocktail Party* occupies a significant place in Eliot's development as a dramatist who uses the medium of the theatre for his personal quest. In the earlier plays it was Christ's Suffering and Sacrifice that he emphasized. From this play onwards Eliot's emphasis shifts towards Christ's loving and compassionate nature—the idea of the Incarnation as the symbol of Divine Love.

## NOTES AND REFERENCES

1. Eliot, Interview, by Lehmann, in Ackroyd 253.
2. Eliot, *Points of View* (London: Faber, 1941) 133.
3. Paul J. Griffiths, *Christianity Through Non-Christian Eyes* (New York: Orbis Books, 1994) 167.
4. Eliot, *The Cocktail Party*, CPP 421.
5. Eliot, *The Cocktail Party*, CPP 417.
6. Fred D. Crawford, "T.S. Eliot," *Dictionary of Literary Biography*, ed. Stanley Weintraub, Vol. 10 (Detroit: Gale Research Co., 1982) 178.
7. Eliot, *The Cocktail Party*, CPP 381.
8. Eliot, *The Cocktail Party*, CPP 364.
9. Eliot, *The Cocktail Party*, CPP 391.
10. Eliot, *The Cocktail Party*, CPP 393.
11. Eliot, *The Cocktail Party*, CPP 395.

12. Eliot, *The Cocktail Party*, CPP 396.
13. Eliot, *The Cocktail Party*, CPP 396.
14. Eliot, *The Cocktail Party*, CPP 397.
15. Eliot, *The Cocktail Party*, CPP 397.
16. Eliot, *The Cocktail Party*, CPP 397.
17. Eliot, *The Cocktail Party*, CPP 403.
18. Eliot, *The Cocktail Party*, CPP 398; Edward's description of Lavinia as a python is reminiscent of Tanner's words about Ann to Ramsden, "You might as well refuse to accept the embraces of a boa constrictor when once it gets round your neck," in George Bernard Shaw's *Man and Superman* (1903; New Delhi: Surjeet, 1978) 13.
19. Eliot, *The Cocktail Party*, CPP 384.
20. Eliot, *The Cocktail Party*, CPP 404.
21. Eliot, *The Cocktail Party*, CPP 407.
22. Eliot, *The Cocktail Party*, CPP 410.
23. Eliot, *The Cocktail Party*, CPP 410.
24. Philip Rahv, *Image and Idea* (Norfolk: New Directions, 1957) 201, qtd. in Sarkar, *T.S. Eliot the Dramatist* 176.
25. Eliot, *The Cocktail Party*, CPP 411.
26. Eliot, *The Cocktail Party*, CPP 425.
27. Eliot, *The Cocktail Party*, CPP 439.
28. Eliot, *The Cocktail Party*, CPP 440.
29. Browne 231.
30. Eliot, *The Cocktail Party*, CPP 440.
31. Browne 231.
32. Dalai Lama, *The Dalai Lama's Book of Wisdom* (London: Thorsons, 1999) 8.
33. Eliot, *The Cocktail Party*, CPP 377.
34. Eliot, *The Cocktail Party*, CPP 380.
35. Eliot, *The Cocktail Party*, CPP 381.
36. Eliot, *The Cocktail Party*, CPP 381.
37. Eliot, *The Cocktail Party*, CPP 382.
38. Eliot, Interview, "The Condition of Man Today," *Horizon* 12.68 (1945): 88.
39. Eliot, *The Cocktail Party*, CPP 413.
40. Eliot, *The Cocktail Party*, CPP 415.

41. Eliot, *The Cocktail Party*, CPP 416-17.
42. Eliot, *The Cocktail Party*, CPP 417.
43. Eliot, *The Cocktail Party*, CPP 418.
44. Eliot, *The Cocktail Party*, CPP 420.
45. Dalai Lama, *The Dalai Lama's Book of Wisdom* 39.
46. Eliot, *The Cocktail Party*, CPP 410.
47. Eliot, *The Cocktail Party*, CPP 436.
48. Eliot, *The Cocktail Party*, CPP 436.
49. Stephen Spender, *Eliot* (Glasgow: Fontana, 1975) 204.
50. Eliot, *The Cocktail Party*, CPP 437-38.
51. Eliot, Interview, "T.S. Eliot Answers Questions," by E.M. Forster, *John O'London's Weekly*, qtd. in Caroline Behr, *T.S. Eliot: A Chronology of His Life and Works* (London: Macmillan, 1983) 66.
52. Eliot, *The Cocktail Party*, CPP 353-65.
53. Eliot, "The Search for Moral Sanction," *The Listener* 446, qtd. in Jones 145-46.
54. Eliot, *The Cocktail Party*, CPP 403.
55. Eliot, *The Cocktail Party*, CPP 410.
56. Eliot, *The Cocktail Party*, CPP 412.
57. Eliot, *The Cocktail Party*, CPP 421.
58. Eliot, *The Cocktail Party*, CPP 422.
59. Eliot, "Poetry and Drama," *On Poetry and Poets* 85.
60. Eliot, "Poetry and Drama," *On Poetry and Poets* 85.
61. Eliot, "Poetry and Drama," *On Poetry and Poets* 85.
62. Matthews 138.
63. Ackroyd 284.
64. Eliot, *Notes Towards the Definition of Culture* (1948: London: Faber, 1962) 64.
65. Matthews 162.
66. Irene Worth, qtd. In the *New York Times,* 21 November 1982, qtd. in Ackroyd 214.
67. Emily Hale, letter dt. 7 August 1947, qtd. in Gordon, *Eliot's New Life* 170.
68. Gordon, *Eliot's New Life* 172-73.
69. Gordon, *Eliot's New Life* 170.
70. Behr 66.

71. Eliot, "Shelley and Keats," *The Use of Poetry and the Use of Criticism* 91.
72. Eliot, answer to question, by Lawrence Durrell, qtd. in Ackroyd 242.
73. Eliot, Interview, *Glasgow Herald* 27 August 1949, qtd. in Browne 236.
74. Eliot, Interview, *Glasgow Herald* 27 August 1949, qtd. in Browne 236.
75. Eliot, Interview, *Glasgow Herald* 27 August 1949, qtd. in Browne 236-37.
76. Eliot, letter dt. 28 August 1949, qtd. in Browne 238-39.
77. Robert Speaight, in *Tablet* 194, September 1949, in Clarke, Vol. 3: 365.
78. Eliot, *The Cocktail Party*, CPP 359.
79. Eliot, *The Cocktail Party*, CPP 359.
80. S.L. Bethell, *Shakespeare and the Popular Dramatic Tradition* (Westminster: P.S. King and Staples, 1944) 29.
81. Eliot, *The Cocktail Party*, CPP 365.
82. Eliot, letter dt. 13 June 1948, qtd. in Browne 173
83. Eliot, *The Cocktail Party*, CPP 353.
84. Eliot, *The Cocktail Party*, CPP 360.
85. Eliot, *The Cocktail Party*, CPP 360-61.
86. Eliot, *The Cocktail Party*, CPP 409.
87. Eliot, *The Cocktail Party*, CPP 386.
88. Eliot, *The Cocktail Party*, CPP 387.
89. Eliot, *The Cocktail Party*, CPP 387.
90. Eliot, *Sweeney Agonistes*, CPP 115.
91. Eliot, *The Cocktail Party*, CPP 437.
92. Eliot, "Shelley and Keats," *The Use of Poetry and the Use of Criticism* 89.
93. Sarkar, *T.S. Eliot the Dramatist* 187.
94. Eliot, "*The Cocktail Party*," in *Playwrights on Play-writing*, ed. Toby Cole (London: Macgibbon and Kee, 1960) 257, in Sarkar, *T.S. Eliot the Dramatist* 162.
95. Eliot, letter dt. 15 March 1949, qtd. in Browne, 219.
96. Eliot, *The Cocktail Party*, CPP 435.
97. Eliot, *The Cocktail Party*, CPP 435.

98. Anne Gage, "The One Work, a Journey Towards the Self," in Happold 83.
99. Eliot, *The Cocktail Party*, CPP 370.
100. Eliot, *The Cocktail Party*, CPP 414.
101. Eliot, "Shelley and Keats," *The Use of Poetry and the Use of Criticism* 90.
102. Eliot, *The Cocktail Party*, CPP 437.
103. *Parinirvana Sutra*, in Happold 79.
104. Eliot, *The Cocktail Party*, CPP 416.
105. Paul O'Prey, Introduction, *Heart of Darkness*, by Joseph Conrad 15.
106. Conrad, *Heart of Darkness* 65.

# 5 The Search for Identity through a Symbolic Quest

When Eliot met William Turner Levy on 29 June 1953 in New York, he described *The Confidential Clerk* to Levy as "less complicated on the surface than *The Cocktail Party* but having much more in layers to be meditated on and thought of as meanings of life."[1] He added that "it will come as a surprise to the audience. It is much simpler than anything I have done and you might say, a departure."[2] The play was staged for the first time on 25 August 1953 at the Lyceum Theatre during the Edinburgh Festival. Soon after the play was completed, Eliot remarked to Mary Trevelyan that a man who had not known his parents was fortunate, and that his own parents had seemed distant, like ancestors.[3] The protagonist of this play is Colby Simpkins, a humble second-rate organist who does not know the identity of his parents. His simplicity is indicated by the ordinariness of his name. His humility is a pointer to the fact which Eliot wished to emphasize in all his plays—that one must surrender oneself to the Divine Will in order to attain self-realization. In this play and the next, Eliot stressed upon the power of God's Grace which redeems mankind. Here he deals with the relation between father and son in both the physical and metaphysical aspects.

When the play begins, it is seen that Colby (whom Sir Claude Mulhammer assumes to be his illegitimate son) has been recruited as Sir Claude's confidential clerk, after the retirement of Eggerson, whose role in the play is a very significant one. From the action of the play it becomes clear that the former employee comes to play an active role as a confidential clerk, probably because Colby was not meant to be one. Sir Claude wanted to familiarize his wife, Lady Elizabeth, with Colby before he broke the assumed secret of Colby's parentage to her. Colby was more interested in his career as an organist than in his present occupation as a confidential clerk. Possibly this is why his role as Sir Claude's confidential clerk is not expressed properly in this play. Eggerson's function in *The Confidential Clerk* serves two purposes: he is Sir Claude's personal secretary on the physical level, but on the metaphysical plane he is almost like a priest, for he will show Colby the way towards self-realization.

It seems that Eliot came to recognize the importance of the role of the confidential clerk in his own life. Valerie Fletcher was an ardent admirer of the poet from the age of fourteen and she was determined to work with him. Her dream was realized when she became his personal secretary in 1950. Her admiration for him and his growing dependence on her may have been one of the sources for the creation of the characters of Eggerson and Colby. Of the two, it is Eggerson who helps Sir Claude in making important decisions by advising him and being available whenever he is wanted.

It is from the dialogue between Sir Claude and his former confidential clerk that the audience comes to know about Colby Simpkins, who has been appointed to the post vacated by Eggerson. Since the Mulhammers are childless, Sir Claude plans to present Colby to Lady Elizabeth as his new confidential clerk in order to prepare the ground for the adoption of Colby as their child. Colby is reluctant to participate in this affair. In order to help him to come to a decision, Sir Claude cites the example of his own life. In his youth Sir Claude wanted to be a potter but his father compelled him to join their family business. Colby has not made up his mind regarding abandoning the idea of being an organist because his present occupation seems unappealing to him. His discomfiture in the present situation is expressed in a sort of confession he makes before Sir Claude when he says that he feels as though he is building his life "upon a deception."[4] Sir Claude failed to assert himself when his father forced him to become a financier. But Colby is not compliant to Sir Claude's wishes. The more Sir Claude interacts with Colby, the greater is his realization that they "hardly know each other at all."[5] A sort of uneasiness troubles Colby who is haunted by the fear that he is becoming a different person. He feels that it would be better if he turned out to be a disappointed organist rather than a successful financier. Colby's higher spiritual awareness prevents him from following the beaten track of social and material success. He knows that the music he plays is a mere shadow of the ideal music which he hears within himself. His exceptional quality lies in his aspiration towards this music which Eliot used as a symbol of the Ultimate Truth. Eliot's experiment with the means of bringing his theme of quest for self-realization within the comprehension of the contemporary audience takes another step forward in *The Confidential Clerk* in which he treats the character of Colby as that of a man who is firmly rooted in the physical world while he reaches up to the Divine (and not as that of a would-be martyr). "It is Colby's unwillingness to accept an imposed identity, to live a divided life in two separate worlds of time and eternity, of matter and spirit, that sets the search for his identity in motion,"[6] observes Spanos. The music of the organ (and also the piano) links the two worlds.

Sir Claude, however, sees the whole thing in a different light. He feels that "truly religious people"[7] and "men of genius"[8] may find some sort of union with God. But all the others have to live in "two worlds—each a kind of make believe."[9] By saying this Sir Claude tries to convince Colby that he has to follow Sir Claude's footsteps. Little does he realize that they do not have the same view of life. Colby sympathizes with the unsuccessful and suppressed potter in Sir Claude whom he accepts as his father. This conception imposes a kind of compulsion on Colby—his sense of filial duty urging him to comply with Sir Claude's desires which are opposed to his own wishes to be an organist. Regarding the choice of a vocation, Grover Smith traces a similarity when he comments: "From Eliot's own background came the alternatives of art and business: his father, a prosperous brick manufacturer, would have preferred that his son devote himself to something less visionary than poetry and criticism."[10] Eliot could present realistically the effect of the contradictory attractions of the two occupations upon Colby since he had undergone the same experiences in his own life. Colby's spiritual self desires to journey blind into the unknown realms in search of his true identity.

The discovery of the identity of his natural parents has little significance for Colby. He is concerned with the quest for self-realization. Right from his infancy he has known that he is an orphan. Now it is difficult for him to adjust to the idea of having parents at this mature age. He explains to Lady Elizabeth that the absence of his mother in his infancy (when he needed her most) has taught him to live without her and now he does not need her any more. Lady Elizabeth claims that she is Colby's mother when she comes to know that Mrs. Guzzard is his aunt. The conflicting claims of parenthood made by the Mulhammers on Colby arouse his curiosity (even if it is in a small measure) to know who his parents are. Colby's quest for his parents is seen by Sarkar as Eliot's "'objective correlative' for the guilt and atonement pattern of his theme."[11] The sense of guilt emanates from Colby's realization that he "should always be haunted / By the miserable ghosts of the other parents."[12] He is caught in a whirlpool created by his desire to know his true parents and a sense of disgust with his present situation. Colby's search for his earthly parents is just a stepping stone in his quest for the Absolute Reality which is presented in *The Confidential Clerk* as his quest for the Father. His higher spiritual awareness provides the impetus for this kind of a quest. Lucasta recognizes his detachment from the material world when she explains that Kaghan and she will need each other (somewhat like Edward and Lavinia in *The Cocktail Party*), whereas Colby is the person who prefers solitude. She points out that none of them can judge Colby because he is different from their known world. Lucasta says to Colby, "We'll mean something to you. But you don't *need* anybody."[13]

Although Colby is curious about his earthly parents he says that the knowledge itself "Is unimportant, once one knows it."[14] It merely enables him to concentrate on his future. The knowledge that Herbert Guzzard, a disappointed organist, was his father satisfies Colby in a way. It helps him in making a decision to begin where his father had left off, which he explains to the others:

> [...] An ordinary man
> Whose life I could in some way perpetuate
> By being the person he would have liked to be,
> And by doing the things he had wanted to do.[15]

*The Confidential Clerk* is a play about the search for the right vocation as well as an identity, about which Colby says, "I must follow my father—so that I may come to know him."[16] The first, or physical, phase of this quest is consummated with Colby's knowledge that his father was a disappointed organist. The second, or spiritual phase begins with this discovery. It is the search for union with God the Father, which is symbolically represented by Colby's quest for the ideal music that he would like to play. Sir Claude makes one last attempt to hold Colby back in the financial world, just as Amy had tried in *The Family Reunion*. He says to Colby, "We have undergone the same disillusionment: / I want us to make the best of it together."[17] Little does he realize that their levels of spiritual understanding are not the same. Colby has made a resolution to become a church organist, which represents "the integration of religion and art on its highest level,"[18] according to Robert A. Colby. It may be said that Colby's art comes to represent his spiritual quest in symbolic terms. Colby explains to Sir Claude that he is content to follow the path which will take him closer to the heavenly Father. He says that he has love for everybody, in order to show them that he is not turning away from those who are on lower levels of spiritual awareness, explaining it in lucid terms to them:

> Now that I've abandoned *my* illusions and ambitions
> All that's left is love. But not on false pretences:
> That's why I must leave you.[19]

With his higher understanding and humility, Colby is capable of shedding illusions and false pretences which is not so easy for the others. So, he leaves their world in order to search for his identity while they try to "make the best of a bad job."[20] He seems to imply that Sir Claude's world is built on illusions, ambitions and false pretences which make this world a potential impediment to the quest for meaning of life. Colby's spiritual inclination separates him from the environment of the Mulhammer house. His quest for identity will take him away from here to Joshua Park where he will join the parish church as organist—a post which Eggerson offers him (quite significantly). Eggerson anticipates a martyrdom when he expresses that Colby will not remain an organist for long because he will become aware of a higher spiritual quest. He says that "Joshua Park may be only a stepping stone / To a precentorship! And a canonry!"[21] This is a very faint hint at Colby's possible martyrdom which is vastly different from the centrality of Becket's martyrdom in *Murder in the Cathedral*. It shows that by the time he was writing *The Confidential Clerk* Eliot had come a long way in his personal quest for self-realization. Grover Smith says that this is "not principally a play about death, but rather about life and its abundance."[22] The reason for the shift in emphasis lies in Eliot's personal quest for self-realization. Colby knows that he must act in patience in order to reach his heavenly Father. He says, "We'll cross the bridge when we come to it, Eggers."[23] His duty is to act in humility and selfless love for his Father. This love is also extended to the other characters which shows that he is not spiritually isolated from them by a sort of "gulf that yawns between Harry and his family, or between Celia and the Chamberlaynes, Peter, etc.,"[24] as Sarkar points out very appropriately. In this play the spheres of the human and divine seem to form part of a single design: a pattern which is represented by the image of the garden and the role played by music in Colby's life in particular, and the entire play in general. Jones, however, is not wholly satisfied with Eliot's portrayal of Colby's character. He alleges that "It is a deeply truthful portrait of a sensitive nature, but hardly a compelling dramatic figure. His experience lacks the urgency of Harry's or Celia's."[25] The urgency is lacking simply because Colby is confident and determined about his vocation. The occupation of being Sir Claude's confidential clerk does not attract him because he is not interested in social and material gains; the corporate world is alien to his nature. The music of the organ beckons him because it is the symbol of his quest for identity. This is noticed by Eggerson who is a highly perceptive man.

Sir Claude values Eggerson's opinion and shares the secrets about his personal affairs with him. Although he has bequeathed his official responsibilities to Colby, Eggerson is available when the Mulhammers need him (coming up to London from Joshua Park). When Browne first talked to Eliot about the new play, the dramatist had said to the director that "Eggerson is the only *developed* Christian in the play."[26] Eggerson's Christianity is symbolized in *The Confidential Clerk* by his garden which he looks after with an eagerness which is comparable with Christian faith. When Eliot calls him a "*developed* Christian," he possibly implies that Eggerson is the man who will guide Colby in his quest for identity. Eggerson is a much more realistic version of the priest-figure who appeared in Eliot's earlier plays. The playwright moulds Eggerson's character with a fine artistry that brings about the "formalist-realist synthesis" in the dramatic presentation of his role in a modern play with a drawing-room setting. Sir Henry Harcourt-Reilly (in *The Cocktail Party*) is a similar figure but his voice is authoritative. In this play, Eggerson is a friendly advisor who is called "Eggy" and "Eggers"[27] by the younger generation. His spiritual understanding enables him to detect the quester in Colby, which is revealed in his observation:

> Some day, he'll want a garden of his own. And yes, a bird bath!
> [..............................................................]
> he told me he was very fond of bird watching.
> [..............................................................]
> I read a letter in *The Times* about wild birds seen in London:
> And I'm sure Mr. Simpkins will find them if anybody.[28]

When Sir Claude entrusts him with the responsibility of promoting Colby in Lady Elizabeth's esteem, he performs the duty diligently, leaving no stone unturned. Eggerson explains to Colby that he has planned to make use of Colby's musical abilities when he presents Colby to Lady Elizabeth. His understanding of her nature helps him to arouse her interest in Colby by mentioning his inclination for music when she returns from Europe that day. Eggerson also functions as the chorus, making observations on the other characters in the play. Regarding Lucasta Angel (Sir Claude's illegitimate daughter), he points out that she is "rather flighty. But she has a good heart."[29] In the end she will marry B. Kaghan who is the only person who can handle a bundle of mischief like her. Eggerson also says that it is Kaghan, a "rough diamond. Very free and easy ways"[30] who will prove himself as successful businessman, although Lady Elizabeth dislikes him.

In the Third Act it is seen that Eggerson is wary of Mrs. Guzzard, interrogating her with the expertise of a professional detective. Even before she arrives from Teddington, he measures the various possibilities regarding her role of looking after other people's children:

> [...] perhaps Mrs. Guzzard made a profession
> of [...] looking after other people's children?[31]

This remark (which appears to be a guess when it is made) turns out to be prophetic when the interrogation reveals truths about Colby and Kaghan which the Mulhammers cannot easily accept.

Eggerson sympathizes with the Mulhammer couple when he says to Sir Claude, "I'm sure it's been a grief to both of you / That you've never had children."[32] There is an element of pain in his voice because he "had a son / Lost in action, and his grave unknown."[33] The Second World War had taken the lives of young soldiers leaving behind thousands of bereaved parents like the Eggersons. Their grief is of one sort, the Mulhammers' is of another. There was every possibility that Lady Elizabeth would be reminded of the child she lost (after she became an unmarried mother) when Sir Claude presented Colby as his illegitimate son and expressed the desire to adopt him as their child. Eliot did have something in mind (about the barrenness in the Mulhammers' lives) when he showed that the Mulhammers have no child in their wedded life although they have illegitimate children. Both men become uncertain about Lady Elizabeth's reactions to the information about Colby. When Sir Claude observes, "it's when you're sure you understand a person / That you're liable to make the worst mistake about him"[34] Eggerson answers. "I must admit there's a lot that *I* don't understand/ About my wife."[35] Their intimate conversation reveals the fact that there is a sort of hiatus in the communication between persons who are apparently very close to each other. This is one of the symptoms of the spiritual malaise of the post-war metropolitan world.

Eggerson is honest and efficient, having some practical hints for the spiritual development of all the other characters. When Colby says to him, "[...] you always contrive to think the best of everyone,"[36] he is making an observation on Eggerson's humility. It is strange that Gardner disapproves of Eliot's portrayal of Eggerson's character when she says, "The theatre exaggerates, and in the glare of the footlights Eggerson may come out as too little a person and too much a character apart."[37] It must be remembered that a successful confidential clerk never exerts himself (or herself) upon the employer. At the same time the confidential clerk must possess the ability to advise the employer whenever his (or her) opinion is sought. Therefore, it is clear from his role in *The Confidential Clerk* that Eggerson possesses the essential qualifications of such an employee which Gardner sees as "too little a person." Eliot's growing dependence on his personal secretary, Valerie Fletcher, during this phase of his life may have enabled him to create the character of Eggerson in so convincing a manner. Eggerson combines in his person the roles of the priest and chorus of Greek drama. He plays a significant part in the formation of Colby's resolution to be an organist in the Parish Church of Joshua Park. To Gardner this seems to appear as "too much a character apart." His garden is symbolic of his function in the play, integrating "the physical world of action and the spiritual world of introspection,"[38] which is pointed out by another critic. The garden protects him from "Mrs. E"[39] who represents the physical level of existence. After he retires from his post, he prefers to spend more time in his garden—his gardening becomes the symbol of Christian faith.

Eggerson's employer, Sir Claude Mulhammer is a successful financier who had been compelled by his father to enter a business which he disliked. Now he can see, with a sense of detachment, that he would have cut a sorry figure as an artist. However, he has a collection of porcelain in a private room which he visits whenever he finds time. This collection seems to represent his desire to be a potter—which was thwarted by the demands of the financial world. Now he is happy to be a successful businessman rather than a second-rate potter. He makes it out to Colby that he expects him to follow his example. However, Colby simply expresses his inability to have the filial attachment for Sir Claude which Sir Claude had for his father. He explains his position to Sir Claude:

> [...] I only wish
> That I had something to atone for!
> There's something lacking, between you and me,
> That you had, and have, and always will have, with your father.[40]

The relationship that Sir Claude aspires to on the physical plane fails to attract Colby who is seeking for identification (on the spiritual plane) with the heavenly Father. From the behaviour of the Mulhammers it appears that they are eager to have a son who will inherit their vast estate.

It is Lady Elizabeth's claim that Colby is her son which brings Mrs. Guzzard to London so that she can testify about Colby's parentage. Lady Elizabeth's spiritual understanding is on a level which is below those of Colby and Eggerson although she prides herself on her training in "mind control."[41] Her "ladylike lunacy"[42] provides delightful comedy every time she appears on the stage. When she comes to Colby's flat in the mews to get acquainted with him, she tries to talk about things that are common to both of them. In the course of their duologue Colby tells her that he is not interested in his relatives. She takes her cue from here and informs him how she disliked her parents in her childhood, had several governesses and swarms of relatives in spite of whom she felt lonely "Because they were so numerous—and so uncongenial."[43] She tries to explain the three obsessions she had at that time:

> The first was, that I was very ugly
> And didn't know it. Then, that I was feeble-minded

And didn't know it. Finally,
That I was a foundling, and didn't know it.[44]

She adds that she "*liked* to believe"[45] that she was a foundling. Later in the play, when Mrs. Guzzard discloses her guarded secret about Colby, Lady Elizabeth's words appear to be a parody of Colby's life. She becomes the "comic butt"[46] when she discovers that Kaghan is her son—a truth she cannot easily accept simply because she cannot stand him. She says to him, "Barnabas, it seems you are my son."[47] He responds to her saying, "Well, I am embarrassed. / If Lady Elizabeth is my mother [...]".[48] They realize that they have to reconcile themselves to their true relationship.

It was not an easy task to represent the elderly Mulhammers on the stage. Very able performers were necessary for the proper portrayal of their emotions and thoughts. Browne was overjoyed to have players like Ina Claire and Claude Rains for the Mulhammers since their interpretation of the characters would add a realistic dimension to the play. He writes about his experiences as the director of *The Confidential Clerk*:

> Ina Clair, most beloved comedienne of the sophisticated audience, had been away from Broadway for seven years. [...] But the idea of a T.S. Eliot play intrigued her into cabling Sherek in London. She was perfectly suited to the part of Lady Elizabeth, and Sherek had a prize that every producer in New York had been longing for.
>
> Claude Rains as Sir Claude was as great a capture.[49]

The Mulhammers appear as elderly representations of the Chamberlaynes (in *The Cocktail Party*), showing a lack of harmony in their conjugal life, which is a sort of symbolic portrayal of the spiritual disintegration that came in the wake of the Second World War. When Sir Claude says, "if you haven't the strength to impose your own terms / Upon life, you must accept the terms it offers you,"[50] he is trying to express how he and his wife can make the best of a bad job, like the Chamberlaynes. Unlike the earlier play, the parent-child relationship is an important part of *The Confidential Clerk*—both on the physical and metaphysical planes.

Lucasta Angel is Sir Claude's illegitimate daughter and Barnabas Kaghan is Lady Elizabeth's son, born before she was married. Lucasta is voracious, jovial, spending money carelessly, losing jobs and falling back on Eggerson, for financial aid, with a disconcerting familiarity. She is the first to arrive at Colby's flat after he occupies it, possibly to get friendly with him because he is the confidential clerk now. She appreciates his music and senses a sort of attraction for Colby. In her excitement she tells him that she is Sir Claude's illegitimate daughter. Colby recoils on hearing this and she feels disgusted with his apparently shabby behaviour. It is only in the final scene that she is able to recognize the reason for his conduct. She says to Sir Claude, "But if he knew that he was your son / He must have been staggered when I said I was your daughter!"[51] Sarkar describes her as a strong character who makes "oracular statements."[52] She feels that Colby neither needs nor depends on anybody. This discovery becomes a significant part of the action of the play and frustrates "the claims of the Mulhammers on Colby and adjudges the human relation on a spiritual plane. But she does it so playfully as to integrate into her character elements of farce and prophecy."[53] In the meantime, she has decided to marry Kaghan (as Eggerson had foretold) whose prospects as a financier are very bright. Unlike Colby, Lucasta and Kaghan are quite satisfied in the knowledge that they have found (and have been accepted by) their earthly parents. Since they are not blood-relations, they can even marry and lead a social life, like their parents. They can also sort things out in a spiritually barren world with a growing awareness of spirituality after coming into contact with people like Colby and Eggerson. The play seems to end on a polyphony created by the Mulhammers and their children:

LADY ELIZABETH. Claude, We've got to try to understand our children.

KAGHAN. And we should like to understand *you* [...]
I mean I'm including both of you,
Claude [...] and Aunt Elizabeth.
You know, Claude, both Lucasta and I
Would like to mean something to you [...]
if you'd let us;

And we'd take the responsibility of meaning it.
[LUCASTA *put her arms around* SIR CLAUDE]

SIR CLAUDE. Don't leave me, Lucasta.
Eggerson! Do *you* really believe her?
[EGGERSON *nods*].[54]

Lucasta's love for her father, shown by her gesture, is developed in great detail in Monica's love for Lord Claverton in *The Elder Statesman*. Therefore, Sarkar's contention that "the playwright sacrifices Lucasta at the altar of his religious 'pattern' and she is mercilessly reduced into a cold insensitive creature,"[55] loses ground because she is the character who bears the potential of the representation of divine love as portrayed through human love, in a way that reminds the auditors of Christ's love for mankind.

The character who shares the role of the priest with Eggerson is Mrs. Guzzard who resembles Athena in Euripedes's *Ion*. Athena's intervention in the lives of the mortals in *Ion* brought order and harmony in their reconciliation. In Eliot's naturalistic play, Mrs. Guzzard is the wife of the Late Herbert Guzzard and Colby's mother (but she chooses to be his aunt). Mathiessen makes an irresistible observation on the portrayal of her character when he writes that she is "a wonderful comic invention—a fairy godmother from the suburbs, with defensive middle-class dignity but a downright, no nonsense manner that soon turns the tables on all the grand people who are hanging on her words."[56] She has the strength of character to bear the impact of her revelation that Colby is *her* son and not Sir Claude's as he was led to believe. Her awareness of the consequences is expressed when she says:

When I gave up my place as Colby's mother
I gave up something I could never have back.
Don't you understand that this revelation
Drives the knife deeper and twists it in the wound?[57]

She has now lost her son as well as the scope of a social position for him towards which she had aspired over the years. Her role in the play is very significant. When Alison Leggatt asked Eliot for help in interpreting the role of Mrs. Guzzard for the London production, he told her that Mrs. Guzzard is "a mixture of Pallas Athene and a suburban house-wife."[58] Pallas Athene was fond of showing great mercy and she took pleasure in settling disputes. Eliot may have kept these attributes of the classical goddess (and her role in *Ion*) in mind when he explained Mrs. Guzzard to Leggatt.

Setting the framework according to the story of a Greek myth is a recurrent feature in Eliot's plays and *The Confidential Clerk* is no exception. This time the source is Euripedes's *Ion*, which is a tragedy with a happy ending. Fred D. Crawford mentions that Eliot had reviewed a translation of *Ion* by Hilda Doolittle for the *Criterion*.[59] The essential features of the plot of *Ion* became typical of Greek New Comedy, particularly that of Menander, to whose play, *Perikeiromene* (shorn hair), *The Confidential Clerk* appears to be indebted in a small measure. Eliot may have read Gilbert Murray's translation of this play which was published in 1942.[60] In Euripedes's *Ion*, Creusa, princess of Athens, was loved by Apollo and bore him a son whom she left in a cave under the Acropolis. Hermes carried the child to Delphi where he was reared as a servant of the temple. Later Creusa marries Xuthus but the couple was childless. So, they went to Delphi to ask for offspring and Apollo ordered Xuthus to accept the first person he met on emerging from the temple as his son. This person turned out to be Ion. Creusa became angry because she thought that her husband was cunningly adopting one of his illegitimate sons. She contrived to kill Ion but was detected. Knowing that her punishment would be death, she took refuge at the altar of Apollo, where she met the priestess who showed Creusa Ion's swaddling clothes. She recognized the child and the Goddess Athene revealed what happened. Ion returned to Athens with Xuthus and Creusa.

In Menander's *Perikeiromene* a poor merchant Pataecus exposes his twin children, a boy and a girl. The boy, Moschio, is adopted by a rich woman who subsequently marries Pataecus who adopts Moschio as his son. The girl, Glycera, becomes the mistress of a soldier, Polemo, who discovers her kissing Moschio whom she knows to be her brother although Moschio is still ignorant of this truth. Polemo cuts off Glycera's hair (which gives the play its title) in jealous wrath and she takes refuge in the house of the now wealthy Pataecus. In the course of the play she shows Pataecus some trinkets she had preserved (which she wore when she was exposed) and he identifies her as his daughter. Moschio also discovers his true identity by eavesdropping. All are reconciled and Glycera marries Polemo.

Eliot makes the necessary modifications in the plots of his sources in order to accommodate them to the naturalistic setting of his play. He splits the character of Ion into those of Colby and Kaghan; Colby goes in search of an identity (with the heavenly Father) and Kaghan is reconciled with his mother, Lady Elizabeth. However, Colby pursues the vocation of Herbert Guzzard, which is that of an organist. Guzzard owes his origin to Apollo, the god of music and poetry. In the formative stages of *The Confidential Clerk* Eliot named Colby 'Ian', but changed it as the play developed, probably because the character of Kaghan also sprang from Ion. Sir Claude owes his origin to both Xuthus and Pataecus, Lady Elizabeth to Creusa and Lucasta to Glycera. Eggerson is the choric character as well as the priest-figure, sharing the latter role with Mrs. Guzzard. When Jones says that Eliot invents a "Bastard daughter"[61] he overlooks Lucasta's similarity with Glycera although he mentions that "Agnoia or Misapprehension, the Prologue [...] tells the audience that she has caused Moschio to fall in love with Glycera so that their true relations as brother and sister may be revealed."[62]

Eliot uses anthropological myth in *The Confidential Clerk*, just as he did in the previous plays. Revelation of secrets involved anthropological rituals and ceremonies and Eliot was attracted by ancient fertility cults towards which C.H. Smith points while discussing Eggerson's role in *The Confidential Clerk*:

> Assisted by Mrs. Guzzard, another spiritual agent in disguise, he enacts the role, present in nearly all of Eliot's plays, of the cook-doctor who assists in the process of rebirth or conducts the spiritual cure. The action of the play takes place, approximately, in the spring of the year and the imagery of planting the new seed, made quite explicit in the

> many references to gardening, suggests the spring fertility ceremonies.[63]

Gardening comes to symbolize a return of fertility (also represented by the release of the life-giving waters in the Quest of the Holy Grail). Eggerson's real garden and Colby's ideal garden come very close to each other in this play, showing a maturity in Eliot's ability to bring these two planes of spiritual understanding within the comprehension of the auditors in lucid terms. This is expressed in the conversation between Lucasta and Colby in the Second Act:

LUCASTA. And *your* garden is a garden
Where you hear a music that no one else could hear,
And the flowers have a scent that no one else could smell.

COLBY. [..............................................]
You know, I think that Eggerson's garden
Is more real than mine
[.........................................................]
If I were religious, God would walk in my garden
And that would make the world outside it real
And acceptable, I think.[64]

Sarkar's observation on this is that "Nowhere else in his plays has Eliot allowed his hero to be so explicit about the relation of the human with the divine which constitutes his idea of reality."[65] This is true because the metaphor of the garden enables him to make a dramatic representation of the two planes of existence—the physical level represented by Eggerson's garden and the metaphysical level represented by Colby's symbolic secret garden. It may be said that the image of the garden has dual function in *The Confidential Clerk*. On one hand it represents physical fertility and on the other, spiritual fertility. So, by using the image of the garden, Eliot has been able to bring these two levels very close to each other. The Holy Grail is the accepted symbol of God's Grace upon mankind. Eliot uses the symbols of the secret garden and ideal music to represent the Holy Grail, making the legend of the Grail relevant in the naturalistic play in which Colby quests for his identity. He chooses the organ as the appropriate musical instrument for Colby because of its association with the Church. Colby abandons the piano when he quits his job as Sir Claude's confidential clerk and he returns to the organ when he accepts the post of organist in the parish church in Joshua Park. This time he knows who his earthly father is, so his quest for union with the heavenly Father is defined and conscious.

It is for the first time in an Eliot play that there are no martyrs (in *The Confidential Clerk)*. Donough also observes this quite correctly when he says that "Colby takes Celia's place in a less spectacular but more convincing role."[66] This is because of a shift in emphasis from the Contemplative Way to the Affirmative Way, which is not sudden but gradual; in *The Cocktail Party* Eliot emphasized the golden mean prescribed by the Buddha (because Christian mysticism does not mention a middle path between the two ways) and in this play he moves closer to the Affirmative Way.

Eliot sees that it is important to begin from the lowest level and gradually rise towards an identity with the heavenly Father. Colby begins his quest for self-realization as an organist in the church. Eggerson merely hints at the possibility of a precentorship and a canonry. Eliot's realization is clearly expressed in what he wrote to Levy in a letter dated 21 August 1954 (nearly a year after the first presentation of this play) when Levy informed him that he had taken Holy Orders:

> It seems to me a very good thing to start in Low Churchmanship and to find oneself moving towards higher churchmanship. For the movement should come from the inside, I think: so that, as one's devotion and one's theological understanding grow, the outer forms will come to appear as the right form of expression.[67]

This statement by the playwright explains his integration of the character of the exceptional person, Colby, much more closely into the pattern of ordinary life. The garden and music are the modes of expressing the inner movement towards union with God, the Father. It is because of his quest for identity as God's son that Colby is satisfied in knowing that his natural father was a disappointed organist. He follows the pattern of the Incarnation when he aspires towards divine union. At the same time his filial piety obliges him to pursue the career of his father in order to reach the goal his father had not been able to attain. So, Colby follows the pattern of Christ's Suffering for others, although he remains innocent of sin, like Christ. Eliot's personal quest for meaning of life enables him to bring Colby closer to the level of understanding of the modern audience.

Although he has committed no sin, Colby suffers from a sense of remorse for which he seeks atonement and salvation, which will be consummated with his union with the heavenly Father. His sense of remorse is somewhat akin to his creator's sense of guilt and remorse during the period that followed Vivienne's death, of which Ackroyd writes:

> Certainly the picture of him during this period is of a man haunted by guilt and remorse; it seems that he felt he had no right to happiness, and the death of his wife had only served to convince him that he had done some irreparable harm to another human being, for which he must undergo a period of punishment.[68]

In the play, Lady Elizabeth says to her husband: "It's a great mistake, I do believe, / For married people to take anything for granted."[69] It is likely that by this time Eliot had realized that Vivienne and he had made this mistake. However, in *The Confidential Clerk* the Mulhammers try to "understand each other, / No matter how late."[70] Earlier, in the First Act, Sir Claude admits:

> My rule is to remember that I understand nobody,
> But on the other hand never to be sure
> That they don't understand me—a good deal better
> Than I should care to think, perhaps.[71]

Clearly, this is the use of the third voice. Eliot's notion that he understood nobody complemented by a lifelong pattern of dismissing people (particularly women) who cared for him may have been the active agent behind his queer behaviour with Emily Hale. Mary Trevelyan proposed to him, her affection for him growing out of a long-standing friendship. His reply of 2 June 1949 made his position clear. He explained to her that "he had never wanted to marry anyone but this one woman"[72] with whom "he had been in love [...] for a great many years."[73] His affection for her "rendered any new relationship impossible for him."[74] Gordon describes Mary Trevelyan's response to Eliot's reply in this way: "She saw Eliot not as a hermit tormented by his dream of divine love but, in her more prosaic way, as a man in a prison largely of his own making"[75] because he failed to fulfill the promise of this love, the failure stemming from his habit of withdrawal from the outside world to his inner self. He used Mary Trevelyan as a prop while he tried to distance himself from Emily Hale, says Gordon,[76] only to distance her in turn. His relationship with Emily Hale could have been much more intimate if he had remained in America. So, Eliot's settling down in England had far-reaching consequences in this respect. He not only distanced himself from Emily when he was free to marry her after Vivienne's death, but married Valerie Fletcher in 1957. This strange behaviour may possibly be the result of a Puritan restraint within himself which he could never overcome in spite of his conversion to Anglo-Catholicism.

Eliot's primary concern was with the idea of the Incarnation, of Christ as "infinitely gentle / Infinitely suffering."[77] Christ was the Son of God born as the Son of Man. Eliot's quest for self-realization makes him understand that he is the son of man aspiring for identification with God, the Heavenly Father. Therefore, Eliot's spiritual movement concerns filial piety which he defines while discussing Aeneas in "Virgil and the Christian World":

> There is personal affection, without which filial piety would be imperfect; but personal affection is not piety. There is also devotion to his father as his father, as his progenitor: this is piety as the acceptance of a bond which one has not chosen. [...] But this filial piety is also the recognition of a further bond, that with the gods, [...] and without gods, or a god, regarded in this way, filial piety must perish. For then it becomes no longer a *duty*: your feelings towards your father will be due merely to the fortunate accident of congeniality, or will be reduced to a sentiment of gratitude for care and consideration.[78]

He adds that *pietas* can be explained in terms of *fatum* or destiny which is "something essentially meaningful."[79] For a man of destiny like Aeneas this is an election which is inexplicable, "a burden and responsibility rather than a reason for self-glorification"[80] implying that "the world, and the course of human history, have meaning."[81] Therefore, Colby, the Christian hero, quests for an identity which leads him to the Parish Church in Joshua Park.

While discussing the love affair between Aeneas and Dido, Eliot remarks that "Virgil, when he wrote [the lines on Aeneas's meeting with the Shade of Dido in Hades], was assuming the role of Aeneas and feeling very decidedly a worm."[82] Colby also feels the same, though in a smaller measure, when Lucasta accuses him, "I can see well enough you *are* shocked,"[83] after he recoils on hearing that she is Sir Claude's daughter. It may be said that for both Aeneas and Colby this is "a very heavy cross to bear."[84] Differentiating between 'love' and *pietas*, Eliot concludes his essay saying:

> Certainly, the love of Aeneas and Dido has great tragic force. [...] But Love is never given, to my mind, the same significance as a principle of order in the human soul, in society and in the universe that *pietas* is given; and it is not love that causes *fatum* [...]. If we are not chilled we at least feel ourselves, with Virgil, to be moving in a kind of emotional twilight.[85]

A detachment from the material world was essential because for Virgil (and for Eliot) the world had order and dignity and history had meaning. These observations on Virgil and Aeneas come from the core of Eliot's inner being, for he felt the same about himself. He showed obvious tendencies of turning away from the materialistic beckonings of the world towards an enrichment of the spiritual being, without resorting to asceticism. As part of this quest for meaning of life he went to St. Stephen's Church every morning at 6.30, all the year round, to "kneel on the cold stone floor"[86] in *pietas*. It may be said that Colby's becoming an organist in a Parish Church in the suburbs of London is the objective correlative for Eliot's personal quest for self-realization. For Colby his music is the expression of a quest for a divinely ordained identity as a son of God; for Eliot it is the music of his poetry—the form of expression.

## II

Eliot wished to devise a form of drama which could bring to the auditors his message of spiritual fertility (which is the basic theme of his plays, symbolically represented by the pattern of the Quest of the Holy Grail). From his personal involvement in the theatrical presentation of the plays he wrote, he knew that drama is purely a form of literature meant for entertainment. Therefore, he sought to provide entertainment to his auditors, living up to the expectations of the commercial theatre, and under the cover of entertainment the message he wished to convey would be blended into it with an artistic finesse. With this aim in mind Eliot used farce which belongs to the central tradition of European Comedy since the times of Aristophanes and Menander. In *The Confidential Clerk*, he uses a simple structure which employs the device of mistaken identities which is one of the salient features of farce. It was not just comedy, but simple, unalloyed humour that Eliot wished to provide for his auditors so that it would be easier for them to accept what he wished to convey to them about the spiritual development of man. C.H. Smith makes a pertinent observation about this aspect of Eliot's plays: "In response to an audience insulated against both religious meaning and poetic method, Eliot has gradually evolved a new kind of religious drama which could introduce both religion and poetry without either being immediately obvious."[87] The obvious layer of the play is formed by the humorous situations created by mistaken identities and the behaviour of Lady Elizabeth who seems to resemble a music-hall comedienne. It is with the help of this outer surface of pure laughter that Eliot wanted to bring the serious message about the necessity of spiritual development for a meaningful existence as human beings.

The simplest level on which the play operates is that of mistaken identities to which there is a hint very early in the play when Sir Claude says about Colby, "He's like me, Eggerson. The same disappointment / In a different form."[88] However, he has no evidence that Colby is his son. On the other hand, in Act Two, Lady Elizabeth gets two names from Colby: a place called 'Teddington' and a person named 'Mrs. Gizzard.' She is overjoyed by this discovery and she excitedly informs her husband that "It's Colby. Colby is my lost child!"[89] The farcical end to this mystery regarding his identity is brought about by Mrs. Guzzard who confirms Colby's parentage: "Registration of birth. To Herbert and Sarah Guzzard / A son."[90] She also informs those present during her interview in Act Three that Barnabas Kaghan is the child the Guzzards had taken in from his father who used to pay for his upbringing, but when the payments stopped the poor Guzzards had to give him away to their childless neighbours, the Kaghans. Coincidences prove that Kaghan is Lady Elizabeth's lost child. This discovery makes mother and son very uncomfortable because they have an open dislike for each other. So, the situation is both realistic (because their opinion about each other cannot change suddenly) and farcical (because of their embarrassment).

Eliot was aware of the experiments with the form of drama which Euripedes and Menander made in *Ion* and *Perikeiromene*. Where Menander's chief device is farce, Euripedes experiments with the combination of tragedy with a happy ending. Just as "Euripedes' loyalty to his tragic conceptions led him further and further from academic standards of dramatic form"[91], Eliot's loyalty to his conception of poetic drama led him onward in his quest for an appropriate dramatic form. Dobree's praise of Eliot's use of farce is appropriate when he calls the experiment "profoundly original"[92] because "he has made a serious thing out of farce"[93] by writing a farce with the texture of comedy.

The choice of *Ion* as the point of reference for *The Confidential Clerk* may have resulted from Eliot's awareness of Euripedes's experimentation with the form of drama in that play. Kitto observes that Euripedes's aim was to create an "effective stagepiece"[94] which would exploit the available resources, not for reaching out to something bigger, but for the sake of art. As a result, the dramatist, for the first time, "can devote himself completely to excellence of workmanship."[95]

Euripedes's tragic-comedies were governed by such conditions like the "absence of a tragic theme, avoidance even of an intellectual theme such as would demand serious advocacy, the adoption of a new standard of reality which, by reducing the tragic to the pathetic, made it possible to combine harmoniously into one theatrical whole a wide range of emotional effects."[96] Events become important for their dramatic value, not for revelation of character. Eliot uses the same conditions for his own purpose—that of searching for an appropriate form that can bear the theme of the quest for self-realization and for identity. The confusion that Euripedes creates around Ion's true identity is repeated by Eliot in the case of Colby. "The dramatist is, as it were, playing cat and mouse with his audience; he erects unforeseen obstacles in order to surmount them with éclat."[97] The new theatrical reality that Euripedes was aiming at brought a touch of naturalism to the *Ion*. Therefore, the *Ion* of Euripedes became the chief source for *The Confidential Clerk*, not only thematically, but also in its form. It could be said that the "formalist-realist synthesis"[98] that Eliot aimed at in his plays was also a return to the traditional European drama, for he was going back to Euripedes's methods which he used in the *Ion*. This is corroborated by what he says in 'Poetry and Drama':

> I have before my eyes a kind of mirage of the perfection of verse drama, which would be a design of human action and of words, such as to present at once the two aspects of dramatic and of musical order. [...] To go as far in this direction as it is possible to go, without losing that contact with the ordinary everyday world with which drama must come to terms, seems to me the proper aim of dramatic poetry.[99]

*The Confidential Clerk* is an amusing comedy but it carries a seriousness that can be equalled only by Eliot's earlier plays. Eliot uses the element of farce in order to make the theme of his play more easily acceptable to an audience which is secularly oriented and materialistic in its pursuits.

In order to come closer to the intellectual and psychological levels of his auditors Eliot continues with his quest for an appropriate poetic medium which would suit the nuances of the common talk of the modern English-speaking world, just as the iambic trimetre of ancient Greece and the blank verse of Elizabeth an England had done. The observations of two critics are quite relevant here. Headings says that "Eliot's concern to approach the language and rhythms of speech seems to have been marvellously achieved in this play,"[100] and Dobree says that "The verse doesn't in any way interfere, but it has its effect on the audience without their knowing it. Here, then, is perfect mastery."[101] The idiom of contemporary conversation continues to dominate the verse of *The Confidential Clerk*, the only exception being the conversation between Colby and Lucasta in the flat in the mews in Act Two. It is lit up by soft incantatory speeches which arouse the romantic instincts of the auditors, as in:

LUCASTA. How afraid one is of [...] being hurt!
COLBY. It's not the hurting that one would mind
But the sense of desolation afterwards.
LUCASTA. I know what you mean. Then the flowers would fade
And the music would stop. And the walls would be broken.[102]

In this long duologue between Lucasta and Colby in Act Two, Eliot makes use of the colloquial idiom to create this beautiful romantic atmosphere.

The playwright makes use of the duologue very often in *The Confidential Clerk*, the aim being the revelation of facts in quick succession before the auditors. The play opens with a very long duologue between Sir Colby and Eggerson on the prospects of Lady Elizabeth's acceptance of Colby as Sir Claude's son. This is soon followed by two duologues between Colby and Eggerson where the latter briefs the former on Kaghan, Lucasta and Lady Elizabeth. The First Act ends with another duologue; this time it is a long one between Sir Claude and Colby in which they lay bare their inner selves, giving us "an insight into the deeper levels of the play's pattern,"[103] as a critic points out.

Act Two opens with the romantic duologue between Colby and Lucasta which has been lauded by many critics. The director of the play, Browne, makes this valuable observation on the duologue:

> In this delicate scene, which may be reckoned the most completely poetic of his post-war drama, the rhythmic pattern is as supple as the feeling of the two young people. Yet it is none the less strong. This is the achievement of Eliot's later dramatic verse at its best: a flexibility which yet never fails to maintain the underlying wholeness of the rhythmic movement.[104]

The entry of Lady Elizabeth compels Lucasta to depart quickly with Kaghan who makes a brief visit to Colby's flat. In the duologue that ensues, Lady Elizabeth discovers that Colby's aunt's name is Mrs. Guzzard and she lives in Teddington. This discovery leads to further complications in the plot. It may be seen that in this play Eliot experiments with the use of the duologue as a dramatic device for revelations which follow in quick succession in tragicomedy. Jones appreciates the innovative use of this device and observes that "For the most part the contrivance goes unnoticed in the theatre, and it is, indeed, an acceptable part of theatrical technique so long as it does not draw attention to itself."[105]

The simple plot of *The Confidential Clerk* depends on the form of farce and the technique of the duologue. It is divided into three Acts of which the first and third are set in the Business Room on the first floor of Sir Claude's London house and the second is set in Colby's flat in the mews.

Act One serves as the exposition, as usual, and introduces all the characters (except Mrs. Guzzard) bringing out their relations to each other through their interactions. It sets the tone of the play which centres on Colby and his future.

Act Two, timed a few weeks later, shows Colby playing the concluding bars of a piece of music when the curtain rises, and Lucasta, seated in an armchair, listening to the music. The famous romantic duologue ensues as soon as the music stops. A section of the conversation between Lucasta and Colby is their discussion on the role of music:

LUCASTA. You seem so secure, to me. Not only in your music—
That's just its expression. You don't seem to me
To need anybody.
COLBY. That's quite untrue.
LUCASTA. But you've something else, that I haven't got:
Something of which the music is a [...] symbol.
I really would like to understand music,
Not in order to be able to talk about it,
But [...] partly, to enjoy it [...] and because of what it stands for.[106]

The way in which Eliot uses the symbol of music here has been possible because of his own deep understanding of the value of the music of words as a way of communicating his inmost experiences. However, the spell is broken when Lucasta says that she is Sir Claude's daughter and Colby is taken aback on hearing this. She asks him, "But why don't you say something? Are you shocked?"[107] to which he replies:

Shocked? No. Yes. You don't understand.
I want to explain. But I can't just yet.
Oh, why did I ever come into this house![108]

She cannot understand his reaction and he cannot tell her who he is (at least, at this stage of the play he knows that he is Sir Claude's son, which makes it impossible for him to have any romantic relation with Lucasta), and he is visibly shattered. But Lucasta misinterprets his queer behaviour as repulsion for an illegitimate offspring. Kaghan arrives right at this moment to find that she is distressed and he rescues her from depression. From here begins a new phase in her life—she begins to realize the significance of Kaghan's attentions towards her and she reciprocates with her growing dependence on him. Eggerson's prophecy in Act One is on the verge of coming true. He had said to Colby:

[...] She'll marry Mr. Kaghan
In the end. He's a man who gets his own way,
And I think he can manage her. If anyone can.[109]

Kaghan and Lucasta leave Colby's flat soon after the arrival of Lady Elizabeth. She discovers the names of Mrs. Guzzard and Teddington during her conversation with him. This makes her think that Colby is her child whom she had abandoned because she was an unmarried mother. When she tells her husband that Colby is her son (in the same Act), he has no alternative but to tell her that Colby is his son by Mrs. Guzzard's sister. He explains to her:

> Colby is the son of Mrs. Guzzard's sister,
> Who died when he was born. Mrs. Guzzard brought him up,
> And I provided for his education.
> I have watched him grow. And Mrs. Guzzard
> Knows he is my son.[110]

This makes it necessary for them to know the truth, for which Mrs. Guzzard has to be summoned from Teddington.

This leads to Act Three which takes place several mornings later. It is the scene of revelations; resolutions are also made in this scene. The irony in this scene emanates from the inversion of roles when Mrs. Guzzard takes over from Eggerson and conducts the proceedings regarding the identities of Colby and Kaghan. From the role that Mrs. Guzzard plays (of looking after other people's children), it is clear that Eliot made use of another recurrent feature of farce: the device of coincidences. This explains her acceptance of Lady Elizabeth's infant boy and the fact that her sister was Sir Claude's lover who bore him a son (supposedly living).

It can be seen that in this play Eliot moves closer to the ideal of integrating the form and theme of drama, for which he uses farce and the duologue as effective devices. The three stress metre is retained in *The Confidential Clerk* because it is the best for bringing the cadence of verse close to that of the contemporary speech rhythm.

## III

In *The Confidential Clerk* Eliot succeeds in forming a fine blend of the colloquial idiom and the music of words. R.A. Colby praises this achievement saying that the play is "virtually a *sinfonia concertante* in its modulations and gradations of a simple, unifying theme."[111] The playwright tries to create a musical structure in this play. He had said in 'Poetry and Drama' that a peculiar range of sensibility "can be expressed by dramatic poetry, at its moments of greatest intensity. At such moments, we touch the border of those feelings which only music can express."[112] In this play, music is the centre of the action. When the play begins, Colby is a disappointed organist who comes to work as the confidential clerk of Sir Claude, his supposed father. When it ends, he leaves Sir Claude and his job in order to become the organist of a Parish Church in the countryside. Therefore, music operates on two levels in the play—in its theme and its form.

Music comes to symbolize both the spiritual and secular levels of the play, as far as its theme is concerned, creating a harmonious co-existence of the two, which is expressed in Sir Claude's exchange with Colby in Act One:

> SIR CLAUDE. I want a world where the form is the reality,
> Of which the substantial is only a shadow.
> It's strange. I have never talked of this to anyone.
> Never until now. Do you feel at all like that
> When you are alone with your music?
> COLBY. Just the same.[113]

Lucasta says nearly the same thing about Colby's ideal music when she talks to him in his flat in Act Two:

> You know, I'm a little jealous of your music!
> When I see it as a means of contact with a world
> More real than any *I've* ever lived in.[114]

Music symbolizes the secular as well as the spiritual worlds; it also represents the difference between the levels of spiritual understanding of Colby and the others. It could be said that Eliot used the piano and organ as symbols of the secular and spiritual levels, respectively. Sir Claude provides Colby with "a really good piano"[115] in the flat so that he can play it during his leisure. It is a temptation to hold him within the bounds of the material world. The piano operates when the hammers of a keyboard strike upon metal strings. The sound of the notes of the piano are high pitched and superficial when it is compared with the deep resonance of the music of the organ which is created by compressing the air in sets of pipes with the help of a keyboard. So, the music of the piano emanates from without the strings, that of the organ comes from within the pipes. The depth of one's spiritual existence is represented by the organ—the musical instrument that accompanies the church choir during Mass.

The actual music which Colby plays represents his quest for the ideal music which he aspires after. Similarly, Eggerson's garden, which exists in reality, serves as a foil to the ideal inner garden of Colby's spiritual quest. Browne makes a pertinent observation on Eliot's use of the symbol of the garden:

> [...] in the scene between Colby and Lucasta in Act Two—which I find the most humanly scene in all his drama; [...] the image of the garden and its door, so familiar in the earlier work both lyric and dramatic, returns with a new poignancy [...].[116]

In *The Confidential Clerk* Eliot has made an innovative use of the image of the garden which has been associated in European literature with the pre-lapsarian state of man. The garden symbolizes Man's longing for the lost glory which he enjoyed in the Garden of Eden before the Fall. Smidt points out that Eliot's "frequent visions of a garden bathed in sunlight [...] obviously stands for a vision of Ultimate Reality. But it only stands for a vision: it is not the vision itself."[117] This observation is absolutely true since the image of the garden is one of the powerful objective correlatives in Eliot's work. In this play Lucasta differentiates between Eggerson's garden and Colby's inner garden when she tells Colby:

> And *your* garden is a garden
> Where you hear a music that no one else could hear,
> And the flowers have a scent that no one else could smell.[118]

The flowers are reminiscent of the Rose as the symbol of the ideal of spiritual perfection which has been referred to by

Christian mystical writings. F.C. Happold observes that like the poet and musician, the mystic has to seek for his own way of communication which is largely the language of symbols which conceal as well as reveal through their symbolism.[119] One such symbol is Dante's final vision of the Rose in *Paradiso* which symbolizes the equality with which every blessed soul experiences God's Grace, regardless of its capacity. Dante writes:

Into the gold of the eternal Rose,
    whose rank of petals fragrantly unfold
    praise to the Sun of everlasting spring.[120]

The image of the "eternal Rose" is one of the striking and oft-quoted symbols in the *Divine Comedy,* and Eliot draws directly from the Dantesque vision of the Rose in *Ash Wednesday* where the Rose and the Garden are shown as representations of the Ultimate Truth:

The single Rose
Is now the garden
Where all loves end
Terminate torment
Of love unsatisfied
The greater torment
Of love satisfied
[......................]
Speech without word and
Word of no speech
Grace to the Mother
For the Garden
Where all love ends.[121]

So, the Garden is the end of the quest—it represents God's Grace.

Right from the early poems Eliot made use of words to create images and symbols as the objective correlatives of the emotions he wished to convey; the words created various layers of meanings by being perfectly arranged in order to convey a harmony of expression. However, this harmony, like Colby's music, was merely a step towards the ideal mode of articulation towards which Eliot persevered in each succeeding play. In

*The Confidential Clerk* Eliot provides his protagonist with the necessary language of communication by the skilful use of poetic symbols, like those of music and the garden. The dramatist deliberately dilutes the poetry of the intense moments in the play in order to give the whole play the effect of a harmonious whole. The perfect measure that Eliot employs in this play makes the poetry sound like ordinary speech. This has been possible for the functional naturalism of the prosaic language which expresses, in a naturalistic style, the complex ideas in a simple manner, employing linguistic devices like digressions, as in the exchange between the Mulhammers:

LADY ELIZABETH. [...] A quiet hour a day
Is most essential, Dr. Rebmann says.
SIR CLAUDE. Rebmann? I thought it was Dr. Leroux.
LADY ELIZABETH. Dr. Leroux is in Lausanne.
I have been in Zurich, under Dr. Rebmann.
SIR CLAUDE. But you were going out to Dr. Leroux
In Lausanne. What made you go to Zurich?
LADY ELIZABETH. Why, I'd no sooner got to Lausanne
Than whom should I meet but Mildred Deverell.
She was going on to Zurich. So she said: 'come to Zurich!
There's a wonderful doctor who teaches mind control.'
So on I went to Zurich.
SIR CLAUDE. So on you went to Zurich.[122]

Interruptions are used for the same purpose as in the final Act:

EGGERSON. What an amazing coincidence!
SIR CLAUDE. That's what it is,
Unless she is mistaken [...]
LADY ELIZABETH. Now, Claude!
SIR CLAUDE. And she came to the conclusion that her child must be Colby,
So I told her the truth. But she cannot believe it.[123]

Another linguistic device is the use of questions and repetitions, as in Mrs. Guzzard's outburst:

> [...] In telling you the truth
> I am sacrificing my ambitions for Colby.
> I am sacrificing also my previous sacrifice.
> This is even greater than the sacrifice I made
> When I let you claim him. Do you think it is a small thing
> For me, to see my life's ambition come to nothing?
> When I gave up my place as Colby's mother
> I gave up something I could never have back.
> Don't you understand that this revelation
> Drives the knife deeper and twists it in the wound?[124]

All these devices make the language of poetry come closer to the colloquial idiom of the contemporary Londoners in particular and the urban English-speaking world of England and America in general.

Eliot's experience of watching the preparations for staging his previous plays helped him when he wrote *The Confidential Clerk*. Right from the beginning (when the play was entitled *Ur-Clerk*) Eliot knew what was expected of him, which Browne mentions in his discussion on *The Confidential Clerk*:

> The script of *Ur-Clerk* is already a complete play. This has never happened before. It indicates, I think, Eliot's greater self-confidence as a playwright, and also is conditioned by the fact that such a plot as he has chosen must be worked out to the end by a single mind.[125]

The harmonious effect of the play in performance was topmost in Eliot's mind when he wrote it. This is confirmed by Headings's observation when he says, "More than any of Eliot's earlier plays, it seems to have verve and vigour realizable only on the stage."[126] Therefore, a mere reading of the play would not be able to convey the message which Eliot was so keen on conveying.

In *The Confidential Clerk* Eliot moves closer to his goal of creating a form of verse dialogue which is musical on one hand and colloquial on the other—a verse that never affects the ears as drab and monotonous. The dramatic structure and characterization of this play follow those in Euripedes's *Ion* and Menander's *Perikeiromene*, blending the two and then creating something new to suit Eliot's purpose of a "formalist-realist synthesis."[127] Sarkar interprets the innovation in this way:

> The plot of Euripedes' play deals with a moral problem, to which Eliot gives a religious solution, while adopting it to the modern naturalistic setting.[128]

It is in this play that Eliot lays greater emphasis on the Affirmative Way of Christian living, for which he uses a simple plot which seems to point towards simple (or humble) living for a better understanding of the meaning of life. The Affirmative Way is treated with greater understanding in the next play, *The Elder Statesman*, the final draft of which was written after Eliot's marriage with Valerie Fletcher, his personal secretary (or, confidential clerk).

## NOTES AND REFERENCES

1. Levy and Scherle 40.
2. Levy and Scherle 41.
3. Gordon 178.
4. Eliot, *The Confidential Clerk*, CPP 462.
5. Eliot, *The Confidential Clerk*, CPP 462.
6. Spanos 227.
7. Eliot, *The Confidential Clerk*, CPP 466.
8. Eliot, *The Confidential Clerk*, CPP 466.
9. Eliot, *The Confidential Clerk*, CPP 466.
10. Grover Smith 237.
11. Sarkar, *T.S. Eliot the Dramatist* 212.
12. Eliot, *The Confidential Clerk*, CPP 491.
13. Eliot, *The Confidential Clerk*, CPP 503.
14. Eliot, *The Confidential Clerk*, CPP 513.
15. Eliot, *The Confidential Clerk*, CPP 513.
16. Eliot, *The Confidential Clerk*, CPP 516.
17. Eliot, *The Confidential Clerk*, CPP 516.
18. Robert A. Colby, "The Confidential Clerk," *Critics on T.S. Eliot*, ed. Sheila Sullivan (1973; New Delhi: Universal Book Stall, 1996) 109.

19. Eliot, *The Confidential Clerk*, CPP 517.
20. Eliot, *The Cocktail Party*, CPP 410.
21. Eliot, *The Confidential Clerk*, CPP 518.
22. Grover Smith 237.
23. Eliot, *The Confidential Clerk*, CPP 518.
24. Sarkar, *T.S. Eliot, the Dramatist* 207-08.
25. Jones 176-77.
26. Browne 167.
27. Eliot, *The Confidential Clerk* 452, 518: Lucasta calls Eggerson "Eggy," Kaghan and Colby (later in the play) call him "Eggers."
28. Eliot, *The Confidential Clerk*, CPP 446.
29. Eliot, *The Confidential Clerk*, CPP 454.
30. Eliot, *The Confidential Clerk*, CPP 451.
31. Eliot, *The Confidential Clerk*, CPP 498.
32. Eliot, *The Confidential Clerk*, CPP 448.
33. Eliot, *The Confidential Clerk*, CPP 448.
34. Eliot, *The Confidential Clerk*, CPP 450.
35. Eliot, *The Confidential Clerk*, CPP 450.
36. Eliot, *The Confidential Clerk*, CPP 457.
37. Gardner, Review, *The New Statesman and Nation*, 20 March 1954: 373-74.
38. Sarkar, *T.S. Eliot the Dramatist* 217.
39. Eliot, *The Confidential Clerk*, CPP 455.
40. Eliot, *The Confidential Clerk*, CPP 467.
41. Eliot, *The Confidential Clerk*, CPP 460.
42. Mathiessen 218.
43. Eliot, *The Confidential Clerk*, CPP 484.
44. Eliot, *The Confidential Clerk*, CPP 484.
45. Eliot, *The Confidential Clerk*, CPP 484.
46. Mathiessen 222.
47. Eliot, *The Confidential Clerk*, CPP 510.
48. Eliot, *The Confidential Clerk*, CPP 511.
49. Browne 291.
50. Eliot, *The Confidential Clerk*, CPP 462.
51. Eliot, *The Confidential Clerk*, CPP 500.

52. Sarkar, *T.S. Eliot the Dramatist* 218.
53. Sarkar, *T.S. Eliot the Dramatist* 218-19.
54. Eliot, *The Confidential Clerk*, CPP 519.
55. Sarkar, *T.S. Eliot the Dramatist* 218.
56. Mathiessen 221.
57. Eliot, *The Confidential Clerk*, CPP 515.
58. Alison Leggatt, "A Postscript from Mrs. Chamberlayne and Mrs. Guzzard," *T.S. Eliot: A Symposium for His Seventieth Birthday*, ed. Neville Braybrook, 79, in C.H. Smith 189 f.n.
59. Crawford 181.
60. Gilbert Murray, trnsl. *Ion*, by Euripedes (London: Unwin, 1942).
61. Jones 157.
62. Jones 158.
63. C.H. Smith 210-11.
64. Eliot, *The Confidential Clerk*, CPP 473-74.
65. Sarkar, *T.S. Eliot the Dramatist* 196.
66. Donough 149.
67. Levy and Scherle 49.
68. Ackroyd 305.
69. Eliot, *The Confidential Clerk*, CPP 495.
70. Eliot, *The Confidential Clerk*, CPP 501.
71. Eliot, *The Confidential Clerk*, CPP 450.
72. Eliot, letter dt. 2 June 1949, qtd. in Gordon, *Eliot's New Life* 215.
73. Eliot, letter dt. 2 June 1949, qtd. in Gordon, *Eliot's New Life* 215.
74. Ackroyd 306.
75. Gordon, *Eliot's New Life* 215.
76. Gordon, *Eliot's New Life* 199.
77. Eliot, "Preludes," CPP 23.
78. Eliot, *On Poetry and Poets* 127.
79. Eliot, *On Poetry and Poets* 128.
80. Eliot, *On Poetry and Poets* 128.
81. Eliot, *On Poetry and Poets* 128.
82. Eliot, *On Poetry and Poets* 129.
83. Eliot, *The Confidential Clerk*, CPP 477.
84. Eliot, *On Poetry and Poets* 129.
85. Eliot, *On Poetry and Poets* 131.

86. Gordon, *Eliot's New Life* 207.
87. C.H. Smith 213.
88. Eliot, *The Confidential Clerk*, CPP 446.
89. Eliot, *The Confidential Clerk*, CPP 487.
90. Eliot, *The Confidential Clerk*, CPP 514.
91. H.D.F. Kitto, *Greek Tragedy* (1939; London: Routledge, 1966) 313.
92. Dobree, "The Confidential Clerk," in Clarke, Vol. 3: 407.
93. Dobree, "The Confidential Clerk," Vol. 3: 407.
94. Kitto 314.
95. Kitto 314.
96. Kitto 320.
97. Kitto 321.
98. Sarkar, *T.S. Eliot the Dramatist* 3.
99. Eliot, *On Poetry and Poets* 87.
100. Headings 193.
101. Dobree, "The Confidential Clerk", in Clarke, Vol. 3: 416.
102. Eliot, *The Confidential Clerk*, CPP 474.
103. Sarkar, *T.S. Eliot the Dramatist* 209.
104. Browne 303-04.
105. Jones 173.
106. Eliot, *The Confidential Clerk*, CPP 474.
107. Eliot, *The Confidential Clerk*, CPP 477.
108. Eliot, *The Confidential Clerk*, CPP 477.
109. Eliot, *The Confidential Clerk*, CPP 455.
110. Eliot, *The Confidential Clerk*, CPP 489.
111. Colby, "The Confidential Clerk," in Sullivan 111.
112. Eliot, "Poetry and Drama," *On Poetry and Poets* 87.
113. Eliot, *The Confidential Clerk*, CPP 464.
114. Eliot, *The Confidential Clerk*, CPP 474.
115. Eliot, *The Confidential Clerk*, CPP 446.
116. Browne 281-82.
117. Smidt 205.
118. Eliot, *The Confidential Clerk*, CPP 473.
119. Happold 68-69.

120. Dante, *Paradiso,* Canto XXX, ll. 124-26, *The Divine Comedy* 356.
121. Eliot, *Ash Wednesday*, CPP 91-92.
122. Eliot, *The Confidential Clerk*, CPP 459-60.
123. Eliot, *The Confidential Clerk*, CPP 497.
124. Eliot, *The Confidential Clerk*, CPP 515.
125. Browne 254.
126. Headings 192.
127. Sarkar, *T.S. Eliot The Dramatist* 3.
128. Sarkar, *T.S. Eliot the Dramatist* 213.

# 6 The Final Quest for Realization through Love

The final draft of *The Elder Statesman* was written after Eliot's marriage with Valerie Fletcher in January 1957. The printed text of the play is preceded by a lyric poem dedicated to her. The carefully chosen words of the poem are a prelude to the scenes between Monica and Charles in the play. These scenes underwent drastic changes, from what Eliot had originally conceived them, owing to a change in his attitude to human love, the redeeming nature of which came to represent divine love. Although Eliot still returned to Greek drama for the foundation of his play (this time it is Sophocles's *Oedipus at Colonus*), the superstructure comprised the naturalistic setting he had been using from *The Family Reunion* onwards. Accordingly, the chief characters belong to the elite society of London.

The protagonist, Lord Claverton, who is the elder statesman of the play, finds at the end of a successful social life that as an individual he is completely alone. This stifling loneliness makes him physically ill and mentally insecure. As a result, he turns for security and assurance towards his only hope, his daughter Monica. Since Lord Claverton disapproves of the lifestyle of his son, Michael, he does not even contemplate sanctuary with Michael. Monica surpasses her father's expectations because of her experience of selfless love which she shares with Charles Hemington, her fiancé. Her love for her father is reminiscent of Shakespeare's heroines in his last great plays.

It may be said that Eliot's personal quest for meaning of life reached a sort of consummation in *The Elder Statesman* for it appears that he could as if hear the laughing ripples of the flowing life-giving waters which fertilized the barren land of the Fisher King in the legend of the Holy Grail. He seems to have understood that selfless love could redeem the spiritually barren modern metropolitan civilization.

Lord Claverton, who represents this world, comes to realize after his retirement at sixty that most of his life has been spent in the pursuit of a materialistic career which was initially designed by his father. He became a successful politician and businessman. However, this success failed to fulfill him. His worldly pursuits had prevented an awareness of the spiritual vacuum that had always occupied his inner being. But on withdrawing from active social life he is overwhelmed by it and he tries to describe it in cognizable terms:

> If I had the energy to work myself to death
> How gladly would I face death! But waiting, simply waiting,
> with no desire to act, yet a loathing of inaction.[1]

This awareness initiates him into a quest for self-realization. So, when a visitor arrives, Lord Claverton decides to see the man himself in spite of his physical weakness. The visitor who announces himself as Frederico Gomez, is actually Fred Culverwell, a crony from his university days. Gomez draws the graph of Lord Claverton's rise from Dick Ferry to the position of the elder statesman:

> When we were up at Oxford, you were plain Dick Ferry.
> Then when you married, you took your wife's name
> And became Mr. Richard Claverton-Ferry;
> And finally, Lord Claverton. [...][2]

This revealing graph of Lord Claverton's ambitiousness helps to define his present state, which, according to the scheme of the play, will lead him towards an awareness of the futility of a materialistic existence. Gomez points out that Lord Claverton has got to pretend, even to his own self, that he is a success — he has to "make up his face before he looks in the mirror."[3] But after his retirement from his business and politics he feels tired of pretending. He seeks peace and prepares to go for a rest-cure to Badgley Court, a home for convalescents modelled on a hotel.

This place is a reminder of the sanatorium in *The Cocktail Party*. The idea of a hospital as a place for cure is also used by Eliot in 'East Coker' where he writes:

> The whole earth is our hospital
> [..............................................]
> Wherein, if we do well, we shall
> Die of the absolute paternal care
> That will not leave us, but prevents us everywhere.[4]

Men suffer for their sins on Earth which also serves as a place where men are treated for their sufferings, through the process of atonement in order to reach salvation. Badgley Court seems to be a microcosmic representation of this idea. Once he is there, Lord Claverton becomes acutely aware of his inner and outer selves. The outer self is accustomed to "prepare a face to meet the faces that you meet."[5] The inner self is critical, judging the outer self impartially. Lord Claverton ponders on an increasing awareness of the presence of his inner being and its significance in his quest for peace in self-realization:

> What is this self inside us, this silent observer,
> Severe and speechless critic, who can terrorize us
> And urge us on to futile activity,
> And in the end, judge us still more severely
> For the errors into which his own reproaches drove us?[6]

Lord Claverton's crisis is summed up very neatly by C.H. Smith when she says, "Neither the pretense of a public personality nor the isolation of a private life filled with unconfessed secrets can give a sense of identity."[7]

Even Badgley Court, fails to provide Lord Claverton with the required protection. Not long after his arrival at this place, Mrs. Carghill intrudes into his privacy, shattering the little complacency which he had managed to regain, by making comments (like Gomez) on his posing as an elder statesman. The mask of a successful man which Lord Claverton wears fails to take in Gomez and Mrs. Carghill: People who have known him when he was just a young man in the university. They appear as representatives of his youthful weaknesses—"ghosts"[8] from his past, as he calls them—who have come to haunt his present and future. They influence Michael, Lord Claverton's son, who is the image of his father as he was in his youth. Lord Claverton recalls his own misadventures and is worried about Michael making the same mistakes like running over a man on the road or getting involved in an affair with a young woman. Michael assures his father that he will not do anything slipshod. Michael's unconcern for his father's anxiety shows that with each passing generation men become more materially oriented, losing the ability to control their desires and show compassion. Lord Claverton cannot resist a warning to Michael for he knows that his son lacks the experience he has acquired over the years. He says to Michael:

> Those who flee from their past will always lose the race.
> I know this from experience. When you reach your goal,
> Your imagined paradise of success and grandeur,
> You will find your past failures waiting there to greet you.[9]

He loves his children and he does not want them to suffer like him by being tormented by the ghosts from their past. The insolent Michael strikes unconsciously upon a very tender spot in his father's inner being when he retorts, saying that he wonders whether his father has lived up to the standards he wishes to set for Michael. The son seems to represent a retrospective alter-ego of Lord Claverton who realizes that he must learn to be humble. He tries to articulate his understanding when he says:

> What I want to escape from
> Is myself, is the past. But what a coward I am,
> To talk of escaping! And what a hypocrite!
> A few minutes ago I was pleading with Michael
> Not to try to escape from his own past failures :
> I said I knew from experience. Do I understand the meaning
> Of the lesson I would teach? Come, I'll start to learn again.
> Michael and I shall go to school together.[10]

In *The Family Reunion*, Harry had tried to escape from his past and Agatha (playing the role of the priestess) had pointed out to him that the clue to the way of his liberation lay in his ability to face the past. A humble submission to the reality which is not "the pastness of the past, but of its presence"[11] and to selfless love and trustworthiness is what Lord Claverton aspires after. At the same time he feels uncertain and turns to his daughter for support and encouragement. His spiritual quest will help him to emerge from the infernal torment he has been suffering as a result of an inability to expose his true self before Monica. He comes to see that the only way towards salvation lies in unmasking himself before Monica—he plucks up courage to lay bare his real self. This is a very important step in his quest and it enables him to face squarely "malicious, petty"[12] people like Gomez and Mrs. Carghill, Lord Claverton admits that the camouflage of a complacent man of the world originated during his difficult marriage. The pretence has continued till the present when he realizes that the pseudo-self, which he has created and nurtured, must be shattered. Monica encourages him towards a disclosure of the secrets which torment him, cajoling him with her comforting words, "It is time to break the silence! Let us share your ghosts!"[13] Lord Claverton feels that he has failed to respect the love which people have shown him. He has abused this expression of love which may have been "vain and selfish."[14] "Here, beyond doubt," says Sarkar, "Eliot has struck a new note in his work. This apotheosis of love is a proof of Eliot's maturity of vision and his liberal understanding of life."[15] In making an uninhibited confession before Monica, whose selfless love for him represents God's Love for mankind, Lord Claverton is relieved of the burden of sin which he has been carrying so long. This confession is the first and most important step towards his spiritual liberation. When Charles asks him how long he will endure this persecution, his reply is precise and brief: "To the end, The place and time of liberation / Are, I think, determind."[16] The persuasions of Lord Claverton and Monica were unsuccessful in changing Michael's decision to go off to San Marco. He prefers to trust Gomez whom he has known for only a few hours. In his self-analysis, Lord Claverton holds himself responsible for such a course of events:

The many many mistakes I have made
My whole life through, mistake upon mistake,

The mistaken attempts to correct mistakes
By methods which prove to be equally mistaken.[17]

He will not be here when Michael returns after five years or so. Like the great sages and mystics he is near his spiritual illumination. So, he is not afraid of death, which he knows is imminent. The cognizance that he is very close to gaining knowledge of the Absolute Truth gives him a sense of peace which "ensues upon contrition / When contrition ensues upon knowledge of the truth."[18] He is happy and contented after recognizing the depth of Monica's selfless love for him. His self-realization arrives with his comprehension of the enormous capacity of love—that between father and daughter, brother and sister, or lovers, as the earthly illustrations of the greater Love of God. The illuminating knowledge of love enables him to declare:

I have been brushed by the wing of happiness.
And I am happy, Monica, that you have found a man
Whom you can love for the man he really is.[19]

Spanos points out that "In progressing from the acknowledgement of sin to the discovery of redemptive love, Lord Claverton achieves authentic sacramental vision,"[20] which enables him to "become genuinely Everyman. The way of redemption has become the human way of the love of created things."[21] Eliot's ability to depict the redeeming quality of love shared by human beings in *The Elder Statesman* obviously draws upon his personal bliss in happy matrimony to which the dedicatory poem, *To My Wife*, bears testimony.

Instead of foisting the staggering personality of the elder statesman upon his children (which he has been doing till now), he begins to appreciate their opinions. This freshly acquired ability develops rapidly as he voluntarily rejects his masked self—the one which Michael also rejected. He experiences satisfaction in the knowledge that Monica and Charles share a strong love for each other. Their selfless love has taught him *damyata* or control—the ability to restrain from excesses and to keep away from the fires that devour the spiritual self. Eliot wrote in 'East Coker':

I said to my soul, be still, and wait without hope
For hope would be hope for the wrong thing;
wait without love
For love would be love for the wrong thing; there is yet faith
But the faith and the love and the hope are all in the waiting.
Wait without thought, for you are not ready for thought:
So the darkness shall be light, and the stillness the dancing.[22]

Once Lord Claverton reaches this stage in his quest, he is prepared to die, for the physical death will qualify the spirit for union with God. However, he does not forget to discharge the vital act of responsibility—that of giving away his daughter in marriage—not in reality, but symbolically. He says to Charles, "I leave Monica to you. Look after her, Charles, / Now and always."[23] Knowing that he will not live to see them married, this is the best that he can do as a loving father. Earlier in the play, Charles had commented on Lord Claverton's possessiveness over Monica, but now Lord Claverton wishes to leave the lovers to themselves. Charles notices this change, describing it to Monica in terms of the image of the Rose Garden:

It's as if he had passed through some door unseen by us
And had turned and was looking back at us
With a glance of farewell.[24]

It seems that Lord Claverton has entered the secret garden Colby spoke about in *The Confidential Clerk*. It is with the protagonist of *The Elder Statesman* that Eliot has at last been able to reach the garden of bliss—his symbol of Paradise. As far as Lord Claverton is concerned, the journey from Inferno, through Purgatorio, to Paradiso, has been consummated. He dies off-stage, under the peace of a beech tree. Monica articulates her understanding of her father's death by saying that "In becoming no one, he has become himself."[25] The physical existence becomes immaterial after Lord Claverton has attained self-realization. Charles explains Monica's strange feeling of happiness at the moment of her father's death, saying that "The dead has poured out a blessing on the living."[26] They are satisfied at their level of spiritual awareness, after witnessing Lord Claverton's peaceful passage. Sarkar seems to contradict himself when he says that Lord Claverton lacks "spiritual anguish"[27] and yet he says that "The spirit of Everyman who gains his spiritual freedom through confession in the medieval Morality *Everyman* is present in Lord Claverton,"[28] which could not be possible without spiritual anguish. He finds salvation and peaceful death only after an uninhibited confession before his daughter. When Hewes asked Eliot in an interview if he read himself in the title role of *The Elder Statesman*, the playwright replied:

> There are three ingredients in all one's characters: (1) observation of other people, (2) pure invention, and (3) something of oneself which includes what Yeats calls the anti-self. But I find that the character is most effective when one is least conscious of putting oneself into it.[29]

It appears that Eliot does put some of himself into the character of Lord Claverton, whom he employs in his own quest for self-realization.

Lord Claverton's past has been spiritually arid and a critic points out that "Senor Gomez and Mrs. Carghill dramatize Lord Claverton's corrupted youth—his deceitfulness and corruption both in friendship and in love. They are merely the voices of his own conscience reminding him of his sinful past."[30] Fred Culverwell, the youth from the provinces, came to Oxford and found himself in the company of the affluent and worldly-wise Dick Ferry who inculcated expensive tastes in Fred. After they parted, Fred was forced to indulge in illegal activities in order to provide himself with means to retain those habits to which he had been addicted; eventually he was imprisoned for forgery. On being released he went away to San Marco and assumed the name of Frederico Gomez, the surname, like Lord Claverton's, belonging to his wife. He explains the surprise visit he pays Lord Claverton as "A natural desire"[31] to trust an old friend. However, Lord Claverton does not want to have anything to do with him. The enforced renewal of friendship veers on the sinister, proving to be quite exhaustive for the already weak Lord Claverton. When the peer points out that Gomez has "been engaged in systematic corruption"[32] Gomez explains that San Marco is a place where corruption is inbred. San Marco is the inverse-Utopia of corruption, selfishness and overambitiousness—the ideal place for most post-war people. In order to achieve his selfish ends, Gomez adjusts to the society of San Marco because he has the advantage of having no spiritual values of his own. He claims that he is capable of adjusting with the morality of every kind of society. He takes Michael away to San Marco, tormenting Lord Claverton by making Michael do the very things his father disapproves. Lord Claverton helplessly witnesses how Gomez entraps the inexperienced Michael.

Senor Gomez is one ghost from Lord Claverton's past and Mrs. Carghill is another. Dick Ferry had had a brief but intense affair with Maisie Batterson. She fell in love with him but was bought off by Dick's father because she was an impediment to his political future. The young girl kept his letters to her in safe custody; now she carries their photostat copies with her. She is none other than Mrs. Carghill who is overjoyed to find him at Badgley Court. He is surprised to discover that she has a better knowledge of his nature then he thinks. She has a hand in Michael's departure with Gomez. The way in which these two characters plot the separation of Michael from his father, seems to anticipate the manoeuvres of certain characters in the plays by Harold Pinter.

Grover Smith finds fault with the characterization of this play, saying that "The liberation of Gomez and Mrs. Carghill from ghostly torment forms no part of Eliot's dramatic design."[33] *The Elder Statesman* was streamlined in order to retain the unity of the theme of Lord Claverton's quest for self-realization. An emphasis on the development of these characters and their relation with the protagonist would lead to unnecessary diversions and complications in the plot.

Mrs. Carghill (alias Maisie Batterson, alias Maisie Montjoy of revue fame) may be said to have borrowed traits partially from Emily Hale and Vivienne Eliot. The revelation that Dick Ferry and Maisie Batterson went "in a punt / On the river"[34] is reminiscent of Eliot and Vivienne's punting on the Thames during their whirlwind courtship. The letters which Mrs. Carghill retains remind us of Emily Hale's careful preservation of Eliot's letters to her, which she gave to Princeton on hearing of his second marriage. She retrieved the letters on Eliot's expiry in 1965 in order to destroy them, "her allegiance to Eliot, and by extension his wife, for whom she now felt sympathy"[35] getting the better of her concern for Eliot-scholars. Herein lies the difference between the nobility of Emily's selfless love and Mrs. Carghill's stratagem of psychologically blackmailing Lord Claverton.[36]

In contrast to Gomez and Mrs. Carghill's selfish designs Eliot presents the young lovers who are prepared to postpone their marriage in order to enable Monica to look after her father. When the play begins we discover that the young lovers, Monica and Charles, have returned from a shopping spree and Charles expresses his possessiveness over Monica, whose company he wishes to enjoy exclusively. He is a fond lover who resents Lord Claverton's intrusions into his affair with Monica. He points out to her that he believes she loves him (this is the first time he says this). In turn she confirms her love for him. The love they share is strong, full of understanding and trust. This expression of love is portrayed by Eliot, says Gordon, with an "unexpected sensitivity to a woman's feeling: he understood the shock of abandoning her reserve, the loss of self in the surrender, the daring of that moment of life-long commitment which is too great to absorb."[37] The vistas of love that originated from his second marriage enabled Eliot to make Monica say to Charles:

> How did this come, Charles? It crept so softly
> On silent feet, and stood behind my back
> Quietly, a long time, a long time
> Before I felt its presence.[38]

Charles is also transformed in the warmth of their mutual love; he feels that they are changing each other as they discover new territories in love. In this private world of theirs the meanings of "*I* and *you*"[39] are different. The lovers exist simultaneously in two worlds—the private and the public—the former comes to have a bearing on the latter. However, Monica's consciousness of her father's dependence on her gives rise to her decision to hold her marriage in abeyance. Lord Claverton surrenders himself to Monica's innocent and selfless love for him and lays bare his true self before her and Charles:

> I've had your love under false pretences.
> Now, I'm tired of keeping up those pretences,
> But I hope that you'll find a little love in your heart
> Still, for your father, when you know him
> For what he is, the broken-down actor.[40]

This is for the first time that he tries to emerge from the pseudo-persona, removing the mask that he had voluntarily put on to advance to the top of the materialistic world. Unlike the elder statesman, Charles has nothing to hide from Monica. Eliot makes use of Lord Claverton's progress towards self-realization to demonstrate the redeeming qualities of love. The love shared by the young lovers inspires him to confess:

> If a man has one person, just one in his life,
> To whom he is willing to confess everything—
> [.............................................................]
> Then he loves that person, and his love will save him.[41]

Monica, who acts as a priestess in the process of her father's spiritual development, encourages him towards a confession saying that she is not afraid of learning anything about Charles or him. Her compassion and understanding help him when he finds it hard to speak about his shady past. She argues that those who love him have the right to know the secrets about him which Gomez and Mrs. Carghill already know. When Michael departs with these persons who hate Lord Claverton, in order to go to San Marco, Monica tries to console her distraught father by explaining to him that "it's not you and me he rejects, / But himself, the unhappy self that he's ashamed of."[42] Eliot had brought about many subtle changes in the dialogue of *The Elder Statesman* (particularly after his marriage) and Browne quotes a speech from ES/ICR, by Monica which is of "much importance to the author"[43]:

> Father, you know I would give my life for you.
> Oh, how silly that phrase sounds!
> But any words are silly between people like ourselves
> Who've no vocabulary for love—but is there one

For love within a family? That love is most in silence,
For it's the love on which all else depends, the love
That stands between us and destruction, love that's lived in
But not looked at, love within the light of which
All else is seen, the love within which
All other human love finds speech—the speech of lovers
Whose speech is nonsense: but the love of father and daughter,
Father and son, brother and sister,
We do not look at that—it is the sight with which we look,
This love is silent, and the deeper is the love
The deeper is the silence. What can I say to either of you?
Except that love within a family should be indestructible?
We're of one blood. If those of one blood quarrel
Then blood is shed, the temple is destroyed,
Whatever Michael has done, Father,
Whatever Father has said, Michael,
You must forgive each other, you must love each other.[44]

Wherever Michael goes, Monica will continue to love him. She tries desperately to bring about a reconciliation between her father and brother. The strength of the love she shares with Charles enables Monica to love her family in spite of the shortcomings of her father and brother. Jones underlines Eliot's objective in *The Elder Statesman* where "the hero finds his salvation not by rejection of ordinary, family life, but by purification of his life within the family. There is, in fact, a new emphasis upon the efficacy of love."[45] Love helps to bridge the divide created by the incapacity to articulate the inmost experiences. Monica understands that her father's death is inevitable. She is secure and happy in Charles's love for her. In the first draft of the play, Eliot had designed a much more explicit duologue between Angela (later changed to Monica) and Charles:

ANGELA. Oh Charles, I love you, love you to the point of agony.
CHARLES. And your love for me, as it unfolds itself,
Discloses new depths, so reveals to me
More and more, the depth of mine for you.

ANGELA. And more frightening intensity.
CHARLES. So love given
Responds to love received.[46]

The alterations in the final draft show that the dramatist wished to make use of expressiveness (and less articulation) in order to convey the impact of Lord Claverton's death upon Monica. Grover Smith regards Charles as a "rather colourless young man"[47] who is no match for Monica. One must not forget that Eliot made use of the relation between Monica and Charles as a plank to highlight the relation between her and Lord Claverton, which he wished to emphasize. The touching warmth of the love shared by the young lovers prompts Crawford to remark that "*The Elder Statesman* differs from earlier plays in its recognition and acceptance of human love as an image of divine love, as opposed to *The Family Reunion*'s rejection of human love."[48] It is to emphasize the filial attachment in this play that Eliot uses the substructure of the mutual love of Monica and Charles.

The playwright must have carefully studied Shakespeare's treatment of the love between father and daughter in his mature comedies, *Pericles* (Pericles and Marina), *Cymbeline* (Cymbeline and Imogen), *The Winter's Tale* (Leontes and Perdita) and *The Tempest* (Prospero and Miranda), which becomes manifest in his essay on John Ford:

> In Shakespeare's plays, this is primarily the recognition of a long-lost daughter, secondarily of a wife; and we can hardly read the later plays attentively without admitting that the father-and-daughter theme was one of very deep symbolic value to him in his last productive years: Perdita, Marina and Miranda share some beauty of which his earlier heroines do not possess the secret.[49]

The same could be said of Lord Claverton and Monica in Eliot's last play. In *The Elder Statesman,* as in Shakespeare's last plays, the young lovers pave the way towards the protagonist's understanding of the meaning of life. Colby's filial piety had taken him on a quest for an identity on a purely spiritual level. But, Monica's love appears to suggest Christ's Love for mankind—He was the Son of God who walked on the Earth, being the exemplar of love and compassion. Although Monica's filial devotion is based on Christianity, there is a hint of Antigone's loyalty to her father, Oedipus, as represented in Sophocles's play, *Oedipus at Colonus.*

Sophocles's play, written some time before his death in 406/5 B.C., recounts the tale in which Oedipus wandered to Colonus, blind and banished from Thebes, attended by his daughter, Antigone. On learning that Colonus is the place where he is destined to die, he appeals to Theseus, King of Athens, seeking permission to remain there against the warnings of the local inhabitants. Theseus is glad because Oedipus's spirit will be a protection for Athens. Oedipus's dead wife, Jocasta's brother and regent of Thebes, Creon, arrives to take him away to Thebes so that the benevolence of his spirit may be enjoyed by the Thebans after his death. Theseus intervenes and Creon's stratagem falls apart. Polynices, Oedipus's son, arrives, seeking his favour in his struggle for power against his brother, Eteocles. Angry with their foolish ambitions Oedipus curses them saying that they will kill each other. Peals of thunder warm him of the time of his death. He withdraws to a lonely spot and dies in the presence of Theseus alone.

Where Antigone vows to carry out the burial rites of her brother Polynices in the ancient Greek play, Monica takes upon herself the responsibility of awaiting Michael's return from San Marco in Eliot's naturalistic drama. C.H. Smith discerns an advancement in Eliot's use of the myth in his play, for he moulds the symbolic ritual of the classical play, weaving it into the texture of his own work, thereby enriching its significance. There is no externalized battle between the old dying god and the new one as in anthropological myth. In *The Elder Statesman* "the struggle is now enacted within the hero himself, who represents both the sin-laden old god and the reborn new god."[50] The complex, yet subtle, treatment of the character of Lord Claverton is definitely a landmark in Eliot's development as a dramatist. The play is a milestone in his personal quest for meaning of life which he appears to have set about behind the façade of the persona of Lord Claverton.

It is within the formalist framework of the ritual of rejuvenation that Eliot makes Lord Claverton undertake his quest for self-realization which, in Christianity, is symbolized by the Quest of the Holy Grail. Eliot had been experimenting in all his previous plays with the means of attaining an understanding of the meaning of life, but none of them were wholly satisfying. *The Elder Statesman* opened new vistas before Eliot, in Lord Claverton's epiphanic realization of the redemptive power of love—his daughter's love, representing divine Love on Earth. In the Turnbull Lectures, Eliot said that "The difference between human and divine love is much subtler than any of the distinctions which modern psychologists are able to draw."[51] Krishna Sen discerns a congeniality between the ancient non-Christian play by Sophocles and Eliot's modern Christian play. The Greek play is "amenable to Christianity. For Sophocles' play deals with suffering, self-knowledge, acceptance of the divine will, and the sacralization of the profane."[52] Eliot's own reflections on the Christian element in his plays have been expressed in a letter to Browne, dated 8 December 1959:

> I have always been most desirous to see ordinary plays *written* by Christians rather than plays of *overtly* Christian purpose. In the theatre, I feel that one wants a Christian mentality to permeate the theatre, to affect it and to influence audiences who might be obdurate to plays of directly religious appeal.[53]

The fundamental significance of Holy Communion in Eliot's perception seems to be reflected in his presentation of the complete and perfect love shared by Monica and Charles. Her devotion to her father helps him to perform a penitential confession before his daughter where she performs the role of the priestess, initiating Lord Claverton's yearning for the higher Communion with God. It appears that in *The Elder Statesman*, Eliot wished to emphasize the redeeming quality of love as exemplified by Christ, for which he underplayed the idea of Original Sin because the idea of the Incarnation automatically implies an awareness of the Fall and its consequences.

Lord Claverton's cognizance of the significant relation between the past and present—that the past comes to have a bearing on the present and is altered by the present—seems to be analogous with the poet's perception in 'The Dry Salvages' where he writes, "It seems, as one becomes older, / That the past has another pattern, and ceases to be a mere sequence."[54] The individual's role in this pattern must follow Krishna's counsels to Arjuna (in the *Gita*) regarding selfless action (*nishkamakarmayoga*), which Eliot hints at in 'The Dry Salvages':

> And do not think of the fruit of action.
> Fare forward.[55]

Such action entails selflessness, dedication and humility. Monica's devotion for her father follows this idea. Matthews comes close to an understanding of this philosophy when he says that "Old men who have been poets, like Eliot, may try to leave us some word—a hint of what they have found, or think they were on the way to finding. What was it that Eliot tried to tell us? That it's all right, really—or that it *will* be all right, when the fire and the rose are one?"[56] Eliot seems to come to a realization that the soul can be possessed of the divine union in spite of the love of created beings, or rather, by virtue of the love of created beings—the love that betokens the ideal love of God for mankind.

In the interview with Hewes Eliot said that "For the Christian there is that perpetual living in paradox. You must lose your life in order to save it. One has to be otherworldly and yet deeply responsible for the affairs of this world. One must preserve a capacity for enjoying the things of this world such as love and affection."[57] In what He did and said, Christ brought about a new understanding of God, His Father, who is loving and compassionate, unlike the Old Testament God who is aloof and angry. In *The Elder Statesman*, Eliot emphasized the divine love which Christ came to personify, setting the example of selfless love and compassion for His fellow beings.

The significance of Christ's love for mankind dawned on Eliot with a new meaning in the aftermath of his experience of conjugal love which he shared with Valerie, his second wife, whom he married in January 1957. Subsequently, the love-duets in the First (completed on 9 February 1958) and Third Acts were revised thoroughly. "More rewriting and cutting went on in the new love scenes than in any other part of the play,"[58] reports Eliot's biographer, Gordon. The relation between Monica and Charles in the play seems to stand for something Eliot looked for in his own married life. Eliot married Valerie when he was sixty-eight and she, thirty. She provided a warm security of love for him enabling him to encounter the myth which his admirers gradually created around his personality. The resultant confidence helped him to look back at his past with a certain detachment. He even commented on his "own shabby behaviour"[59] by using the third voice of Mrs. Carghill in the play:

> Men live by forgetting—women live on memories.
> Besides a woman has nothing to be ashamed of:
> A man is always trying to forget
> His own shabby behaviour.[60]

He is possibly reflecting on his conduct with Emily Hale. To marry his secretary, "in a wedding that seemed to her almost as hurried and clandestine as the first"[61] was too much for Emily to bear. "The man of whom she had been so sure now stood revealed as a rather unpleasant stranger."[62] Gordon attempts an explanation regarding Eliot's rejection of Emily:

> Though Eliot still loved Emily Hale, he preferred not to see her, and felt embarrassed and unhappy when he did. He was irritated by a man's sense of being in the wrong, and decided that they now had little in common. It was, he repeated, 'too late.' He had become fixed, however much he rebelled against the fixing. He was burnt out, a haunted man.[63]

Seen in the light of his second marriage, this explanation appears to be partial and inadequate. Faced with the embarrassment of being connected with Eliot in spite of his disregard for her, Emily wrote to him on 12 September 1963, "I think you will be aware that for me to consider my life as important because of its relationship to you—a noted world figure—is very difficult."[64] Unlike Mrs. Carghill in *The Elder*

*Statesman*, Emily had no intention of using their relationship, about which she says, "[...] from *my own* feeling for shielding the association with the man I loved, and who I think, did not respond as he should have to my long trust, friendship and love."[65] Gordon refers to the period preceding Eliot's second marriage as "another phase of hollowness"[66] when his secretary, a young woman, came forward to rejuvenate the aged poet. It seems strange that he did not seek psychological asylum with the faithful friend who had helped him to recover from the period of hollowness that followed his broken marriage with Vivienne. The Unitarian constraint, the inability to take the first step—the "daring of a moment's surrender"[67]—possibly hindered Eliot's advancement towards marrying the woman who waited faithfully for him all her life. It seems that the contrition Eliot experienced at this mature age came to cast a shadow on the character of Lord Claverton whose reminiscence of his affair with Maisie Batterson appears to harp on Eliot's relation with his former wife:

> In fact we were wholly unsuited to each other,
> Yet she had a peculiar attraction
> Which no other woman has had. [...][68]

On approaching his twilight years Eliot appears to have reached a position from where he could look back at his past, analyzing his own behaviour with people who trusted him and whom he had possibly let down miserably. When Matthews defines *The Elder Statesman* as Eliot's "final public statement [in which he] allowed himself, although with perfect propriety and no risk of being unmasked, a few lines which, if not from the heart, are assuredly from the memory,"[69] he has certain speeches by Lord Claverton in mind, like the one he makes before Monica and Charles in the Third Act:

> [...] How open one's heart
> When one is sure of the wrong response?
> How make a confession with no hope of absolution?
> It was not her fault. We never understood each other.
> And so we lived, with a deep silence between us,
> And she died silently. She had nothing to say to me.[70]

This seems to be a clear reference to Eliot's conjugal life with Vivienne, whose obsession with her own interests prevented him from opening up his inner self before her. Lord Claverton's self-analysis is much more explicit in the first manuscript draft of the play:

> That was not her fault. I should have risked it
> Rather than live, as we lived, in silence [...][71]

The unfulfilled expectations of Eliot's first marriage had to wait for a long time until Valerie Eliot brought a sense of completeness to the elderly poet. Her devotion was like the life-giving waters that rejuvenated the barren land of the Fisher King. In the interview with Hewes, Eliot said that "Love reciprocated is always rejuvenating. Now I feel younger at seventy than I did at sixty. Any man if he is alone becomes more aware of being lonely as he ages. An experience like mine makes all the more difference because of its contrast with the past."[72] This unprecedented happiness enabled Eliot to describe his seventy-first birthday as "the happiest birthday I've ever known."[73]

It is towards the end of his life-long quest for self-realization that Eliot comes to experience the saving quality of love—that which is cradled in the tender affection of a daughter for her father—Antigone's for Oedipus, Miranda's for Prospero, Monica's for Lord Claverton, and perhaps, Valerie's for Eliot (which seems to be an intricate blend of filial and conjugal love). Gordon indicates that "Slowly, he came to recognize that this contained young woman was a disciple with the absolute dedication of an ideal heir. It was a special kind of devotion, the rare, voluntary bond between generations."[74] Eliot's satisfaction is reported by Gordon when she cites a minor incident at a social gathering, where, after Mrs. Eliot was "borne off to be introduced, Gwen Watkins sat down next to Eliot and said: 'You look as if, like Dante, you'd passed into paradise.' 'Exactly,' he said, pleased."[75] The marriage, conducted in a very private ceremony at 6.15 in the morning of 10 January 1957 at St. Barnanabas' Church in Kensington, came as a surprise to Eliot's closest friends. Soon after his marriage he declared, "I'm the luckiest man in the world."[76] Ever since he left America, Eliot missed the loving care of his mother and elder sisters. This resulted in a sense of insecurity and a sort of anxiety that was reflected in his works. Therefore, it was quite natural that the knowledge of conjugal bliss which he experienced after his second marriage, would cast a light upon the play Eliot was writing at that time. He describes the conscious artistry that was involved in the writing of the final draft of *The Elder Statesman*:

> I can only say that it is a very different play (and I believe a better one) for so much of it having been written during this last year, than it would have been if I had finished it before our marriage.[77]

In his first full-length play, *Murder in the Cathedral*, Eliot had emphasized the way of the martyr. Here, in *The Elder Statesman*, he upholds the way of the Affirmative, which shows that the dramatist has made a spiritual journey in which he has come to see the idea of the Incarnation in a new light which makes it more meaningful and fulfilling. Eliot expresses his contentment in a letter to Levy:

> It is a wonderful thing, my dear William, to be happily married, and a very blessed state for those who are called to it, even at my age. I have a very beautiful and good and sensitive wife, with a very good mind as well and a passionate love of poetry—she has everything to make me happy, and I am humbly thankful.[78]

Earlier, in 'East Coker,' Eliot has harped on the notes of conjugal love as portrayed in the poetry of the seventeenth century metaphysical poets:

> The association of man and woman
> In daunsinge, signifying matrimonie—
> A dignified and commodious sacrament.
> Two and two, necessarye coniunction,
> Holding each other by the hand or the arm
> Which betokeneth concorde. [...][79]

The intentional retention of the seventeenth century spellings by Eliot links his poem with the tradition of the metaphysical poets, who used various conceits to represent the fresh entity that was created by the union of selfless lovers (which was usually spiritual). The dedicatory poem, *To My Wife*, expresses this very idea in a more direct (even unabashed) manner:

To whom I owe the leaping delight
That quickens my senses in our wakingtime
And the rhythm that governs the repose of our sleepingtime,
    The breathing in unison
Of lovers [...][80]

This public admission of his love for his wife makes his most simple play the most personal, too. As a sequel to the dedicatory poem, Charles says to Monica at the end of the play:

So that now we are conscious of a new person
Who is you and me together.[81]

*The Elder Statesman*, complemented by the poem *To My Wife*, seems to demonstrate how Valerie's selfless love helped Eliot to arrive at "The awful daring of a moment's surrender."[82] At the same time, the dedicatory poem tempts the reader to pause for thought about the openness of the poet who had been using personae and voices in all his poetical works until he came to this short personal poem. It seems to be incongruous with the tenor of his previous accomplishments. Charles and Monica, in this play, represent the fulfillment of selfless love shared by lovers, a relationship which Eliot would possibly have liked to have with his wife, who was over thirty years younger than him. Eliot's dependence on Valerie seems to be reflected in Lord Claverton's reliance on Monica. It could be said that the relationship of the Eliot couple is a combination of filial and conjugal love which gave the private individual in Eliot a sense of satisfaction which came to illuminate the relationship between Charles, Monica and Lord Claverton.

## II

The unprecedented bliss of his second marriage was the driving force behind Eliot's successful creation of the characters of Lord Claverton, Monica and Charles, whose speeches ring with a delicate harmonious lilt. It was as though Eliot could hear the music of the spheres like Dante did in his vision of Paradise, as he expressed a sense of peace and tranquility that man experiences on being one with God and His creation—"the love that moves the sun and the other stars."[83] Dante combined in his epic the Franciscan world of love with the Dominican world of law in the interpretation of a spiritual world. In the *Paradiso* "his stupendous genius apprehends and shows to us a beatific vision in which the symbolic systems of all great mystics [...] are included and explained."[84] The music of the spheres which Dante envisions in *Paradiso* represents an organic unity. Eliot chose to express his recently acquired state of conjugal bliss in the play which he was writing during this time, by organizing *The Elder Statesman* in a way which would represent the movements of a symphony. In a talk broadcast in 1936, Eliot had pointed out that:

> To work out a play in verse is to be working like a musician as well as like a prose dramatist: it is to see the thing as a whole musical pattern. [...] The verse dramatist must operate on you on two levels at once, dramatically, with the characters and plot. The requirements for a good plot are just as severe as for a prose play. [...] It is fatal for a poet trying to write a play, to hope to make up for defects in the movement of the play by bursts of poetry which do not help the action. But underneath the action, which should be perfectly intelligible, there should be a musical pattern which intensifies our excitement by reinforcing it with feeling for a deeper and less articulate level. Everybody knows that there are things that can be said in music that cannot be said in speech. And there are things which can be said in poetic drama that cannot be said in either music or ordinary speech.[85]

This speech, delivered about a year after he wrote *Murder in the Cathedral*, expresses Eliot's concern with the music of poetry which he strove towards in every successive play he wrote, coming closest to it in *The Elder Statesman* in which he portrayed his own experience of reciprocated love.

The first of the three Acts of the play is set in the drawing-room of Lord Claverton's London home, at four o'clock in the afternoon. It begins with a long duologue between Monica and Charles which conveys their deep love for each other; this duologue is a significant dramatic device which Eliot employs in order to lay the foundation of the play. The conversation that ensues on Lord Claverton's entry, reveals him as a sensitive, dissatisfied and broken-down man. An element of the sinister is introduced in the First Act when Gomez returns from San Marco and contacts Lord Claverton, posing as a threat to the already distraught elder statesman, by talking primarily about certain unpleasant experiences during their acquaintance in their youth. When the Second Act opens, it is seen that Monica and Lord Claverton are rapt in conversation on the terrace of Badgley Court—for the first time in Eliot's plays a scene is set in the open, quite significantly. About a fortnight's stay in this modified 'hotel' has enabled him to regain much of his confidence, which is evident from his happiness on this bright sunny morning. But as soon as Monica leaves him to take a walk around the grounds of Badgley Court, Mrs. Carghill intrudes upon his privacy and introduces herself as Maisie Batterson, the girl with whom he had a brief affair in his youth. In a very sophisticated manner she informs him that she still carries copies of his letters to her—the intention to shatter his sense of security becomes temporarily successful. Mrs. Piggot's timely intervention prevents her from plaguing Lord Claverton any further. Soon there is a conversation between Lord Claverton, Monica, Michael, Gomez and Mrs. Carghill which ends with Michael's decision to go abroad. The Third Act shows Monica seated on the terrace in the late afternoon of the following day when Charles enters, followed soon after by Lord Claverton who had been "Standing under the great beech tree."[86] The enlightenment which he gains on witnessing the love of his daughter and her fiancé, enables him to unravel before them the mystery about his past which Gomez and Mrs. Carghill were trying to intensify and complicate. This disclosure paves the way for his self-realization. So, when Michael comes back with Gomez to declare that he is going to San Marco with Gomez, Lord Claverton tries his best to prevent Michael's association with Gomez. However, he has to give in to his son's wishes and realizes that he wanted to "mark out a narrow path for Michael"[87] which was a wrong step. He accepts Michael's departure as part of the design and dies in peace under his favourite beech tree. This simple and clear plot-structure is a reflection of the transparency of Eliot's own understanding of personal bliss.

For Eliot, poetic drama meant drama with a spiritual design—a pattern that represented an intrinsic order in a way similar to that in Dante's *Paradiso*. In the Preface to Wilson Knight's *The Wheel of Fire*, Eliot pointed out that the task of the poetic dramatist is different from that of the poet or the prose dramatist, for "his pattern is more complex and more dimensional. [...] Shakespeare's pattern was more complex, and his problem more difficult, than Dante's."[88] He explains his observation elaborately:

> The genuine poetic drama must, at its best, observe all the regulations of the plain drama, but weave them *organically* (to mix a metaphor and to borrow for the occasion a modern word) into a much richer design. But our first duty as either critics or 'interpreters,' surely must be to try to grasp the whole design, and read *character* and *plot* in the understanding of this subterrene or submarine music.[89]

The music of poetry does not imply merely that of the verse; it is the effect of the play as a whole. Characterization, plot, action, form and dialogue—all these harmonize into the music of a play like Shakespeare's *The Tempest* or Eliot's *The Elder Statesman*. Eliot had noticed that "In the plays of Shakespeare a musical design can be discovered in particular scenes, and in his more perfect plays as wholes. It is a music of imagery as well as sound. [...] the properties in which music concerns the poet most nearly are the sense of rhythm and the sense of structure."[90] When he was writing *The Elder Statesman*, Eliot had come a long way since he made these observations, in 1942, on the last great poems of Shakespeare in which that great dramatist was "experimenting to see how elaborate, how complicated, the music could be made without losing touch with colloquial speech altogether, and without his characters ceasing to be human beings [...] the music of verse is not a line by line matter, but a question of the whole poem."[91] This is exactly the impetus that instigates the musicality of *The Elder Statesman*, a play that expresses Eliot's love for his wife through the shared bond between Lord Claverton, Monica and Charles. The love-duets, like the one in the beginning of the Third Act, are the first of their kind in Eliot's plays:

> MONICA. Oh Charles, how I've wanted you! And now I *need* you.
> CHARLES. My darling, what I want is to know that you needed me.
> On that last day in London, you admitted that you loved me,
> But I wondered. […] I'm sorry, I couldn't help wondering
> How much your words meant. You didn't seem to need me then.
> And you said we weren't engaged yet […]
> MONICA. We're engaged now
> At least *I'm* engaged. I'm engaged to you for ever.[92]

The music that flows through the colloquialism of this duologue of sophisticated twentieth century lovers seems to draw inspiration from Shakespeare's *The Tempest* which, according to Knight, is "the most perfect work of art and the most crystal act of mystic vision"[93] in English literature. The expression of love in Eliot's play gives the impression of being stimulated by the profession of love in the duologue between Miranda and Ferdinand in the Third Act of *The Tempest:*

> MIRANDA. I am your wife, if you will marry me;
> If not, I'll die your maid: to be your fellow
> You may deny me; but I'll be your servant,
> Whether you will or no.
> FERDINAND. My mistress, dearest;
> And I thus humble ever.
> MIRANDA. My husband then?
> FERDINAND. Ay, with a heart as willing
> As bondage e'er of freedom: here's my hand.
> MIRANDA. And mine, with my heart in't:[94]

Their words illustrate humility, innocence, faith, purity, simplicity and sincerity. Eliot discloses in the Introduction to *The Wheel of*

*Fire* that while he was mulling over the late plays of Shakespeare as a separate group, he was impressed by what seemed to him "important and very serious recurrences of mood and theme"[95] for the plays had a pattern which was in addition to its verbal beauty—a pattern which was elaborate, extensive and inscrutable. In *The Elder Statesman,* Eliot achieves a verse and mode of articulation which, while imitating the rhythms of contemporary speech and distinguishing one character from another, naturally insinuates into that speech a multivocal effect of feeling and meaning. He was aiming at a sublime state of humility which he finally reaches in the "subterranean music that reaches beyond the limits of words"[96] in *The Elder Statesman.* The "music from a farther room"[97] which Prufrock heard but failed to reach because of his state of spiritual barrenness has at last become the encompassing symbol of *The Elder Statesman*, in which human love, as the earthly manifestation of divine love, comes to rejuvenate Lord Claverton and paves the way for his self-realization.

### III

Poetic language is itself an incarnation of thought arising from the conditions of the deepest self-realization, attempts to objectify which lead to a visionary conception explained by an unmetaphoric and crystal-clear style found in the *Divine Comedy, The Tempest* and, it may be said, *The Elder Statesman.* In his essay on Dante, Eliot concludes that "gradually we come to admit that Shakespeare understands a greater extent and variety of human life than Dante; but that Dante understands deeper degrees of degradation and higher degrees of exaltation."[98] According to Eliot, who draws inspiration from both, Shakespeare and Dante complement each other, and Eliot throws light upon their works saying, "And take the *Comedy* as a whole, you can compare it to nothing but the *entire* dramatic work of Shakespeare."[99] Eliot found that for Dante the language had to be direct, every single word and line had to be completely disciplined to the purpose of the whole, for in this austere and bare style, every word had to be 'functional', leaving no scope for vagueness or imprecision.[100] He sums up Dante's influence on him under two points: first, he says that "Dante seems to me to teach that the poet should be the servant of his language, rather than the master of it."[101] And second, the "*width of emotional range*"[102] which Dante displays in the *Divine Comedy*—it is a quest for articulation which Eliot analyses:

> The Divine Comedy expresses everything in the way of emotion, between depravity's despair and the beatific vision, that man is capable of experiencing. It is therefore a constant reminder to the poet, of the obligation to explore, to find words for the inarticulate, to capture those feelings which people can hardly even feel, because they have no words for them; and at the same time, a reminder that the explorer beyond the frontiers of ordinary consciousness will only be able to return and report to his fellow-citizens, if he has all the time a firm grasp upon the realities with which they are already acquainted.[103]

It is obvious that the two points are inseparable. Therefore, a poet must have extensive linguistic resources in order to engender in the readers a comprehension of the ordinarily incomprehensible. This task turns out to be challenging when the poet is writing for the theatre, where the mode of communication is audio-visual. The efforts to make the characters in his plays articulate the deepest experiences of spiritual awareness, which Eliot made in each successive play, give the impression of reaching a sort of consummation in *The Elder Statesman*. There is a serenity in this play which seems to be absent in the earlier plays. *The Elder Statesman* comes closest to Eliot's desired goal of precise articulation. He writes in detail about the conscious use of poetry in the theatre in 'The Three Voices of Poetry':

> In a verse play, you will probably have to find words for several characters differing widely from each other in background, temperament, education, and intelligence. You cannot afford to identify one of these characters with yourself, and give him (or her) all the 'poetry' to speak. The poetry (I mean, the language at those dramatic moments when it reaches intensity) must be as widely distributed as characterization permits; and each of your characters, when he has words to speak which are poetry and not merely

> verse, must be given lines appropriate to himself. When the poetry comes, the personage on the stage must not give the impression of being merely a mouthpiece for the author. Hence the author is limited by the kind of poetry, and the degree of intensity in its kind, which can be plausibly attributed to each character in his play. And these lines of poetry must also justify themselves by their development of the situation in which they are spoken.[104]

From this interpretation of the role of the poet in the theatre it is clear that Eliot was conscious about restricting himself while undertaking his quest for articulation because his chosen form of literature—drama—has no place for any kind of excess which destroys the world the play creates for itself, and thereby for its auditors. This does not mean that the use of imagery was debarred from use in poetic drama. Hulme has justified the use of imagery in literature in *Speculations*:

> Creation of imagery is needed to force language to convey over this *freshness* of impression. The particular kind of art we are concerned with here, [...] can be defined as an attempt to convey over something which ordinary language and ordinary expression lets slip through.[105]

Eliot seems to abide by this statement in the use of symbols and imagery in his poetic plays. The images of the Garden and Rose of Light prevail upon the play—they are hinted at when Lord Claverton says to Monica and Charles, "I've only just now had the illumination / Of knowing what love is."[106]

The enlightenment that Eliot received after his second marriage enabled him to add an extra dimension, maybe a different one, to the scenes in which Monica and Charles's love for each other is expressed. The manifestation of this love in *The Elder Statesman* stands in sharp contrast to its absence in the previous plays by Eliot. The drafts of the love scenes underwent maximum revision (in the light of Eliot's firsthand experience of conjugal bliss), in order to accommodate an enveloping tenderness hitherto absent in the tone of the play. For Eliot it was a difficult task, considering the fact that "underneath this diffident and subdued exterior, there was a passionate temperament which he was generally at pains to control."[107]

A hint at Eliot's awareness of the immense value of precise articulation is made in one of the drafts in which Monica says to Charles:

> But words are only the final way of knowing;
> I loved you, long before the words came;
> And when the words came, I knew that I'd loved you
> For a very long time....[108]

Besides the lyric duets for Monica and Charles's voices, Eliot also had soft music for Monica's compassionate words to her father, particularly when he needed her assurance after his self-revelation:

> Oh Father, I've always loved you,
> But I love you more since I have come to know you
> Here, at Badgley Court. And I love you the more
> Because I love Charles.[109]

On the other hand, the rhythm of Lord Claverton's final speech in the play, after he comes to possess an understanding of the meaning of life, seems to synchronize with the cadence of the peace chant which comprises the formal ending to an *Upanishad*: "Shantih shantih shantih,"[110] when he says:

> I've been freed from the self that pretends to be someone;
> And in becoming no one, I begin to live.
> It is worth while dying, to find out what life is.[111]

In his twilight years Eliot came to have an understanding of human love that brought about a complete awareness of the significance of the idea of Incarnation as an epitome of love and compassion. The satiation which he experienced in the wake of his marriage with Valerie enabled Eliot to reflect his newly discovered bliss in *The Elder Statesman*, the play which bears testimony to his arrival at a proximity of his envisaged ideal of form and articulation. He has been able to mould a form of verse drama which accommodates the colloquial idiom and yet retains the austerity of poetry in the theatre. *The Elder Statesman* helps us to arrive, "through a fusion of impressions [...] at a personal understanding of an intense experience of life."[112] This perception of love comes to unite the human and divine in the idea of the Incarnation which represents the supervision of the divine over the human.

## NOTES AND REFERENCES

1. Eliot, *The Elder Statesman,* CPP 530.
2. Eliot, *The Elder Statesman,* CPP 533.
3. Eliot, *The Elder Statesman,* CPP 540.
4. Eliot, "East Coker," *Four Quartets*, CPP 181.
5. Eliot, "The Love Song of J. Alfred Prufrock," CPP 14.
6. Eliot, *The Elder Statesman,* CPP 545.
7. C.H. Smith 219.
8. Eliot, *The Elder Statesman*, CPP 569.
9. Eliot, *The Elder Statesman*, CPP 561.
10. Eliot, *The Elder Statesman*, CPP 565.
11. Eliot, "Tradition and the Individual Talent," *The Sacred Wood* 49.
12. Eliot, *The Elder Statesman*, CPP 569.
13. Eliot, *The Elder Statesman*, CPP 570.
14. Eliot, *The Elder Statesman*, CPP 571.
15. Sarkar, *T.S. Eliot the Dramatist* 248.
16. Eliot, *The Elder Statesman*, CPP 573.
17. Eliot, *The Elder Statesman*, CPP 578.
18. Eliot, *The Elder Statesman*, CPP 581.
19. Eliot, *The Elder Statesman*, CPP 581.
20. Spanos 235-36.
21. Spanos 231.
22. Eliot, "East Coker", CPP 180.
23. Eliot, *The Elder Statesman*, CPP 582.
24. Eliot, *The Elder Statesman*, CPP 582.
25. Eliot, *The Elder Statesman*, CPP 583.
26. Eliot, *The Elder Statesman*, CPP 583.
27. Sarkar, *T.S. Eliot the Dramatist* 231.
28. Sarkar, *T.S. Eliot the Dramatist* 228-29.
29. Henry Hewes, "Eliot on Eliot: An Interview," in Clarke 3: 428.
30. Sarkar, *T.S. Eliot the Dramatist* 229.
31. Eliot, *The Elder Statesman*, CPP 535.
32. Eliot, *The Elder Statesman*, CPP 533.

33. Grover Smith 248.
34. Eliot, *The Elder Statesman*, CPP 549.
35. Gordon, *Eliot's New Life* 185.
36. Eliot's letters to Hale were with Princeton when *The Elder Statesman* was being written. So, the threat of publication lured over their very private correspondence.
37. Gordon, *Eliot's New Life* 244.
38. Eliot, *The Elder Statesman*, CPP 526.
39. Eliot, *The Elder Statesman*, CPP 526.
40. Eliot, *The Elder Statesman*, CPP 569.
41. Eliot, *The Elder Statesman*, CPP 568.
42. Eliot, *The Elder Statesman*, CPP 580.
43. Browne 325.
44. Eliot, ES/ICR, in Browne 325.
45. Jones 192-93.
46. Eliot, ES/III MS, in Browne 336.
47. Grover Smith 247.
48. Crawford, in Weintraub 183.
49. Eliot, "John Ford," *Selected Essays* 194-95.
50. C.H. Smith 231.
51. Eliot, "Turnbull Lectures," *The Varieties of Metaphysical Poetry* 276.
52. Krishna Sen, *Negotiating Modernity: Myth in the Theatre of Eliot, O'Neill and Sartre* (Culcatta: Minerva, 1999) 75.
53. Eliot, letter dt. 8 Dec. 1959, to Browne, in Browne 312.
54. Eliot, "The Dry Salvages," *Four Quartets*, CPP 186.
55. Eliot, "The Dry Salvages," *Four Quartets*, CPP 188.
56. Mathews 170.
57. Hewes, in Clarks 3: 428.
58. Gordon, *Eliot's New Life* 250.
59. Eliot, *The Elder Statesman*, CPP 551.
60. Eliot, *The Elder Statesman*, CPP 550-51.
61. Matthews 149.
62. Matthews 149.
63. Gordon, *Eliot's New Life* 179.
64. Gordon, *Eliot's New Life* 183.
65. Gordon, *Eliot's New Life* 186.

66. Gordon, *Eliot's New Life* 188.
67. Eliot, "What the Thunder Said," *The Waste Land*, CPP 74.
68. Eliot, *The Elder Statesman*, CPP 572.
69. Matthews 168-69.
70. Eliot, *The Elder Statesman*, CPP 570.
71. Eliot, ES/III MS, in Browne 332.
72. Eliot, in an interview with Hewes, *Saturday Review* 13 Sept. 1958, in Ackroyd 326.
73. Rupert Hart-Davies, letter dt. 28 Sept. 1958, to George Lyttleton, *The Lyttleton Hart-Davies Letters*, Vol. 3, in Ackroyd 326.
74. Gordon, *Eliot's New Life* 243.
75. Gordon, *Eliot's New Life* 248.
76. Robert Giroux's report, in Ackroyd 321.
77. Eliot, qtd. in Gordon, *Eliot's New Life* 246.
78. Eliot, letter to Levy, in Levy 98-99.
79. Eliot, "East Coker," CPP 177-78.
80. Eliot, *The Elder Statesman*, CPP 522.
81. Eliot, *The Elder Statesman*, CPP 583.
82. Eliot, "What the Thunder Said," CPP 74.
83. Dante, *The Divine Comedy*, Paradiso, canto XXXIII, verse 42, trans. Mark Musa (1971; New York: Penguin, 1984) 394.
84. Evelyn Underhill, *Mysticism* (1911; London: Methuen, 1977) 551.
85. Eliot, "The Need for Poetic Drama," *The Listener*, 25 Nov. 1936: 994.
86. Eliot, *The Elder Statesman*, CPP 568.
87. Eliot, *The Elder Statesman*, CPP 581.
88. Eliot, Introduction, *The Wheel of Fire*, by Knight xix.
89. Eliot, Introduction, *The Wheel of Fire*, by Knight xix.
90. Eliot, "The Music of Poetry," *On Poetry and Poets* 36-38.
91. Eliot, "The Music of Poetry," *On Poetry and Poets* 36.
92. Eliot, *The Elder Statesman*, CPP 567.
93. G. Wilson Knight, *The Crown of Life* (London: Methuen, 1947) 28.
94. William Shakespeare, *The Tempest*, III. i. 83-90 *The Complete Works of Shakespeare,* ed. and Introduction by Peter Alexander (1951; London: Collins, 1985)15.
95. Eliot, Introduction, *The Wheel of Fire*, by Knight xviii.

96. Spanos 245.
97. Eliot, "The Love Song of J. Alfred Prufrock," CPP 14.
98. Eliot, "Dante," *Selected Essays* 252.
99. Eliot, "Dante," *Selected Essays* 264.
100. Eliot, "What Dante Means to Me," *To Criticise the Critic and Other Writings* 129.
101. Eliot, "What Dante Means to Me," *To Criticise the Critic and Other Writings* 133.
102. Eliot, "What Dante Means to Me," *To Criticise the Critic and Other Writings* 134.
103. Eliot, "What Dante Means to Me," *To Criticise the Critic and Other Writings* 134.
104. Eliot, "The Three Voices of Poetry," *On Poetry and Poets* 92-93.
105. Hulme 163.
106. Eliot, *The Elder Statesman* 581.
107. Ackroyd 324.
108. Eliot, ES/Edin., in Browne 331.
109. Eliot, *The Elder Statesman*, CPP 581.
110. Eliot, "What the Thunder Said," CPP 75.
111. Eliot, *The Elder Statesman*, CPP 582.
112. Sarkar, *T.S. Eliot the Dramatist* 257.

# Conclusion

The poetry and plays of Eliot show how, in the process of his development as a dramatist, he has been able to evolve his own idiom of drama, and the manner in which he treats the theme of quest in each work, establishes him as a dramatic artist. His consciousness regarding the social responsibility of the artist can be discerned from his critical writings, in which he spoke about his objectives. However, he was also aware of the problems of creative writing and the chances of a disparity between his aims and achievements. "It would appear," he wrote, "that while I maintain the most correct opinions in my criticism, I do nothing but violate them in my verse; and thus appear in a double, if not double-faced role. I feel no shame in this matter."[1] Eliot explains himself saying, "I should say that in one's prose reflexions one may be legitimately occupied with ideals, whereas in the writing of verse one can only deal with actuality."[2] By adopting and treating his theme very deftly and carefully and by incorporating his personal experiences to these, Eliot has evolved a drama which arises from his personal obligation to life. His consciousness of tradition and the role of the poet in his society helped Eliot to seek for an appropriate form to express the quest for self-realization which is undertaken by the various characters in his plays. This quest for form and expression can be traced back to his earliest poetic endeavours. Although Eliot was aware of the presence of the past in the work of an artist, he also knew that the poet was obliged to cater to the needs of his society. Therefore, as an artist, he felt that he would have to create a form of expression which could communicate his ideas and experiences to his readers and auditors. He aimed at bringing about "poetic naturalism"[3] in his poetry and plays. Each successive play is an advance towards the creation of a form of verse whose rhythm comes closer to the idiom of the everyday intercourse of the modern urban civilization. By the time Eliot wrote *The Elder Statesman*, the poetry of his plays sounded like prose and yet possessed a cadence and music which was unparalleled in modern English drama. The poetry enabled him to use meaningful symbols which could not be used in prose; these symbols served as the necessary equipment for implying layers of meaning which could reach the various cognitive levels of his readers and auditors. This technique brings Eliot close to Rabindranath Tagore, another Nobel Laureate, who could effortlessly convey various layers of meaning in his poems.

Eliot had begun writing plays with an emphasis on the Way of the Contemplative, but his view of life changed with his growing experiences in his personal life, which enabled him to emphasize the Way of the Affirmative in *The Elder Statesman*. In doing so, he came to express his realization that selfless love follows the example of Christ's Love for men because it represents God's Love for mankind. Sarkar refers to this aspect of Eliot's poetry and compares it with Tagore's works: "In fact there is a personalized vision in Tagore's *Gitanjali* which is very close to Eliot's representation of his personal vision of the eternal through the temporal. It is a sort of religious awareness that binds the creator with the creature."[4] The symbolic representation of divine love in the love shown by Monica to all her loved ones, especially Lord Claverton and Charles, resembles Tagore's understanding of the meaning of life.

In the Hibbert Lectures which Tagore delivered at Manchester College, Oxford, in 1930 (when he was about sixty-nine), he explained his understanding of the religion of Man as one in which "the infinite became defined in humanity and came close to [Tagore] so as to need [his] love and co-operation."[5] The understanding of the Infinite as his "Jivandevata", or as he calls it, "the Lord"[6] of his life, helped him to realize the relation of the individual with the Supreme One as one of love which is the most perfect relationship for, according to Tagore's translation of a *baul* song, "Love is the magic stone that transmutes by its touch greed into sacrifice."[7] Tagore conceives that though the Supreme Man is "infinite in his essence, he is finite in his manifestation in us the individuals."[8] A basic similarity can be discerned in the cognitive faculties of the two poets (particularly in their mature years). For Eliot, as for Tagore, the gradual development in his understanding of the meaning of life was closely linked with an expression of his inmost experiences in his creations. Tagore's observation is equally relevant where Eliot's perception is concerned: "We suffer from the sense of sin, which is the sense of discord,"[9] and Tagore goes on to explain his comprehension of music:

> For music, though it comprehends a limited number of notes, yet represents the infinite. It is for man to produce the music of the spirit with all the notes which he has in his psychology and which through inattention or perversity, can easily be translated into a frightful noise. In music man is revealed, and not in a noise.[10]

Therefore, it may be said that both poets undertook a lifelong quest for the form of poetry which would express their experiences to their readers and auditors, and one aspect of this search was that for a cadence in their poetry which only music can produce. Eliot writes about this music: "The music of poetry, then must be a music latent in the common speech of its time. And that means also that it must be latent in the common speech of the poet's *place*."[11]

Just as Eliot used the conversational idiom of the contemporary urban world in his creative works, he used the voice of the interlocutor to convey his perceptions. He created the personae in his poems, and later, the characters in his plays, for the purpose of undertaking his personal quest for self-realization. These dramatis personae helped the creator in Eliot to achieve a certain amount of detachment on one hand, allowing the private individual in him to be involved in the action of the drama, on the other. Eliot wrote about this in his essay on Ben Jonson:

> The creation of a work of art, we will say the creation of a character in a drama, consists in the process of transfusion of the personality, or, in a deeper sense, the life, of the author in the character. [...] The ways in which the passions and desires of the creator may be satisfied in the work of art are complex and devious.[12]

After making some early excursions into the realm of drama, Eliot wrote plays for the theatre.

The first of his complete plays, *Murder in the Cathedral*, is a study of Becket's religious quest for self-realization through suffering and death which represents a complete and conscious surrender to the Will of God. Eliot wrote the play for performance at the Canterbury Festival of 1935—a totally religious occasion. This gave him the scope for the dramatic presentation of a theme already treated by Tennyson, but in a different manner. Eliot deals with the theme of martyrdom, showing the professional precision of a dramatist by rendering the storyline with a double interest where the auditor is concerned. The first is the important aspect of martyrdom which is a Christian concept intended for the auditors who have an orientation in Christian doctrine. The other necessitates murder (for the martyrdom to take place) which adds the colour of a detective thriller to the play, making it equally enjoyable to the secular auditors. However, Eliot remained dissatisfied with the formal sombreness of *Murder in the Cathedral* and when he ventured to write the next play, he intended to bring the characters closer to the world of his auditors.

Eliot's persistent search for an effective mode of communication in poetry led him to the theatre—a highly beneficial association—for which he wished to create an individual form of drama that is capable of integrating poetry and drama as well as restoring the lost links between religion and drama, thereby making the great tradition of religious and poetic drama relevant for the contemporary urban audience. Eliot found that in the absence of an accepted centre of adherence and lack of faith in the essential values of life, there is a corresponding reflection in the mode of communication which turns out to be ill-equipped for conveying the complicated situation in which the modern city-dweller finds himself. However, he preferred to work within the accepted norms of literature, for which he would "take a form of entertainment and subject it to the process that would leave it a form of art."[13] In this respect, the music-hall comedian was his ideal. He decided upon a scheme of synthesis of realism and formalism in his plays as a daring experiment towards the orientation of the theatre on traditional lines.[14] Eliot did not approve of the excessive realism which he considered to be the "great vice of English drama from Kyd to Galsworthy."[15] He was aware of the competition he was going to face in the commercial theatre where all other dramatists preferred prose as their form of expression, and he prepared himself accordingly. So, in his second full-length play, Eliot picks on the modern aristocracy for his characterization. The protagonist, Harry Monchensey, is a young man who is dissatisfied with his family and feels the urgent need to purge the ills of his family through his own suffering in his quest for salvation which implies a quest for meaning of life, and articulation. Here, Eliot introduces the very interesting theme of the man-woman relationship—something he could not afford to present in *Murder in the Cathedral*. In *The Family Reunion*, Eliot treats this ever-intriguing relationship on two planes. The first is that between Harry and his dead wife along with the relationship between Harry and Mary. The second is revealed to the auditors as the play unfolds the past of Dowager Lady Monchensey, Harry's mother, where lay the buried secret of a relationship between her husband, the late Lord Monchensey, and her sister, Agatha. Harry's quest is treated from both the psychological and naturalistic perspectives. For this Eliot converts the classical concept of the Furies, which turn into the Eumenides (as in Orestes), in order to set the play in the framework of naturalistic drama. Harry's mental processes are externalized by dramatization in *The Family Reunion*, rendering the spiritual and psychological aspects of his quest with a realistic, audio-visual and intellectual presentation. However, the play has its flaws and Eliot discusses them in 'Poetry and Drama.'

*The Cocktail Party* was Eliot's next dramatic venture. Here, the element of psychology is complemented by philosophy, which is largely Oriental. In this transitional phase in the development of his understanding, Eliot turned to the Buddhistic doctrine of the two-fold path towards *Nirvana*: one path is that of the quest on the social level which is followed by Edward and Lavinia Chamberlayne, the other is that of the quest on the higher spiritual level—the one preferred by Celia. Sir Henry Harcourt-Reilly is a character who combines the rôle of the psychiatrist and Father-Confessor—the psychological and spiritual guide of people like the Chamberlaynes and Celia. Reilly also serves as Eliot's spokesman in presenting the philosophy of the Buddha's teachings before the auditors. The combination of the roles of psychiatrist and chorus makes Reilly conform to the "formalist-realist synthesis"[16] which his creator was aiming at. While writing *The Cocktail Party*, Eliot kept in mind a few important points necessary for a dramatist, which he speaks about in 'Poetry and Drama':

> I tried to keep in mind that in a play, from time to time, something should happen; that the audience should be kept in the constant expectation that something is going to happen; and that, when it does happen, it should be different, but not too different, from what the audience has been led to expect.[17]

Just like his previous plays. Eliot scrutinized *The Cocktail Party* in order to discern its flaws so that he would be able to do away with them in his next play. He speaks about this in the same essay, where he says that "the desire to write something which will be free of the defects of one's last work is a very powerful and useful incentive."[18]

In the next play, *The Confidential Clerk*, the quest for self-realization which is undertaken by the protagonist, Colby Simpkins, is given a symbolic representation in the image of the garden and in music. The quest for identity as the son of God is conveyed with the help of these symbols which are used to stand for both the natural and supernatural aspects that Eliot wished to represent in the naturalistic drama of this play. The symbolic garden of Colby's inner self is used here as the conceptualized consummation of his quest, as well as an indication of the journey he is to undertake in order to reach the goal of self-realization. So, also, his music is a companion and a means which provides his sustenance in his quest. The music is the legacy from his earthly father, Herbert Guzzard, and a perfection of its melody is all that he aspires after. Eliot hints at the use of music in this play in 'Poetry and Drama':

> I should not like to close without attempting to set before you, though only a dim outline, the ideal towards which poetic drama should strive. It is an unattainable ideal: and that is why it interests me, for it provides an incentive towards further experiment and exploration. Beyond any goal there is prospect of attaining. It is a function of all art to give us some perception of an order in life, by imposing an order upon it. [...] This peculiar range of sensibility can be expressed by dramatic poetry, at its moments of greatest intensity. At such moments, we touch the border of those feelings which only music can express. We can never emulate music, because to arrive at the condition of music would be the annihilation of poetry, and especially of dramatic poetry.[19]

Colby feels that his quest for an identity will be successful if he is associated with the Church as an organist. Here, the ideal music he would like to play represents the Chalice and his relentless endeavours to perfect his music symbolically represent his search for an identity as God's son.

Lord Claverton, in *The Elder Statesman*, is a martyr for the cause of love—temporal love as the representative of eternal love which affirms the Christian belief that God is love and love is God, as rejoiced by the devotional song:

> Love it was that made us and it was love that saved us.
> Love was God's plan when He made man; God's divine nature is Love.
> Born of God's love we must love Him, that's why He made us—to love Him.

> But only when we love all men, can we partake of God's love.[20]

Lord Claverton wished to atone for his past deeds by being spiritually purified through the process of personal suffering. He dies in peace after overcoming the difficult hurdle of confessing before his innocent and loving daughter, Monica, whose angelic presence in the play is a striking contrast to the selfish designs of Gomez and Mrs. Carghill. Lord Claverton's acceptance of the love shared by Monica and Charles as the human representation of divine Love paves the way for his self-realization. He discovers the meaning of life only after his self-revelation before Monica in a confession which enables him to discard the impediment of a false personality which he had constructed for the world as well as himself. He finds life easier and happier in being able to articulate his inmost thoughts before Monica. So, his peaceful death is seen by the auditors as a natural culmination of his bliss.

The idea of the Incarnation courses through Eliot's poetry and plays. Christ's martyrdom for the salvation of mankind comes to occupy a pivotal position in Eliot's works. With his development as a creative artist, Eliot moulded his own understanding of the significance of the Incarnation, so that it could be congruent with the realistic aspect of his plays. Being a priest, Becket follows the Way of Contemplation towards martyrdom. There is a different inner struggle in Harry, who is a man with a secular lifestyle. He needs guidance which is provided by Agatha, who shows him the way towards self-realization. Harry's quest takes him away from the frame of the drama—his martyrdom is implied. Celia follows the path of asceticism and leaves her familiar world after being counselled by Reilly. Her martyrdom, reported by Alex, is once removed from the direct experience of the auditors. Colby's martyrdom is merely hinted at by Eggerson, who offers him the post of organist in the parish church; Colby's love for God comes to have greater significance in *The Confidential Clerk*. Lord Claverton's death in *The Elder Statesman* is a martyrdom which indicates the consummation of his quest for self-realization. Monica plays the role of the priestess in this play by initiating

Lord Claverton's understanding of the efficacy of love. It may be seen that by the time he wrote *The Elder Statesman*, Eliot had come to a realization of the loving and compassionate nature of the Incarnation, for which Christ's Suffering was possible.

Eliot wished to convey this understanding to his readers and auditors, since he believed that all poets would like to have a social relevance. In each of his works there can be felt the presence of a conscious artist who makes use of the third voice. Eliot was aware of the technical aspect of playwriting and the difference between writing poetry and drama. Poetry allows a free expression on the part of the poet but the playwright will have to overcome the temptation of subjugating the characters he creates in order to express his own views directly before the audience. Subtlety is the key-word where a dramatist's technique of presentation is concerned, about which Eliot writes in 'Poetry and Drama':

> But in the theatre, the problem of communication presents itself immediately. You are deliberately writing verse for other voices, not for your own, and you do not know whose voice they will be. You are aiming to write lines which will have an immediate effect upon an unknown and unprepared audience, to be interpreted to that audience by unknown actors rehearsed by an unknown producer. And the unknown audience cannot be expected to show any indulgence towards the poet. [...] Hence one finds out that many of the things one likes to do, and knows how to do, are out of place; and that every line must be judged by a new law, that of dramatic relevance.[21]

At the same time, Eliot was aware of the importance of having realistic characters in his plays. It is for this reason that he saw the flaw in the presentation of the Eumenides in *The Family Reunion*. He says that the only way to make a character realistic is to "have a profound sympathy with that character."[22] It also enables the playwright to undertake his personal quest for which he used the characters in his plays. This is expressed by Eliot in 'The Three Voices of Poetry':

> It seems to me that what happens, when an author creates a vital character, is a sort of give-and-take. The author may put into that character, besides its other attributes, some trait of his own, some strength or weakness, some tendency to violence or to indecision, some eccentricity even, that he has found in himself. Something perhaps never realized in his own life, something of which those who know him best may be unaware, something not restricted in transmission to characters of the same temperament, the same age, and least of all, of the same sex. Some bit of himself that the author gives to a character may be the germ from which the life of that character starts. On the other hand, a character which succeeds in interesting its author may elicit from the author latent potentialities of his own being. I believe that the author imparts something of himself to his characters, but I also believe that he is influenced by the characters he creates.[23]

These lines, written by Eliot, show that he undertook his personal quest for meaning of life, form and articulation, besides the search for an understanding of the man-woman relationship, behind the facade of the playwright's objectivity, which was a perfect veil for his purpose. He was successful in writing a play like *The Elder Statesman* only after his happy marriage with Valerie Fletcher, which shows that the personal bliss which he enjoyed, enabled him to write a play that revolves around the element of human love as an earthly representation of Divine Love.

Though the desire to create another play remained unfulfilled owing to his death in 1965, there is no doubt that Eliot had reached a sort of consummation in his quest for self-realization, form and articulation. In *The Elder Statesman*, Eliot portrayed the essence of Christianity—the supremacy of love experienced in human life—something that brings him almost close to Tagore, as an artist, who in the last phase of his literary career, points out that God resides in man. Like Dante, Petrarch, and other poets before him, Eliot came to a realization that an understanding of the Ultimate Truth can be attained through human love. His plays express a consummation of his search for a meaning of life which had begun in his poetry. The last play is the supreme example of how one can attain excellence in art while adhering to his personal religious feelings and impulses.

## II

The voice of the interlocutors and the device of the "internal monologue"[24] serve as indicators of Eliot's persistent search for an effective mode of communication. The poets of the early seventeenth century came to have a profound influence on him in this regard, about which he writes in 'To Criticize the Critic': "I think that if I wrote well about the metaphysical poets, it was because they were poets who had inspired me."[25] While acknowledging his debt to the French Symbolist poets, Eliot confessed, "I have written about Baudelaire, but nothing about Jules Laforgue, to whom I owe more than to any one poet in any language."[26] These were the primary influences on Eliot's poetic technique in the early phase of his literary career. For his inspiration while writing dramatic poetry, Eliot turned to the dramatists who were the contemporaries and immediate successors of Shakespeare. He says, "Just as the modern poet who influenced me was not Baudelaire but Jules Laforgue, so the dramatic poets were Marlowe and Webster and Tourneur and Middleton and Ford, not Shakespeare"[27] because Shakespeare's greatness can only be imitated. Eliot's search for an effective mode of communication was imperative in the absence of any accepted code of conduct in the present age of unbelief.

At the same time, Eliot realized that the best method he could employ in order to reach out to his target readers was to be culled from the popular forms of entertainment and the conversational idiom of the modern metropolis. His enterprise was "to take a form of entertainment and subject it to a process that would leave it a form of art."[28] In keeping with this scheme, he slowly turned towards drama which is the most popular form of literary entertainment, reaching out at one and the same time, to the highest and lowest strata of understanding. Eliot gave most of his plays a naturalistic surface and yet integrated them into the framework of ritual, both classical and Christian. In doing so, he has "performed the difficult feat of weaving the elements of plain drama organically into a richer design,"[29] which have been effectively rendered by the use of poetry in the theatre because Eliot believed that:

> [...] a verse play is not a play done into verse, but a different kind of play: in a way more realistic than 'naturalistic drama,' because, instead of clothing nature in poetry, it should remove the surface of things, expose the underneath, or the inside, of the natural surface appearance. It may allow the characters to behave inconsistently, but only with respect to a deeper consistency.[30]

The verse of Eliot's poetic drama is a remarkable contribution to the modern theatre because ever since Shakespeare, no other poet has been able to vitalize dramatic poetry by bringing it close to the conversational idiom of the contemporary society and giving it a wide range of communication. The use of symbols and images has made it possible to convey various (and sometimes, subtle) layers of meaning in the plays.

As a reflection of the development of Eliot, the dramatist, there is a noticeable transformation from the formal dignity of *Murder in the Cathedral* to the graceful ease of *The Elder Statesman*. "The wide variety of its diction almost gives the dialogue of Eliot's plays an alabaster-like smoothness and cameo-like precision,"[31] points out a critic. Eliot used the Anglo-Saxon line with three to four stressed and a varying number of unstressed syllables, and a caesura, to its maximum advantage because he found that this line was most suited to the cadence of the speech-rhythm of the modern urban conversational idiom. Thus, he was able to bring the lilt of the dialogue in his verse plays close to the rhythm of everyday speech.

The present study has attempted to trace the graph of Eliot's development as a literary artist, showing how he came to mould an appropriate form and idiom which could express the quest for meaning of life he undertook in his poetry and plays.

## NOTES AND REFERENCES

1. Eliot, *After Strange Gods* 28.
2. Eliot, *After Strange Gods* 28.

3. Sarkar, *T.S. Eliot the Dramatist* 78.
4. Sarkar, "Tagore and Eliot: Poetry of Tradition, Religion and Suffering," *Rabindra Bharati Journal* (1995) 20.
5. Rabindranath Tagore, *The Religion of Man* (1931; London: Unwin, 1961) 60.
6. Tagore 60.
7. Tagore 69.
8. Tagore 74.
9. Tagore 77.
10. Tagore 80.
11. Eliot, "The Music of Poetry," *On Poetry and Poets* 31.
12. Eliot, "Ben Jonson," *Selected Essays* 157-58.
13. Eliot, "The Possibility of a Poetic Drama," *The Sacred Wood* 70.
14. Sarkar, *T.S. Eliot the Dramatist* 261.
15. Eliot, "Four Elizabethan Dramatists," *Selected Essays* 111.
16. Sarkar, *T.S. Eliot the Dramatist* 3.
17. Eliot, "Poetry and Drama," *On Poetry and Poets* 85.
18. Eliot, "Poetry and Drama," *On Poetry and Poets* 85.
19. Eliot, "Poetry and Drama," *On Poetry and Poets* 86-87.
20. Anonymous. This song was taught when we were in Loreto Convent, Darjeeling, to be sung during Prayers.
21. Eliot, "Poetry and Drama," *On Poetry and Poets* 79.
22. Eliot, "The Three Voices of Poetry," *On Poetry and Poets* 93.
23. Eliot, "The Three Voices of Poetry," *On Poetry and Poets* 93-94.
24. Sarkar, "'The Love Song of J. Alfred Prufrock' as a Modernist Poem," *The Journal of English Studies Association*, 1. 1: 1.
25. Eliot, "To Criticize the Critic," *To Criticize the Critic and Other Writings* 22.
26. Eliot, "To Criticize the Critic," *To Criticize the Critic and Other Writings* 22.
27. Eliot, "To Criticize the Critic," *To Criticize the Critic and Other Writings* 18.
28. Eliot, "The Possibility of a Poetic Drama," *The Sacred Wood* 70.
29. Sarkar, *T.S. Eliot the Dramatist* 263.
30. Eliot, Introduction, *Shakespeare and the Popular Dramatic Tradition* 9.
31. Sarkar, *T.S. Eliot the Dramatist* 263.

# Bibliography


Ackroyd, Peter. *T.S. Eliot*. London: Hamish Hamilton, 1984.

Aeschylus. *The Oresteia*. Trans. Robert Eagles. Rev. ed. London: Penguin, 1979.

Andreach, Robert. *Studies in Structure*. n.p.: Fordham UP, 1964.

Antrim, Harry T. *T.S. Eliot's Concept of Language*. Gainesville: University of Florida P, 1971.

Arnold, Edwin. *The Light of Asia*. 1879. New Delhi: Srishti, 1999.

Augustine, Saint. *'The Confessions,' 'The City of God,' 'On Christian Doctrine'*. Gen. Ed. Robert Maynard Hutchins. *Great Books of the Western World*. 18. Chicago: *Encyclopaedia Britannica*, 1952.

Baudelaire, Charles. *Poems of Baudelaire*. Trnsl. of *Les Fleurs du Mal*. By Roy Campbell. London: Harvill, 1952.

Becket, Samuel. *Waiting for Godot*. 1956. 2nd ed. London: Faber, 1965.

Behr, Caroline. *T.S. Eliot: A Chronology of His Life and Works*. London: Macmillan, 1983.

Bergonzi, Bernard. *T.S. Eliot*. Ed. Louis Kronenberger. *Masters of World Literature Series*. New York: Macmillan, 1972.

*Bhagavad Gita*. Trnsl. Sarvepalli Radhakrishnan. 1948. New Delhi: Harper Collins, 1993.

Bible, The Holy. King James Version. Nashville: Thomas Nelson, 1977.

Blackmur, R.P. *Language as Gesture*. London: George Allen and Unwin, 1954.

Bloom, Harold, Ed. "T.S. Eliot's 'Murder in the Cathedral'". *Modern Critical Interpretations*. New York: Chelsea House, 1988.

Bodkin, Maud. *The Quest for Salvation in an Ancient and a Modern Play*. London: Oxford UP, 1941.

*Brhadaranyaka Upanishad*. Trnsl. Swami Madhavananda. Calcutta: Advaita Ashrama, 1965.

Brooks, Cleanth. *The Hidden God*. New Haven: Yale UP, 1963.

Browne, E. Martin. *The Making of T.S. Eliot's Plays*. Cambridge: Cambridge UP, 1969.

Browning, Robert. *'Men and Women' and Other Writings*. Ed. J.W. Harper. London: J.M. Dent, 1975.

Calder, Angus. *T.S. Eliot*. Harvester New Readings. Brighton: Harvester P, 1987.

Chatterjee, A.K. *Facets of Buddhist Thought*. Calcutta: Sanskrit College, 1975.

Chatterjee, Sati. *Encounters With Reality*. Calcutta: Papyrus, 1990

Chatterjee, Viswanath. "T.S. Eliot and Buddhism." *Thoughts on American Literature*. Ed. Goutam Ghosal. Calcutta: Subarnarekha, 1988.

Clarke, David R., Ed. "Murder in the Cathedral," *Twentieth Century Interpretations*. New Jersey: Prentice Hall, 1971.

Clarke, Graham, Ed. *T.S. Eliot: Critical Assessments*. 4 Vols. London: Christopher Helm, 1990.

Coghill, Nevill, Ed. and Introduction. *The Family Reunion*. By T.S. Eliot. Oxford: Oxford UP, 1963.

——. Ed. and Introduction. *Murder in the Cathedral*. By T.S. Eliot. Oxford: Oxford UP, 1963.

"Congress for Cultural Freedom." *T.S. Eliot: Papers and Proceedings of a Seminar*. Bombay: Manaktalas, 1965.

Conrad, Joseph. *Heart of Darkness*. Ed. and Introduction Paul O'Prey. 1902. London: Penguin, 1973.

Coomaraswamy, Ananda K. *Buddha and the Gospel of Buddhism*. New Delhi: Munshiram Manoharlal, 1974

Cornford, F.M. *The Origin of Attic Comedy*. London: Edward Arnold, 1914.

Crawford, Fred D. "T.S. Eliot," *Dictionary of Literary Biography*. Ed. Stanley Weintraub. Vol. 10. *Modern British Dramatists—1900-1982*. Detroit: Gale, 1982. Many Vols.

Dalai Lama, His Holiness. *The Dalai Lama's Book of Wisdom*. London: Thorsons, 1999.

Dante. *The Divine Comedy*. Transl. Mark Musa. 1971. New York: Penguin, 1984.

Davidson, John. *The Poems of John Davidson*. Ed. Andrew Turnbull. Vol. 1. Edinburgh: Scottish Academic P. 1973.

Davison, Peter. *Contemporary Drama and the Popular Dramatic Tradition*. London: Macmillan, 1982.

Dobree, Bonamy. *The Lamp and the Lute*. New York: Barnes and Noble, 1929.

Donaldson, Evelyn and Terry Donaldson. *Principles of Tarot*. 1996. New Delhi: Harper Collins, 1999.

Donough, Denis. *The Third Voice*. Princeton: Princeton UP, 1959.

Doyle, Arthur Conan. *Sherlock Holmes: The Complete Facsimile Edition*. Hertfordshire: Wordsworth, 1996.

Drabble, Margaret, Ed. *The Oxford Companion to English Literature*. 1932. Oxford: Oxford UP, 1995.

Eliot, T.S. *After Strange Gods*. London: Faber, 1934.

——. Ed. and Introduction. *A Choice of Kipling's Verse*. London: Faber, 1951.

——. *The Complete Poems and Plays*. London: Faber, 1969.

——. Ed. and Introduction. *Ezra Pound: Selected Poems*. London: Faber, 1928.

——. *For Lancelot Andrewes*. London: Faber, 1928.

——. *The Idea of a Christian Society and Other Writings*. London: Faber, 1939.

——. *Knowledge and Experience in the Philosophy of F.H. Bradley*. London: Faber, 1964.

——. *The Letters of T.S. Eliot.* Ed. Valerie Eliot. Vol. 1.—1898-1922. London: Faber, 1988.

——. "Preface." *The Need for Roots*, By Simone Weil. London: Routledge, 1952.

——. *Notes Towards the Definition of Culture*. London: Faber, 1948.

——. *On Poetry and Poets*. London: Faber, 1957.

——. *Points of View*. London: Faber, 1941.

——. *The Rock*. London: Faber, 1934.

——. *The Sacred Wood*. London: Methuen, 1920.

——. *Selected Essays*. 3rd ed. London: Faber, 1951.

——. *Selected Prose*. Ed. Frank Kermode. London: Faber, 1975.

——. "Introduction." *Shakespeare and the Popular Dramatic Tradition*. By S.L. Bethell. Westminster: King and Staples, 1944.

——. "Introduction," *The Wheel of Fire*. By G. Wilson Knight. London: Methuen, 1930.

——. *To Criticise the Critic and Other Writings*. London: Faber 1965.

——. *The Use of Poetry and the Use of Criticism*. London: Faber, 1964.

——. *The Varieties of Metaphysical Poetry*, Ed. and Introduction. Ronald Schuchard. London: Faber, 1993.

Eliot, George. *God is Spirit, God is Love: A Treatise on Spiritual Unitarianism*. London: Philip Green, 1895.

Enright, D.J. *The Apothecary's Shop*. London: Secker, 1957.

Evans, Gareth Lloyd. *The Language of Modern Drama*. London: J.M. Dent, 1977.

*Everyman*. Trnsl. C.G. Child. Calcutta: Avantgarde, 1995.

Feather, Leonard, Ed. *The Encyclopaedia of Jazz*. New York: Horizon, 1955.

Frazer, James G. *The Golden Bough*. 1922. Hertfordshire: Wordsworth, 1993.

Gallup, Donald. *T.S. Eliot: A Bibliography*. London: Faber, 1969.

Gardner, Helen. *The Art of T.S. Eliot*. 1949. London: Faber, 1964.

——. Ed. *The Metaphysical Poets*. 1957. London: Penguin, 1987.

Gaskell, Ronald. *Drama and Reality*. London: Routledge, 1972.

Ghosh, P.C. *Poetry and Religion as Drama*. Calcutta: World Press, 1965.

Gordon, Lyndall. *Eliot's Early Years*. Oxford: Oxford UP, 1977.

——. *Eliot's New Life*. Oxford: Oxford UP, 1988.

Grant, Michael, Ed. "T.S. Eliot." *Critical Heritage*. Vol. 1. London: Routledge, 1982.

Graves, Robert. *The Greek Myths*. Combined ed. 1955. London: Penguin, 1992.

Griffiths, Paul J. *Christianity Through Non-Christian Eyes. Faith Meets Faith Series*. New York: Orbis, 1994.

Guthrie, Donald. *New Testament Theology*. Leister: Inter-Varsity P, 1981.

Halverson, Marvin, Ed. *A Handbook of Christian Theology. Living Age Books*. New York: Meridian, 1958.

——. *Religious Drama. Living Age Books*. New York: Meridian, 1957.

Happold, F.C. *Mysticism: A Study and an Anthology*. Middlesex: Penguin, 1963.

Harben, Niloufer. *Twentieth Century English History Plays: From Shaw to Bond*. Basingstoke: Macmillan, 1988.

Harrison, Everett F., Ed.-in-Chief. *Baker's Dictionary of Theology*. Michigan: Baker, 1960.

Hartnoll, Phyllis, Ed. *The Concise Oxford Companion to the Theatre*. 1972. Oxford: Oxford UP, 1986.

Headings, Philip R. *T.S. Eliot*. New York: Twayne, 1964.

Hemingway, Ernest. *The Old Man and the Sea*. 1952. London: Triad Grafton, 1988.

Hinchliffe, Arnold P. *Modern Verse Drama. Critical Idiom Series*. London: Methuen, 1977.

——. Ed. *T.S. Eliot's Plays. Casebook Series*. Basingstoke: Macmillan, 1985. Rpt. 1993.

Hulme, T.E. *Speculations*. Ed. Herbert Read. London: Routledge, 1924. Rpt. 1954.

Isaacs, J. *An Assessment of Twentieth-Century Literature*. London: Secker, 1951.

Jones, David E. *The Plays of T.S. Eliot*. London: Routledge, 1960.

Kearns, Cleo McNelly. *T.S. Eliot and Indic Traditions*. Cambridge: Cambridge UP, 1987.

Kennedy, Andrew. *Six Dramatists in Search of a Language*. London: Cambridge UP, 1975.

Kenner, Hugh. *The Invisible Poet: T.S. Eliot*. New York: McDowell, Obolensky, 1959.

——. Ed. *T.S. Eliot: Collection of Critical Essays*. New Jersey: Prentice Hall, 1962.

Keown, Damien. *Buddhism: A Very Short Introduction*. Oxford: Oxford UP, 1996.

Kitto, H.D.F. *Greek Tragedy*. 1939. London: Routledge, 1966.

Knight, G. Wilson. *The Crown of Life*. London: Methuen, 1947.

——. *The Golden Labyrinth*. London: Phoenix, 1962.

——. *Neglected Powers: Essays on Nineteenth and Twentieth Century Literature*. London: Routledge, 1971.

Leeming, Glenda. *Poetic Drama. Macmillan Modern Dramatists Series*. Hampshire: Macmillan, 1989.

Levy, William Turner and Victor Scherle. *Affectionately T.S. Eliot*. London: J.M. Dent, 1968.

Lucy, Sean. *T.S. Eliot and the Idea of Tradition*. London: Cohent West, 1960.

Mackinnon, Lachlan. *Eliot, Auden, Lowell: Aspects of the Baudelairean Inheritance*. London: Macmillan, 1983.

MacNicholas, John, Ed. *Twentieth Century American Dramatists*. Vol. 7. of *Dictionary of Literary Biography*. Detroit: Bruccoli Clark, 1981. Many Vols.

March, R. and Tambimuttu, Ed. *T.S. Eliot: A Symposium*. London: Frank Cass, 1948. 3rd Imprint 1965

Marlowe, Christopher. *Doctor Faustus*. Ed. John D. Jump. London: Methuen, 1960.

Martin, Graham, Ed. *Eliot in Perspective: A Symposium*. London: Macmillan, 1970.

Martin, Mildred. *A Half-Century of Eliot Criticism*. Lewisburg: Bucknell UP, 1972.

Mathiessen, F.O. *The Achievement of T.S. Eliot*. New York: Oxford UP, 1959.

Matthews, T.S. *Great Tom*. New York: Harper and Row, 1973.

McCann, Justin, Ed. *The Cloud of Unknowing*. By an English mystic of the Fourteenth Century. London: Burns and Oates, 1924.

Menand, Louis. *Discovering Modernism: T.S. Eliot and His Context*. Oxford: Oxford UP, 1987.

Menander. *Perikeirome*. Trnsl. *The Rape of the Lock*. By Gilbert Murray. London: Allen, 1942 (The Fragments translated and the Gaps conjecturally filled in by Gilbert Murray).

Milton, John. *Samson Agonistes*. Ed. and Introduction by H.M. Percival. Calcutta: Radha, 1985.

Molland, Einar. *Christendom*. London: A R. Mowbray, 1961.

Moody, A.D. *Thomas Stearns Eliot: Poet*. Cambridge: Cambridge UP, 1979.

Moorman, Charles. *Arthurian Triptych: Mythic Materials in Charles Williams, C.S. Lewis, and T.S. Eliot*. London: Cambridge UP, 1960.

Olney, James, Ed. *T.S. Eliot: Essays from the 'Southern Review'*. Oxford: Clarendon, 1988.

Otto, Rudolf. *Mysticism East and West*. London: Macmillan, 1932.

Paz, Octavio, *Children of the Mire*. Trnsl. By Rachel Phillips. Massachussets: Harvard UP. 1974.

Peacock, Ronald. *The Poet in the Theatre*. London: Macgibbon and Kee, 1961.

Pinion, F.B.A. *T.S. Eliot Companion*. London: Macmillan, 1986.

Pollard, Arthur. *English Sermons*. London: Longmans, 1963.

Rajan, B., Ed. *T.S. Eliot: A Study of His Writings by Several Hands*. London: Dennis Dobson, 1947.

Ramaiah, L.S. *Indian Response to T.S. Eliot: A Bibliographical Guide*. Calcutta: Writers' Workshop, 1988

Ray, Mohit Kumar. *Studies in Literary Criticism*. New Delhi: Atlantic, 2001.

——. *T.S. Eliot: Search for a Critical Credo*. Calcutta: Firma, 1978.

Richardson, Alan, Ed. *A Theological Word Book of the Bible*. London: SCM Press, 1950.

Rosenthal, N.L. *Sailing into the Unknown: Yeats, Pound and Eliot*. New York: Oxford UP, 1978.

Roy, Virendra Kumar. *T.S. Eliot: Quest for Belief*. New Delhi: Ajanta, 1979.

Sarkar, Subhas. *The Chorus in Eliot's Plays and Other Essays*. Calcutta: Rupa, 1993.

——. *Eliot and Yeats: A Study*. Calcutta: Minerva, 1978.

——. *T.S. Eliot the Dramatist*. Calcutta: Minerva, 1972; New Delhi: Atlantic, 2006.

Schneider, Elisabeth. *T.S. Eliot: The Pattern in the Carpet*. California: University of California P, 1975.

Sen, Krishna. *Negotiating Modernity: Myth in the Theatre of Eliot, O'Neill and Sartre*. Calcutta: Minerva, 1999.

Seymour-Smith, Martin, Ed. *The English Sermon: Vol. I: 1550-1650. An Anthology*. Cheshire: Carcanet, 1976.

Shakespeare, William. *The Complete Works*. Ed. and Introduction. Peter Alexander. London: Collins, 1951.

Sharpe, Tony. *T.S. Eliot: A Literary Life. Literary Life Series*. Gen. Ed. Richard Dutton. London: Macmillan, 1991.

Sherek, Henry. *Not in Front of the Children*. London: William Heinemann, 1959.

Smidt, Kristian. *Poetry and Belief in the Works of T.S. Eliot*. London: Routledge, 1949.

Smith, Carol H. *T.S. Eliot's Dramatic Theory and Practice*. Princeton: Princeton UP, 1963.

Smith, Grover. *T.S. Eliot's Poetry and Plays: A Study in Sources and Meaning*. Chicago: University of Chicago P, 1956.

Southam, B.C., Ed. *T.S. Eliot: 'Prufrock,' 'Gerontion,' 'Ash Wednesday' and Other Shorter Poems*. Casebook Series. Gen. Ed. A. E. Dyson. Basingstoke: Macmillan, 1978. 3rd rpt. 1985.

Spanos, William V. *The Christian Tradition in Modern British Verse Drama*. New Brunswick: Rutgers UP, 1967.

Spencer, Theodore, Ed. *A Garland for John Donne*. 1931. Gloucester: Peter Smith, 1958.

Spender, Stephen. *The Creative Element*. London: Hamish Hamilton, 1953.

——. *The Destructive Element*. Philadelphia: Albert Saifer, 1953.

——. *Eliot*. Glasgow: Fontana, 1975.

——. "T.S. Eliot and the Writers of the Thirties." *Prof. M.M. Bhattacharyya Memorial Lectures*. Calcutta: University of Calcutta, 1990.

St. John of the Cross. "The Dark Night of the Soul." *Studies of the Spanish Mystics*. Vol. I. Ed. E. Allison Peers. London: Sheldon P, 1927.

Stead, C.K. *Pound, Yeats, Eliot and the Modernist Movement*. London: Macmillan, 1986.

Styan, J.L. *The Elements of Drama*. 1960. New Delhi: Vikas, 1979.

Sullivan, Sheila, Ed. *Critics on T.S. Eliot*. 1973. *Critics on Series*. New Delhi: Universal Book Stall, 1996.

Symons, Arthur. *The Symbolist Movement in Literature*. 1899. New York: Dutton, 1919.

Tagore, Rabindranath. *The Religion of Man*. 1931. London: Unwin, 1961.

Tate, Allen, Ed. *T.S. Eliot: The Man and His Work*. London: Chatto, 1967.

Thouless, Priscilla. *Modern Poetic Drama*. Oxford: Basil Blackwell, 1934.

Tomlin, Frederick. *T.S. Eliot: A Friendship*. London: Routledge, 1988.

Ulanov, Barry. *A Handbook of Jazz*. New York: Viking, 1960.

Underhill, Evelyn. *Mysticism*. 1911. London: Methuen, 1977.

Unger, Leonard. "T.S. Eliot." *American Writers: A Collection of Literary Biographies*. Ed-in-Chief Leonard Unger. Vol. 1. New York: Scribner's, 1974. 4 Vols.

——. *T.S. Eliot: Moments and Patterns*. Minneapolis: University of Minnesota P, 1956.

Virgil. *The Aeneid*. Trans. John Dryden. Introduction by James Morwood. Hertfordshire: Wordsworth, 1997.

Wakefield, Gordon S., Ed. *A Dictionary of Christian Spirituality*. London: SCM Press, 1983.

Ward. David. *T.S. Eliot Between Two Worlds*. London: Routledge, 1973.

Warren, Henry Clarke. *Buddhism in Translations*. *Harvard Oriental Series*. Vol 3. 1896. Delhi: Motilal Banarsidass, 1986.

Weales, Gerald, *Religion in Modern English Drama*. Philadelphia: University of Pennsylvania P, 1961.

Weston Jessie L. *From Ritual to Romance*. 1920. New York: Doubleday, 1957.

——. *The Quest of the Holy Grail*. 1913. London: Frank Cass, 1964.

Williams, Raymond. *Drama from Ibsen to Eliot*. 1952. London: Peregrine, 1964.

Wilson, Edmund. *Axel's Castle*. 1931. London: Fontana, 1962.

Worth, Katharine J. *Revolutions in Modern English Drama*. London: Bell, 1972.

Woods, James Haughton. *The Yoga System of Patanjali*. Harvard Oriental Series. Vol.17. 1914. Delhi: Motilal Banarasidass, 1966.

**Periodicals**

Banerjee, Sumita. "The Sea in Shakespeare's Last Plays." *Literature and Criticism* 1.1 (2001): 116-124.

Clutton-Brock, Alan. "T.S. Eliot and Conan Doyle." *Times Literary Supplement* 2555 (19 Jan. 1951): 37.

Eliot, T.S. "The Condition of Man Today: An Interview with T.S. Eliot." *Horizon* 12.68 (1945).

——. Ed. *The Criterion*. London: Faber, 1967.

*Indian Journal of American Studies*. Special Issue on T.S. Eliot 18.2 (Summer 1988).

Moore, Marianne. "Review of *Sweeney Agonistes*, by T.S. Eliot." *Poetry*. May 1933: 106-09.

Pellegrini, Alessandro. "A London Conversation with T.S. Eliot." *Sewanee Review* 57 (Spring 1949): 287-92.

Popkin, Henry. "Theatre Letter." *Kenyon Review* 12 (Spring 1950) 337-39.

Ray, Mohit Kumar, "T.S. Eliot and the Gita." *Journal of the Department of English* (University of Burdwan) 5-6.1 (1989-90): 80-89.

Sarkar, Subhas. "'The Love Song of J. Alfred Prufrock' as a Modernist Poem." *Journal of English Studies Association* 1.1 (1998): 1-10.

——. "A Modernist Quest for Martyrdom: Hemingway's 'The Old Man and the Sea' and T.S. Eliot's 'Murder in the

Cathedral.'" *West Bengal.* Hemingway Birth Centenary No. 16 Dec. 1999.

——. "T.S. Eliot and Ezra Pound: An Intercontinental Creative Encounter." *Literature and Criticism* 1.1 (2001): 18-21.

——. "T.S. Eliot: A Poet in Quest of His Roots." *Manual of First UGC Sponsored Refresher Course, Benares Hindu University* (1999).

——. "Tagore and Eliot: Poetry of Tradition, Religion, and Suffering." *Rabindra Bharati Journal* (1995) 16-24.

——. "Tagore and T.S. Eliot: Poets of Religion and Humanism." *Special-Lecture Series.* Vol.1 Kolkata: Rabindra Bharati V, 2001.

——. "The Vedas, Oriental Culture and T.S. Eliot." *Bulletin of the Ramkrishna Mission Institute of Culture* 51: (7 July 2000): 316.

Sayers, Michael. "Mr. T.S. Eliot's 'The Rock,'" *New English Weekly* 21 June 1934: 230-31.

Wimsatt, W.K. Jr. "Eliot's Comedy." *Sewanee Review* 58 (Autumn 1950): 669-78.

Zabel, Morton D. "A Modern Purgatorio." *Commonweal* 19 April 1933: 696-97.

# Index

## D

## N



## O

## P



## Q



## R

## S

## T



## U

**V**



**W**



**X**



**Y**



**Z**